STAR WARS

DARTH VADER

VADER

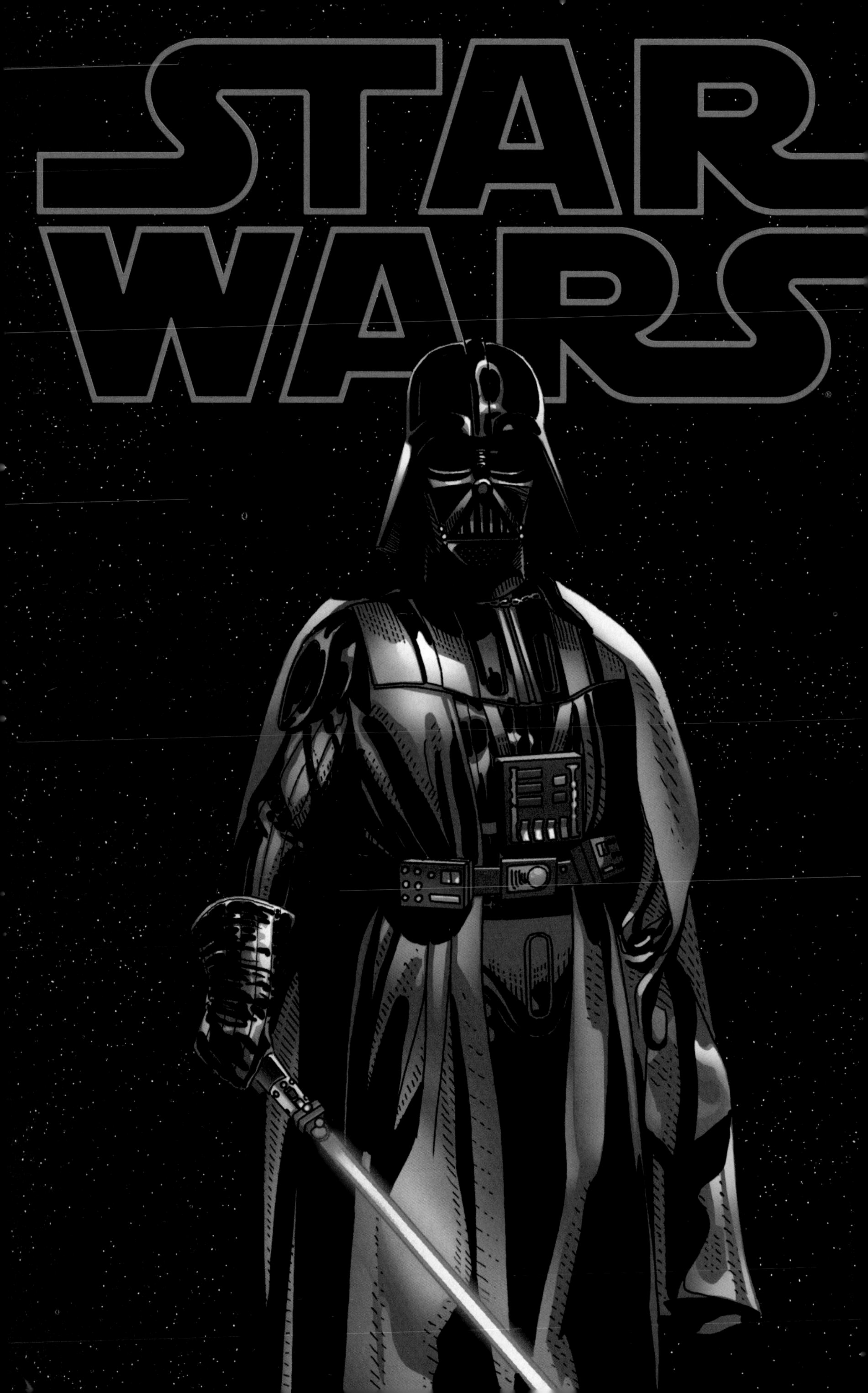
STAR WARS

DARTH VADER

VADER

Writer	**KIERON GILLEN**
Artist	**SALVADOR LARROCA**
Colorist	**EDGAR DELGADO**
Letterer	**VC's JOE CARAMAGNA**
Cover Art	**ADI GRANOV**
Assistant Editors	**CHARLES BEACHAM** & **HEATHER ANTOS**
Editor	**JORDAN D. WHITE**
Executive Editors	**C.B. CEBULSKI** & **MIKE MARTS**
Editor in Chief	**C.B. CEBULSKI**

For LucasFilm:

Creative Director	**MICHAEL SIGLAIN**
Senior Editors	**JENNIFER HEDDLE, FRANK PARISI**
Lucasfilm Story Group	**RAYNE ROBERTS, PABLO HIDALGO, LELAND CHEE**

Collection Editor	**JENNIFER GRÜNWALD**
Assistant Editor	**DANIEL KIRCHHOFFER**
Assistant Managing Editor	**MAIA LOY**
Assistant Managing Editor	**LISA MONTALBANO**
VP Production & Special Projects	**JEFF YOUNGQUIST**
SVP Print, Sales & Marketing	**DAVID GABRIEL**
Book Designer	**ADAM DEL RE**

STAR WARS: DARTH VADER VOL. 1 — VADER. Contains material originally published in magazine form as DARTH VADER #1-6. Fifth printing 2021. ISBN 978-0-7851-9255-8. Published by MARVEL WORLDWIDE, INC., a subsidiary of MARVEL ENTERTAINMENT, LLC. OFFICE OF PUBLICATION: 1290 Avenue of the Americas, New York, NY 10104. STAR WARS and related text and illustrations are trademarks and/or copyrights, in the United States and other countries, of Lucasfilm Ltd. and/or its affiliates. © & TM Lucasfilm Ltd. No similarity between any of the names, characters, persons, and/or institutions in this magazine with those of any living or dead person or institution is intended, and any such similarity which may exist is purely coincidental. Marvel and its logos are TM Marvel Characters, Inc. **Printed in Canada.** KEVIN FEIGE, Chief Creative Officer; DAN BUCKLEY, President, Marvel Entertainment; JOE QUESADA, EVP & Creative Director; DAVID BOGART, Associate Publisher & SVP of Talent Affairs; TOM BREVOORT, VP, Executive Editor; NICK LOWE, Executive Editor, VP of Content, Digital Publishing; DAVID GABRIEL, VP of Print & Digital Publishing; JEFF YOUNGQUIST, VP of Production & Special Projects; ALEX MORALES, Director of Publishing Operations; DAN EDINGTON, Managing Editor; RICKEY PURDIN, Director of Talent Relations; JENNIFER GRÜNWALD, Senior Editor, Special Projects; SUSAN CRESPI, Production Manager; STAN LEE, Chairman Emeritus. For information regarding advertising in Marvel Comics or on Marvel.com, please contact Vit DeBellis, Custom Solutions & Integrated Advertising Manager, at vdebellis@marvel.com. For Marvel subscription inquiries, please call 888-511-5480. **Manufactured between 2/19/2021 and 3/23/21 by SOLISCO PRINTERS, SCOTT, QC, CANADA.**

1 0 9 8 7 6 5

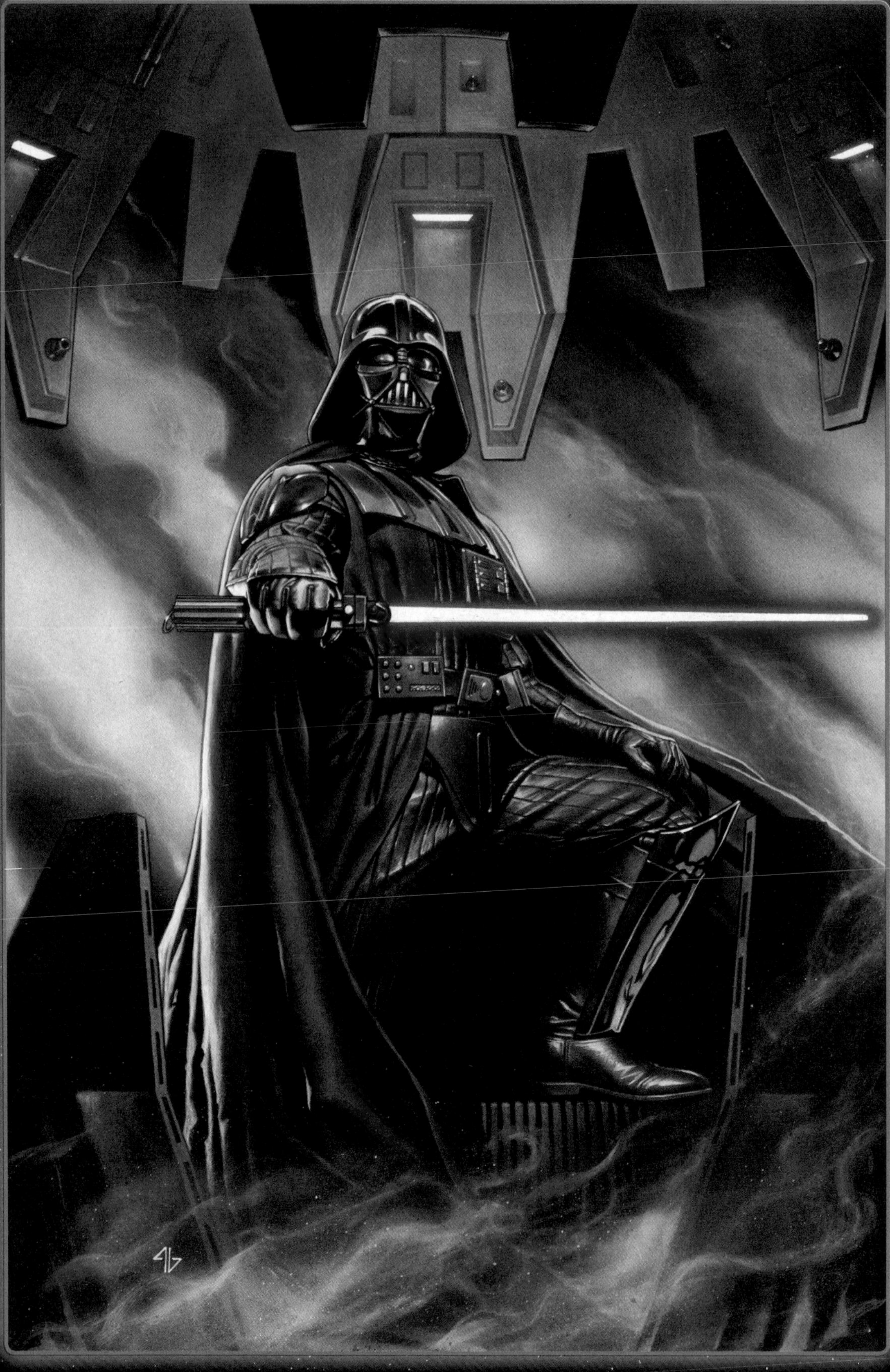

A long time ago in a galaxy far, far away....

STAR

DARTH

WARS®

VADER

Book I
VADER

It is a period of insurgence. Rebel spaceships, striking from a hidden base on a moon of Yavin, have won a shocking surprise victory against the rightful reign of the Galactic Empire.

The Empire's ultimate peacekeeping force, THE DEATH STAR, was destroyed due to an unforeseen design flaw. Without this deterrent, the rule of law is in danger. Chaos looms!

For the nineteen years after the vanquishing of the Jedi and his painful rebirth on volcanic Mustafar, Sith Lord DARTH VADER has faithfully served his master. But now, he has failed the Emperor and must pay the price....

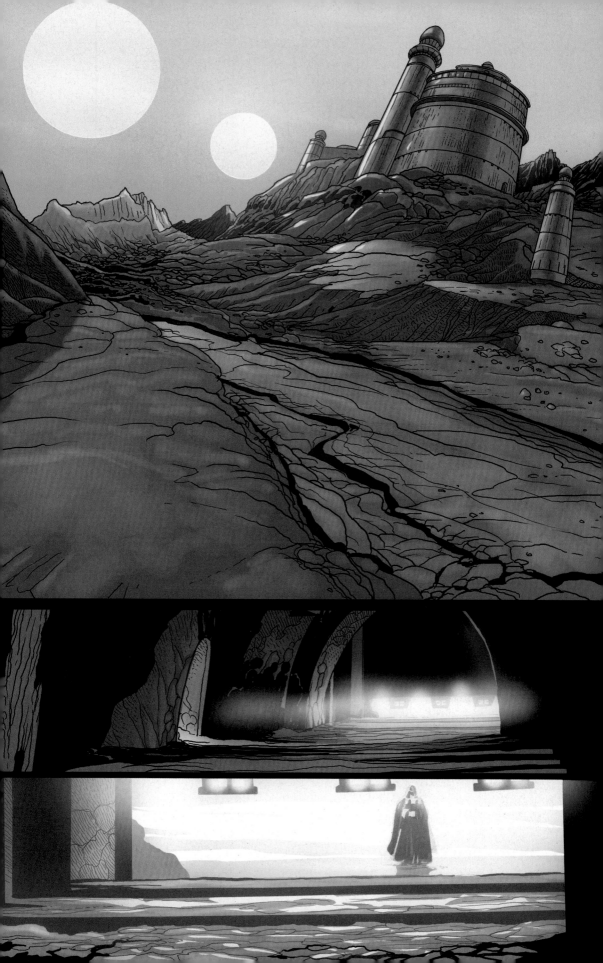

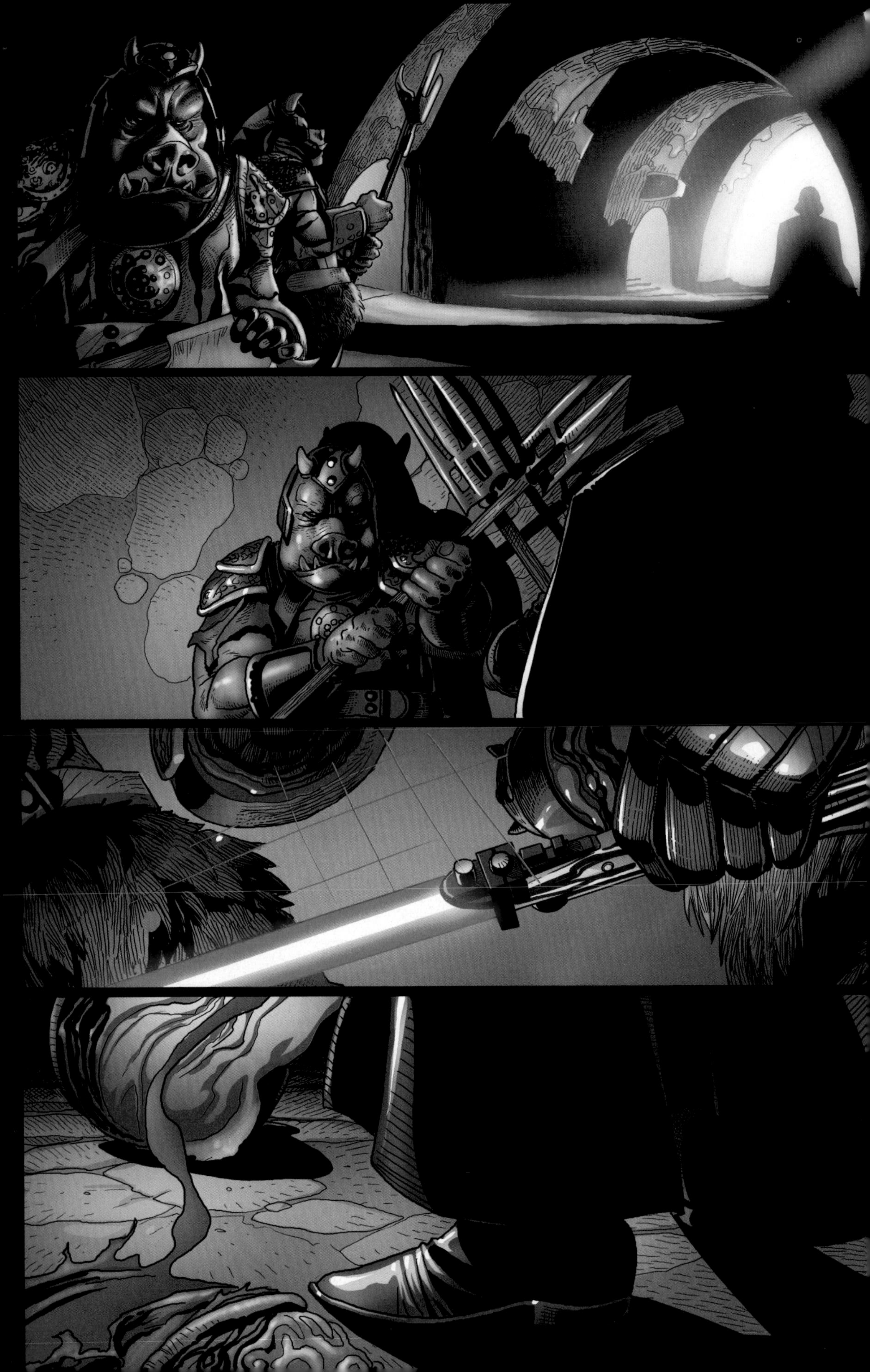

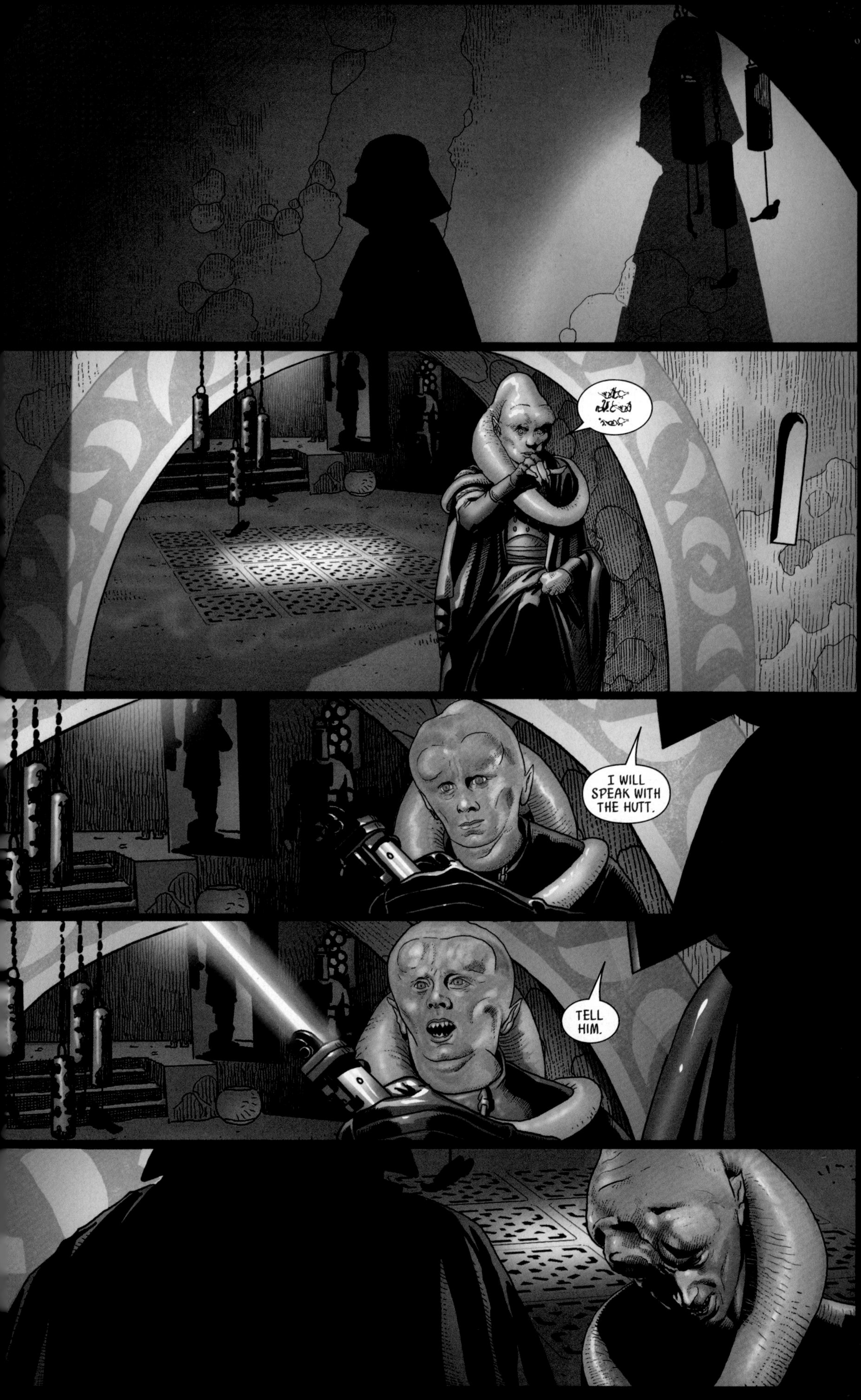
I WILL SPEAK WITH THE HUTT.
TELL HIM.

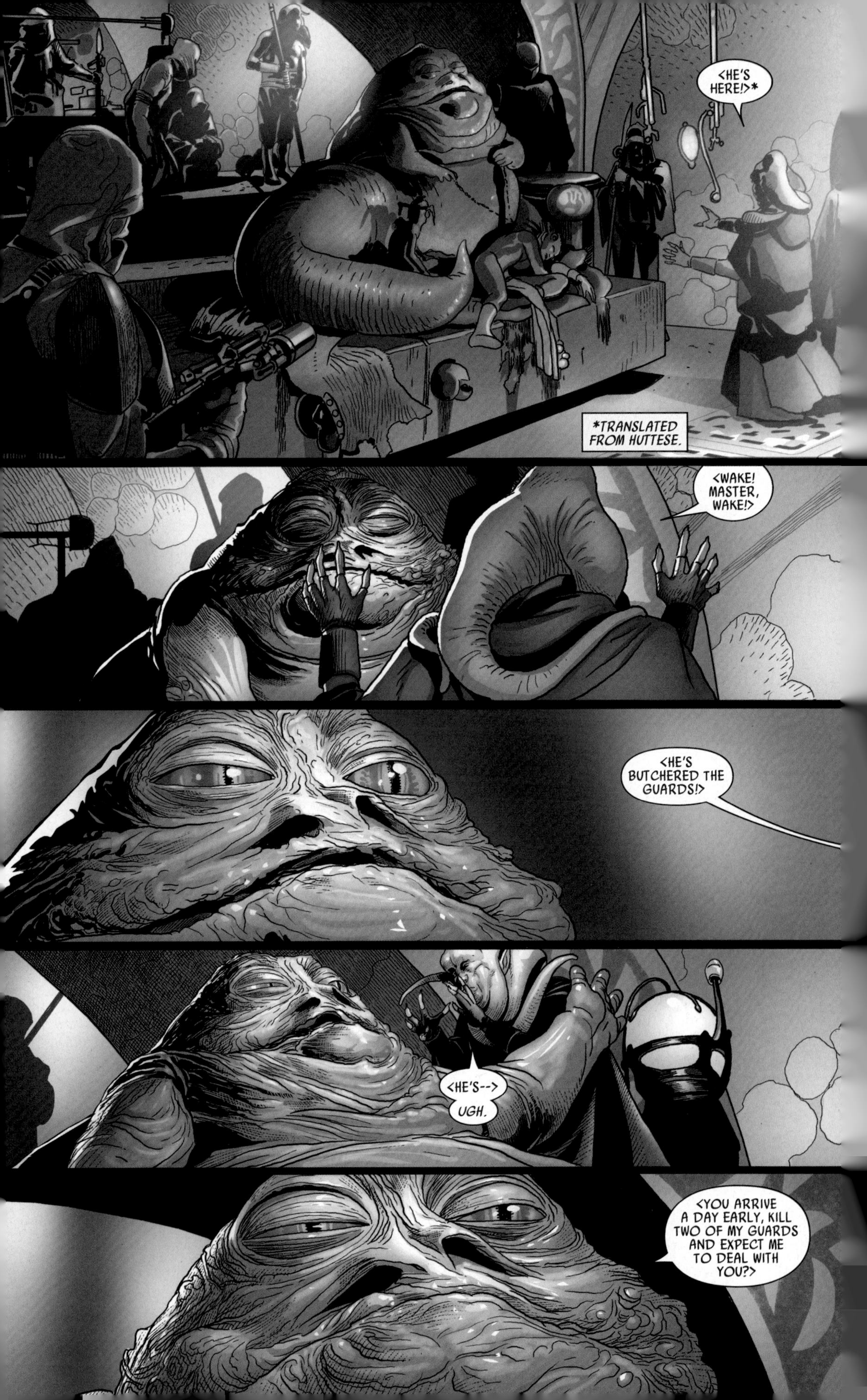
<HE'S HERE!>*
*TRANSLATED FROM HUTTESE.
<WAKE! MASTER, WAKE!>
<HE'S BUTCHERED THE GUARDS!>
<HE'S-->
UGH.
<YOU ARRIVE A DAY EARLY, KILL TWO OF MY GUARDS AND EXPECT ME TO DEAL WITH YOU?>

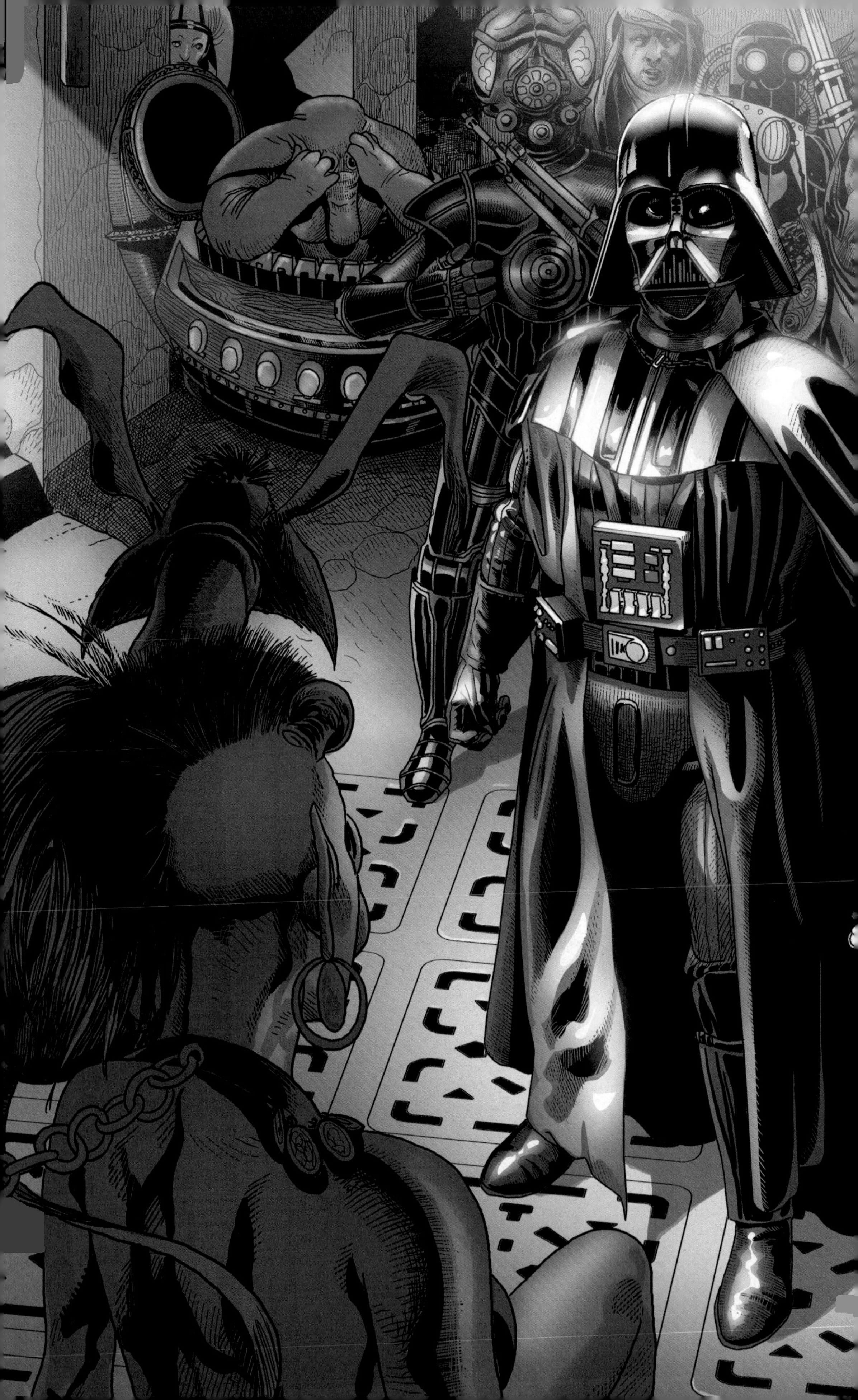

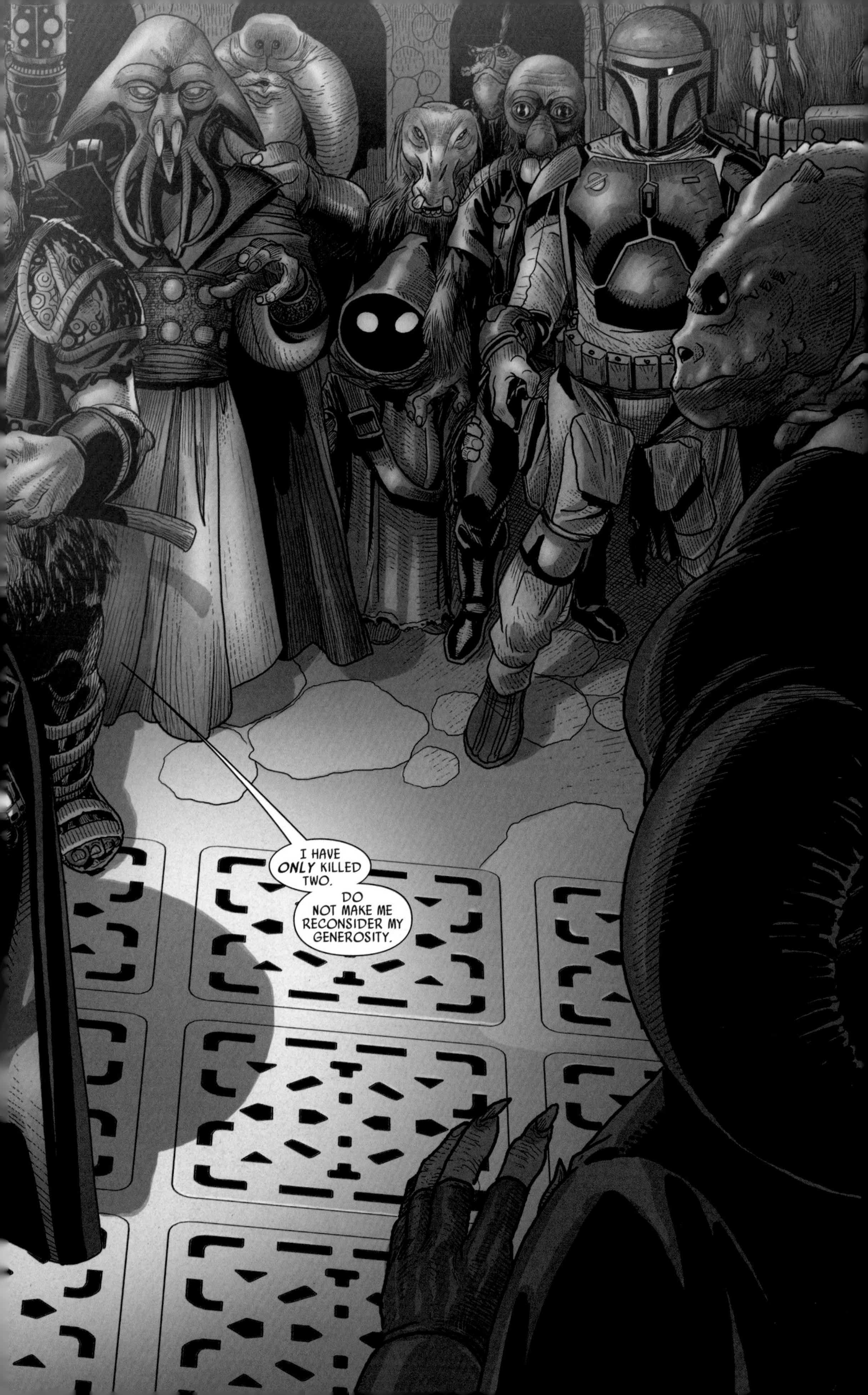
I HAVE ONLY KILLED TWO.
DO NOT MAKE ME RECONSIDER MY GENEROSITY.

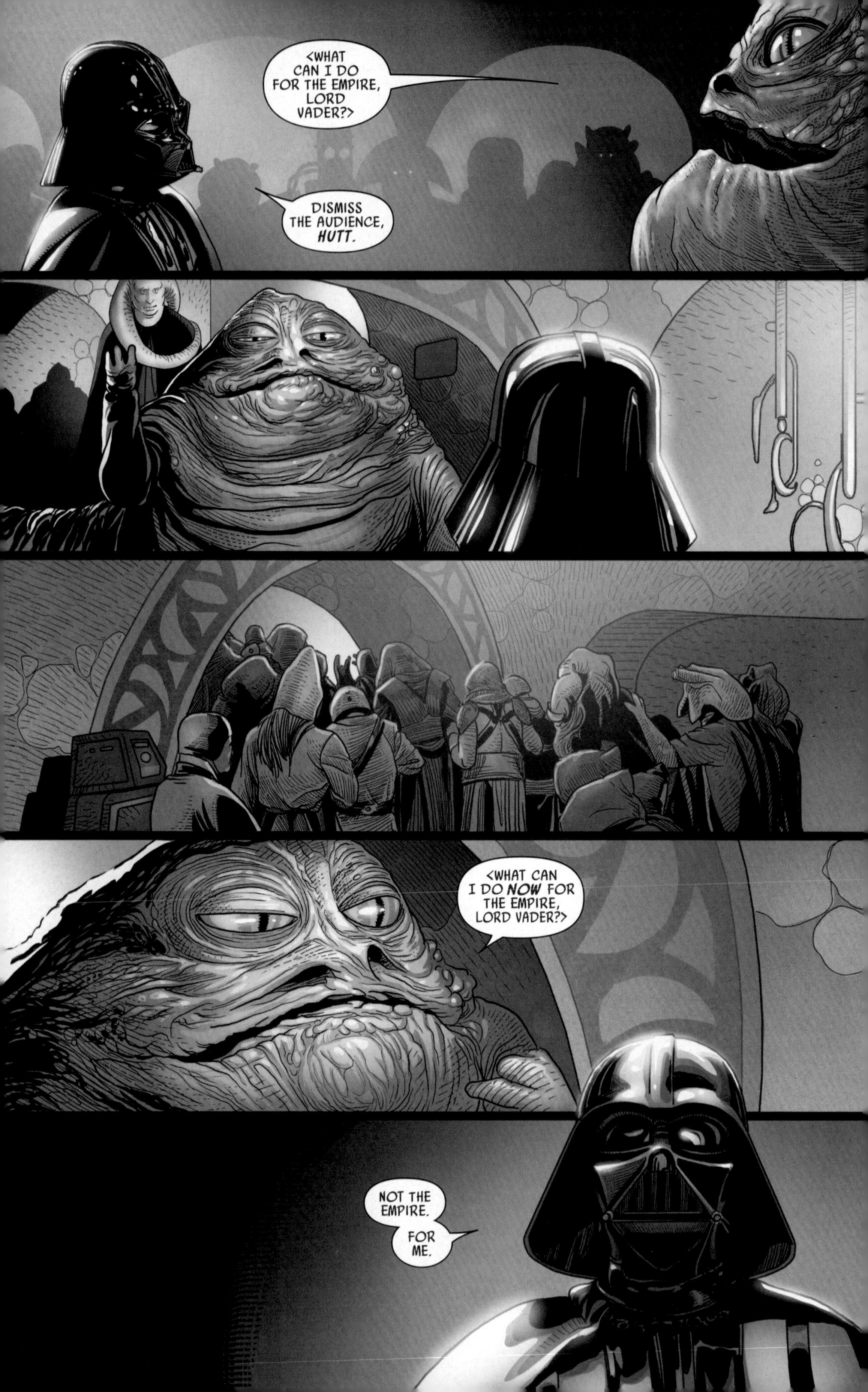
<WHAT CAN I DO FOR THE EMPIRE, LORD VADER?>
DISMISS THE AUDIENCE, *HUTT*.
<WHAT CAN I DO *NOW* FOR THE EMPIRE, LORD VADER?>
NOT THE EMPIRE.
FOR ME.

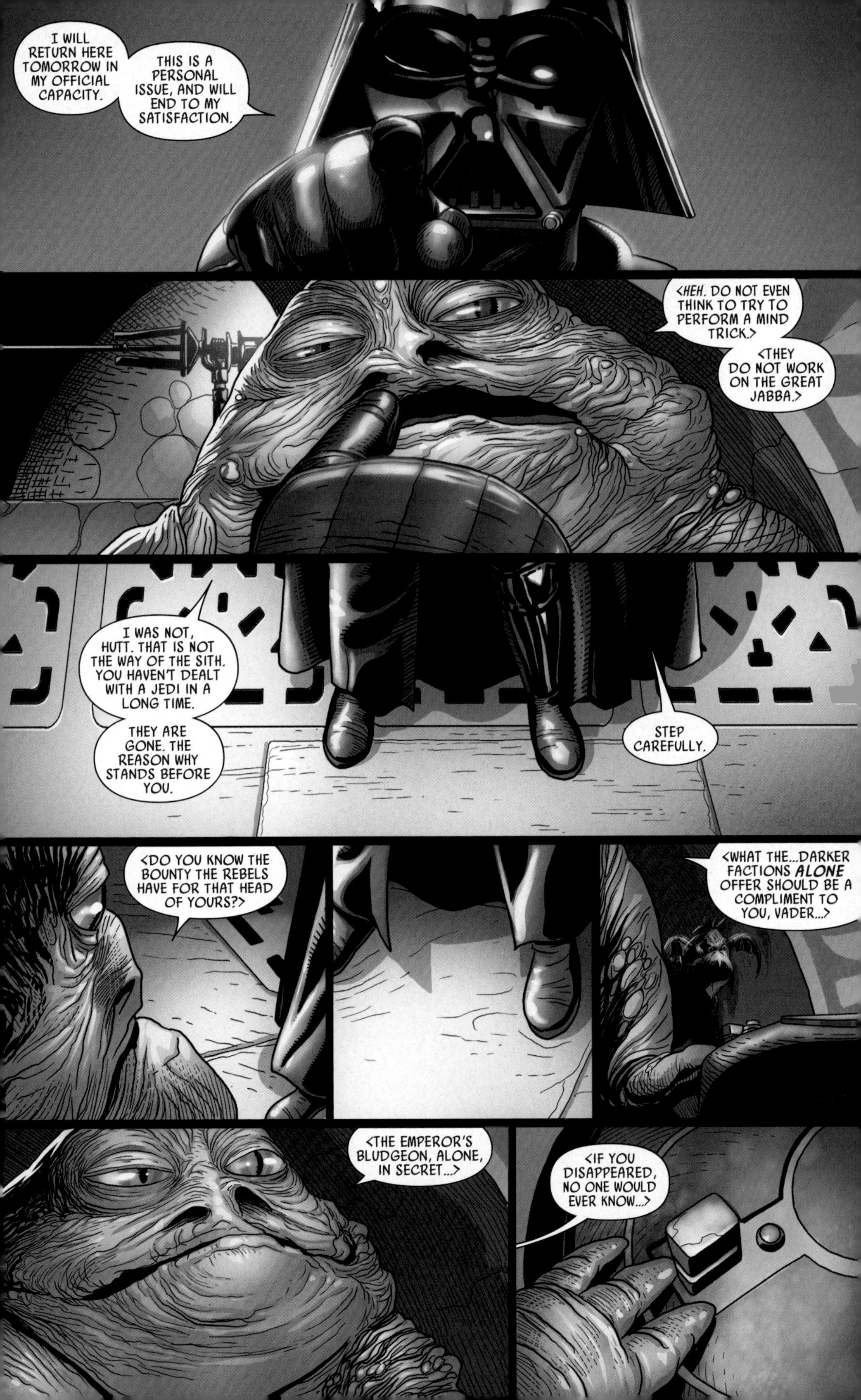
I WILL RETURN HERE TOMORROW IN MY OFFICIAL CAPACITY.
THIS IS A PERSONAL ISSUE, AND WILL END TO MY SATISFACTION.
<HEH. DO NOT EVEN THINK TO TRY TO PERFORM A MIND TRICK.>
<THEY DO NOT WORK ON THE GREAT JABBA.>
I WAS NOT, HUTT. THAT IS NOT THE WAY OF THE SITH. YOU HAVEN'T DEALT WITH A JEDI IN A LONG TIME.
THEY ARE GONE. THE REASON WHY STANDS BEFORE YOU.
STEP CAREFULLY.
<DO YOU KNOW THE BOUNTY THE REBELS HAVE FOR THAT HEAD OF YOURS?>
<WHAT THE...DARKER FACTIONS ***ALONE*** OFFER SHOULD BE A COMPLIMENT TO YOU, VADER...>
<THE EMPEROR'S BLUDGEON, ALONE, IN SECRET...>
<IF YOU DISAPPEARED, NO ONE WOULD EVER KNOW...>

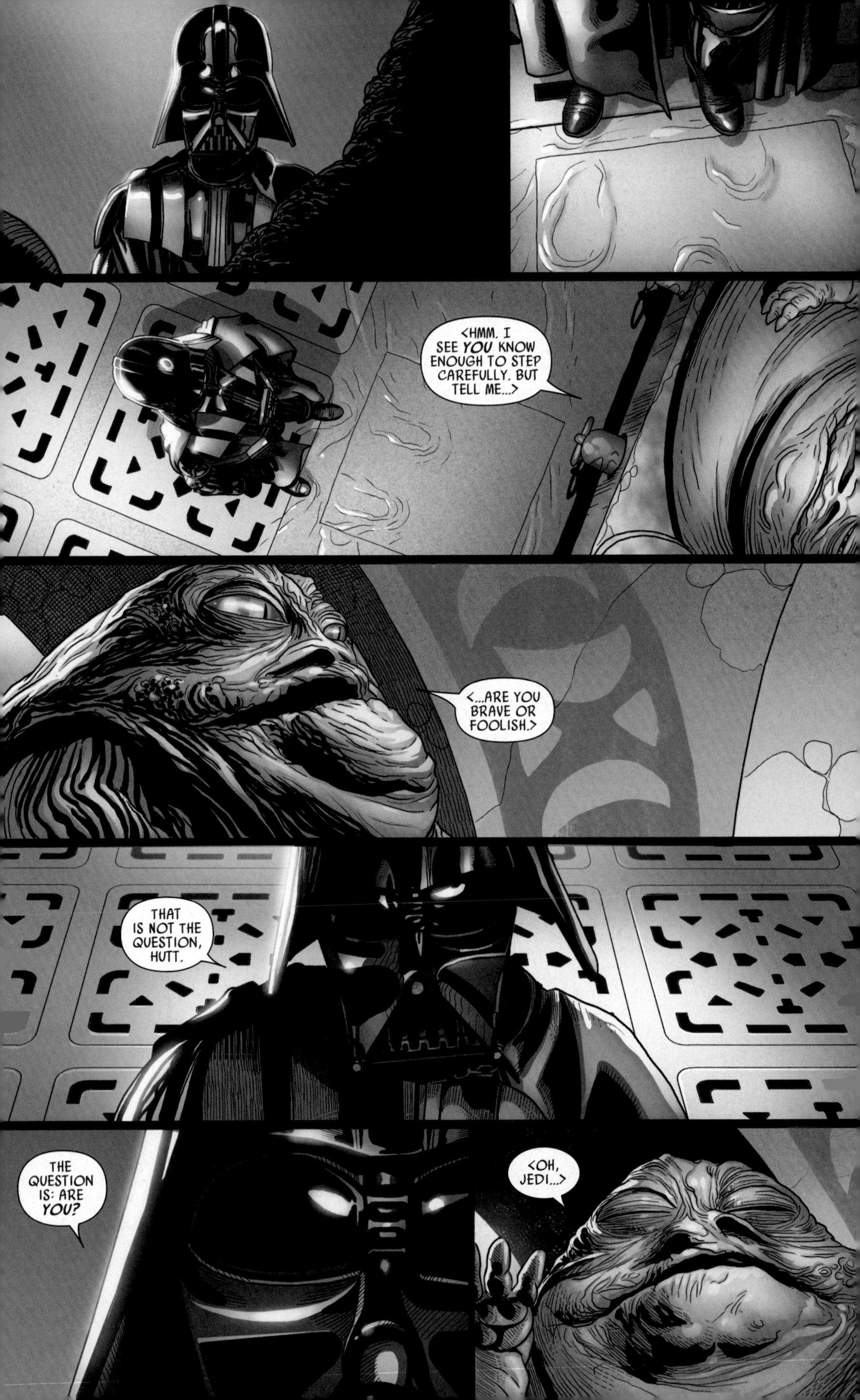
<HMM. I SEE YOU KNOW ENOUGH TO STEP CAREFULLY. BUT TELL ME...>
<...ARE YOU BRAVE OR FOOLISH.>
THAT IS NOT THE QUESTION, HUTT.
THE QUESTION IS: ARE YOU?
<OH, JEDI...>

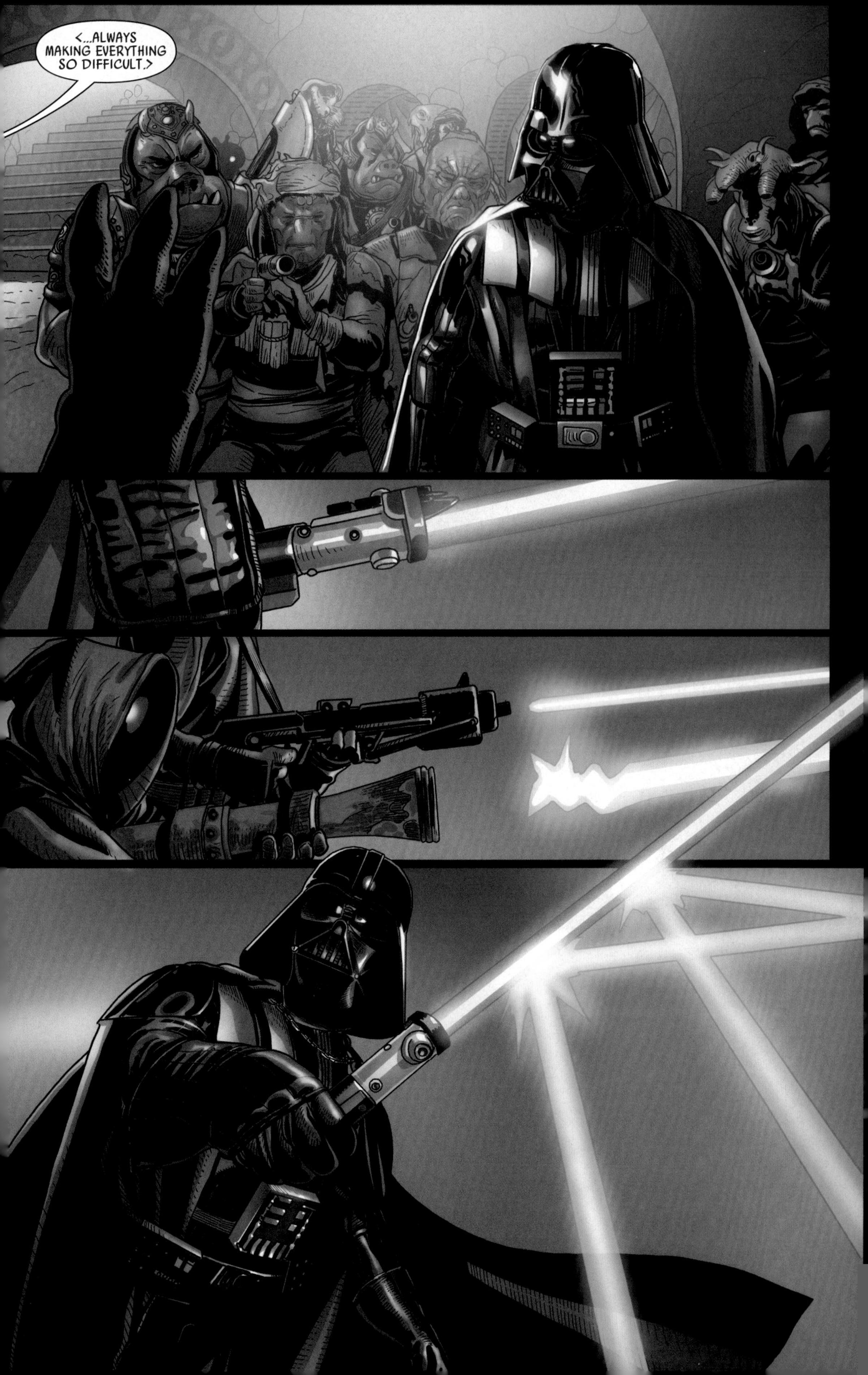
<...ALWAYS MAKING EVERYTHING SO DIFFICULT.>

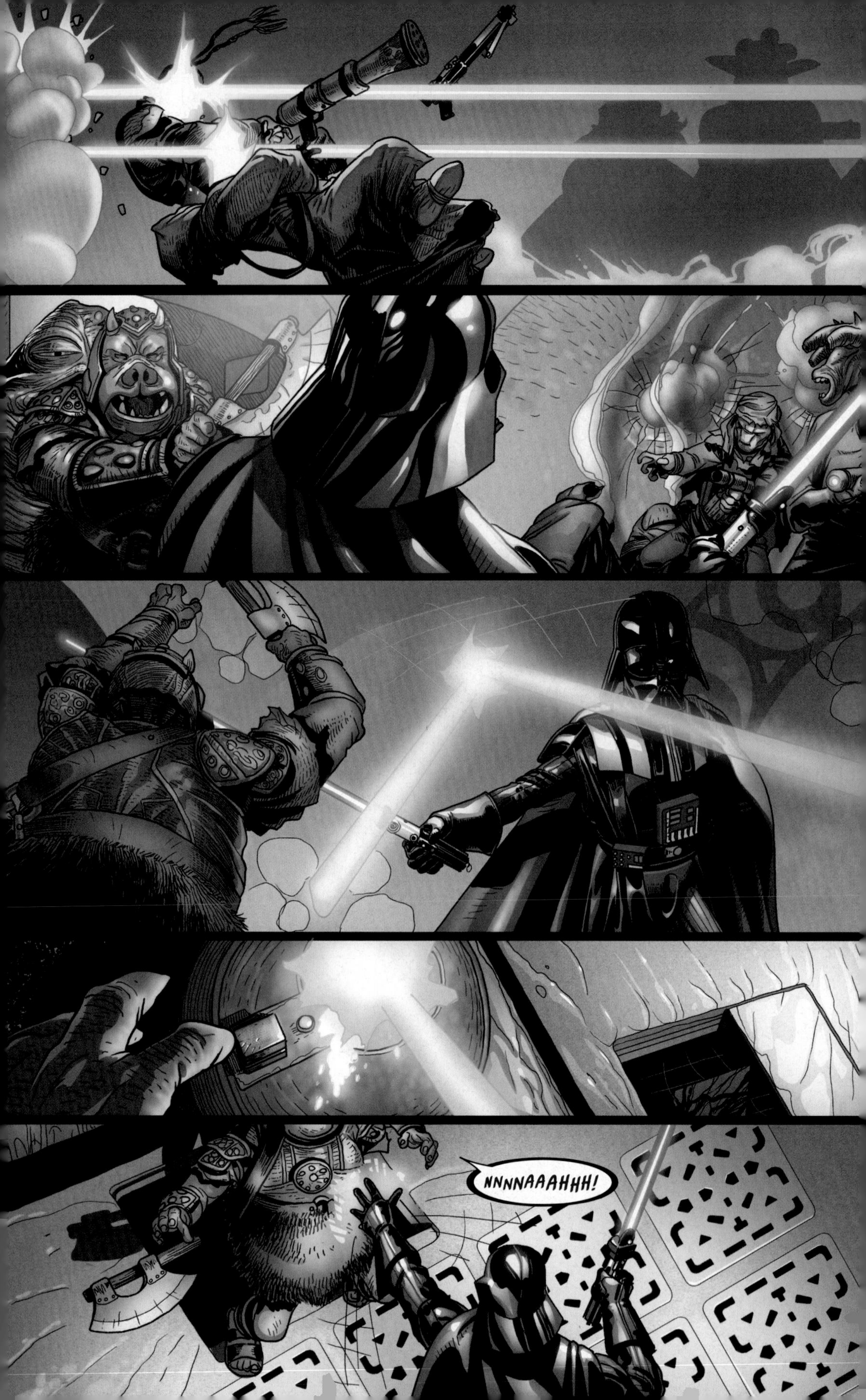
NNNNAAAHHH!

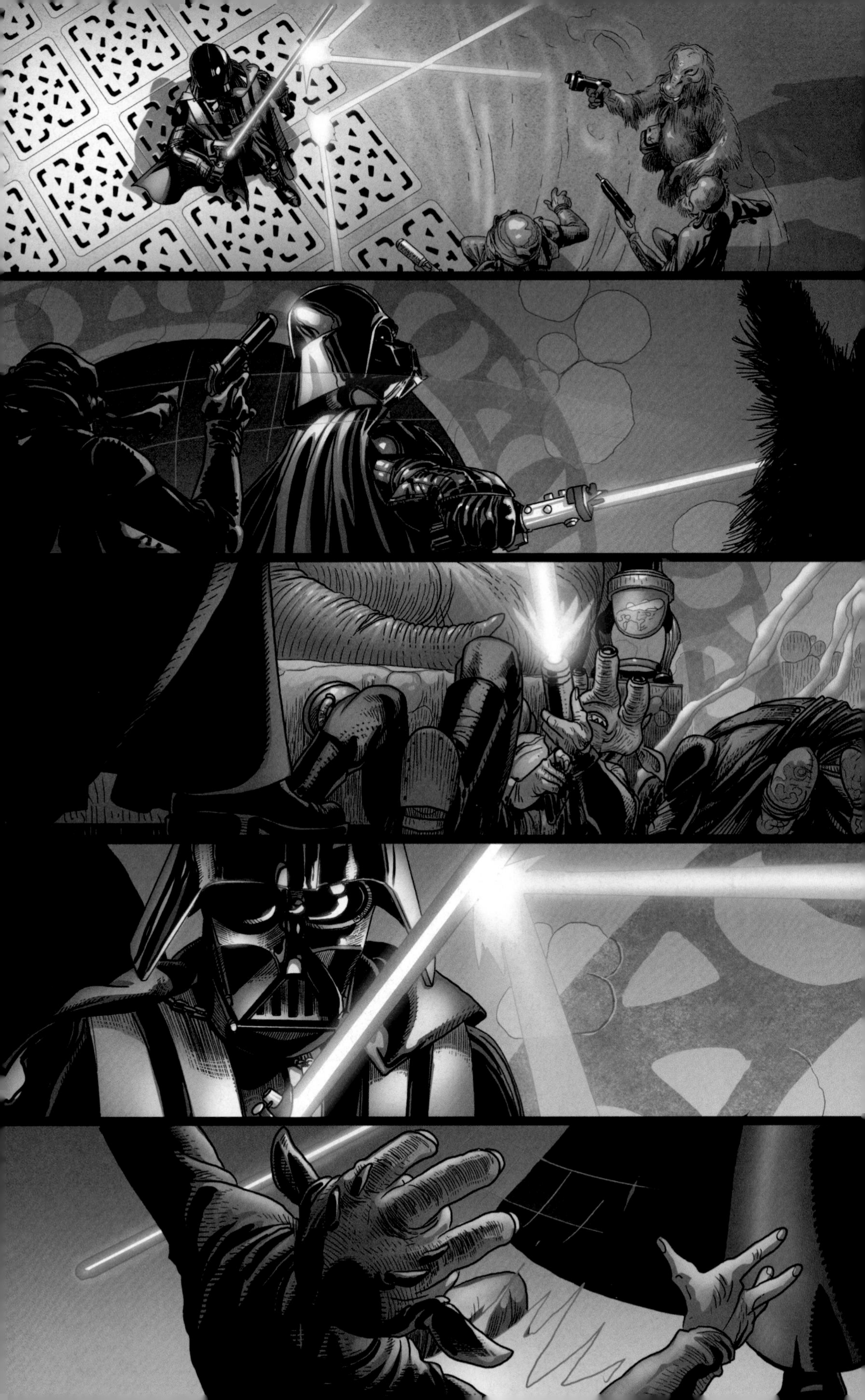

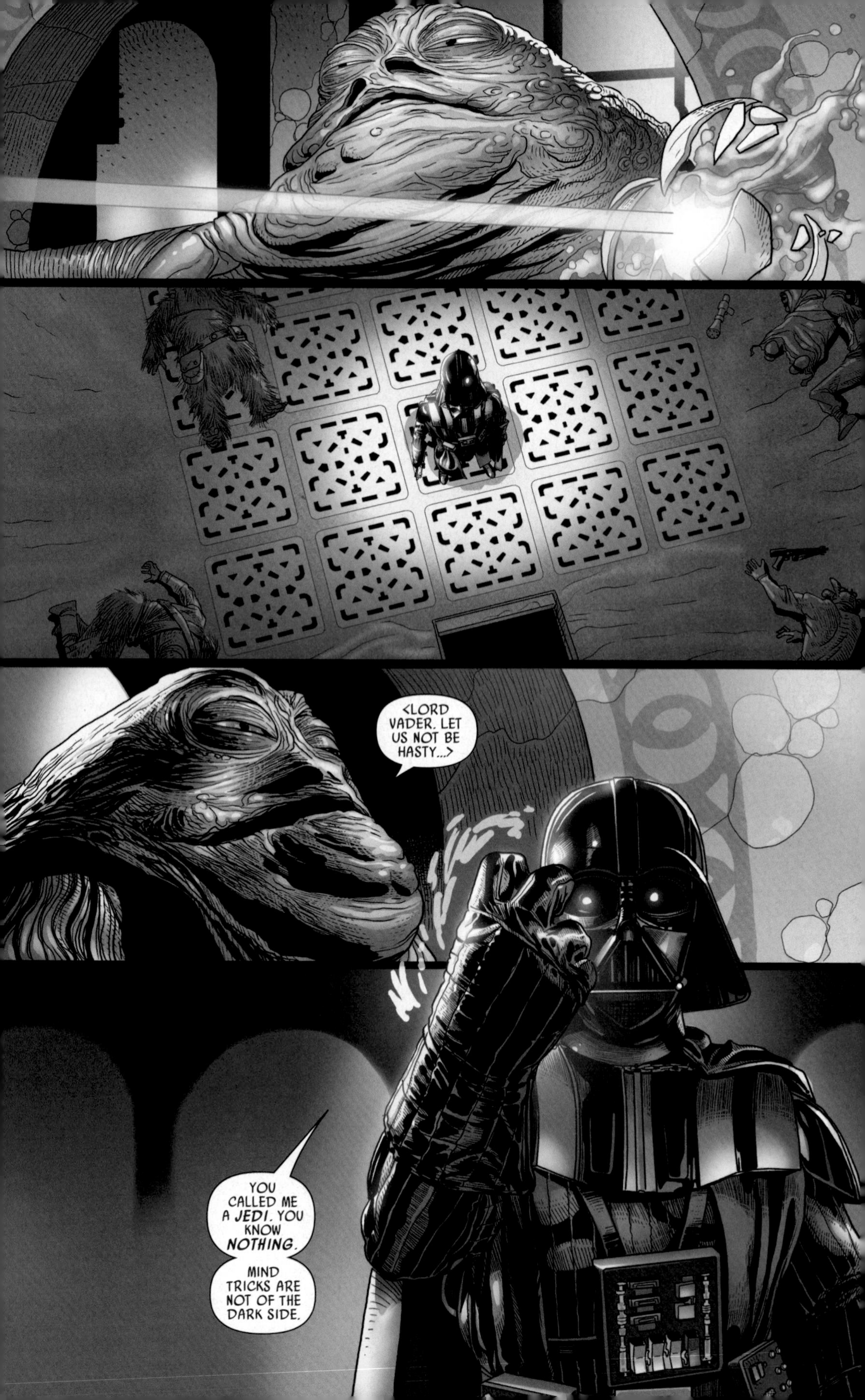
<LORD VADER. LET US NOT BE HASTY...>
YOU CALLED ME A JEDI. YOU KNOW NOTHING.
MIND TRICKS ARE NOT OF THE DARK SIDE.

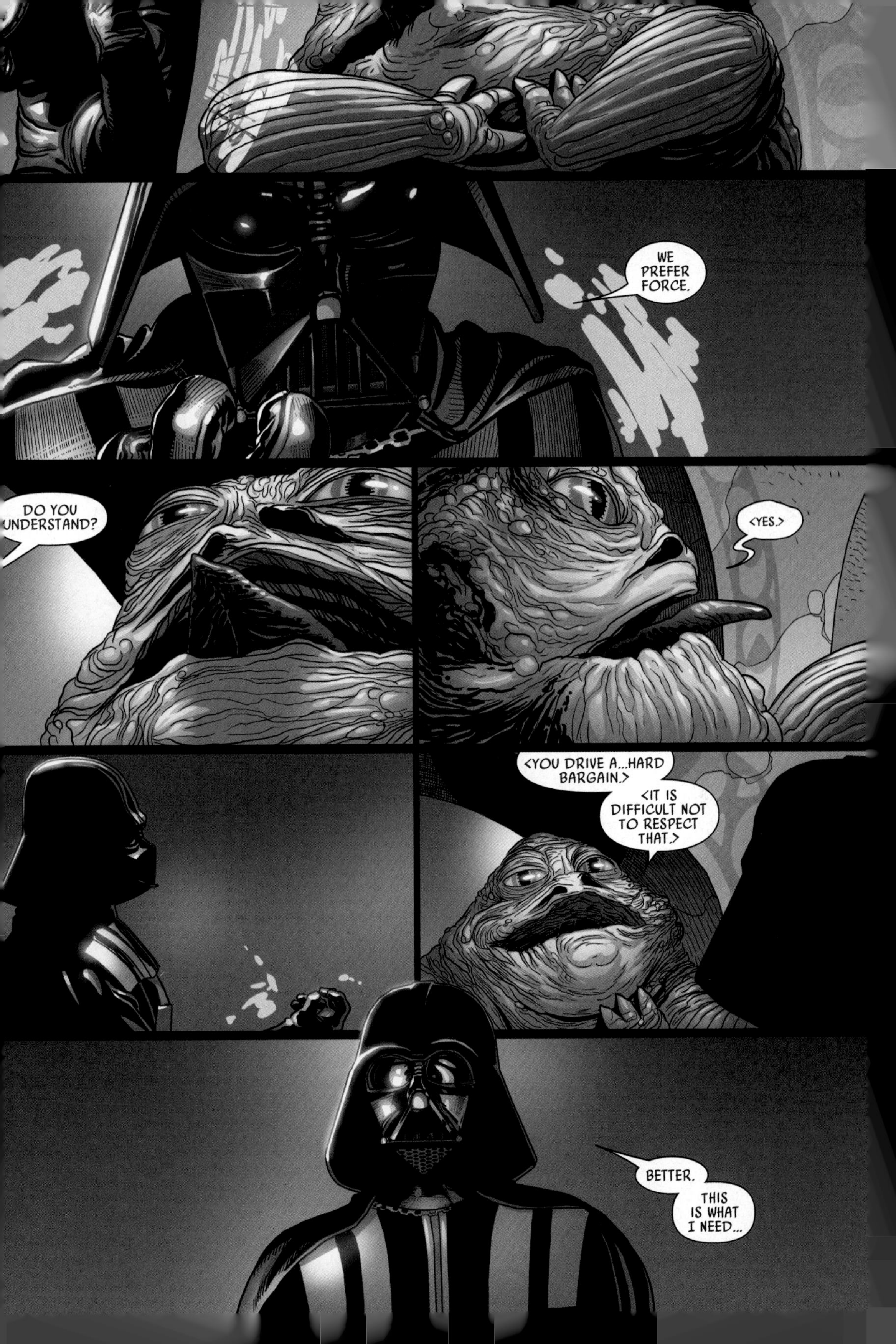
WE PREFER FORCE.
DO YOU UNDERSTAND?
<YES.>
<YOU DRIVE A...HARD BARGAIN.>
<IT IS DIFFICULT NOT TO RESPECT THAT.>
BETTER.
THIS IS WHAT I NEED...

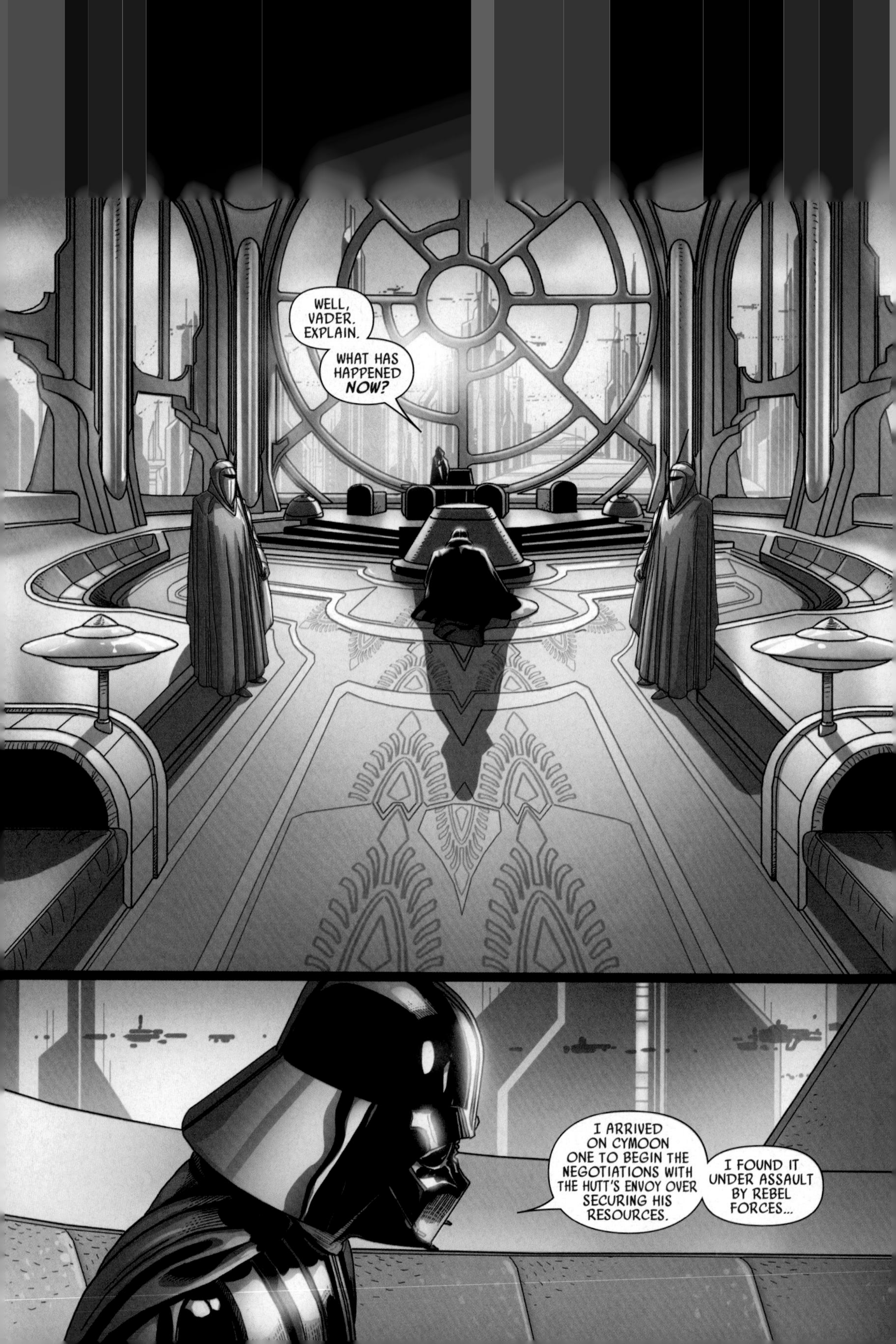
WELL, VADER. EXPLAIN.
WHAT HAS HAPPENED NOW?
I ARRIVED ON CYMOON ONE TO BEGIN THE NEGOTIATIONS WITH THE HUTT'S ENVOY OVER SECURING HIS RESOURCES.
I FOUND IT UNDER ASSAULT BY REBEL FORCES...

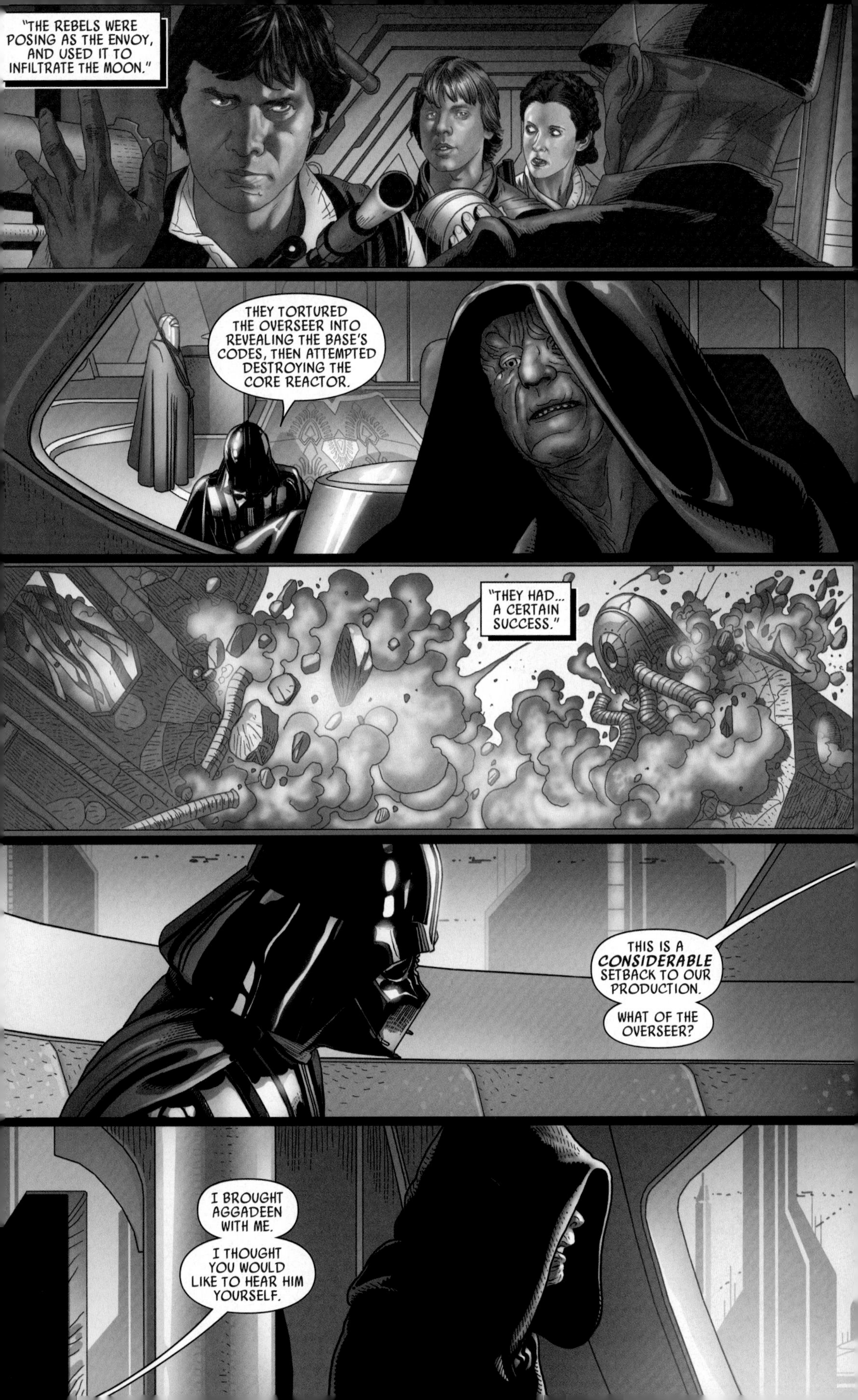
"THE REBELS WERE POSING AS THE ENVOY, AND USED IT TO INFILTRATE THE MOON."
THEY TORTURED THE OVERSEER INTO REVEALING THE BASE'S CODES, THEN ATTEMPTED DESTROYING THE CORE REACTOR.
"THEY HAD... A CERTAIN SUCCESS."
THIS IS A CONSIDERABLE SETBACK TO OUR PRODUCTION.
WHAT OF THE OVERSEER?
I BROUGHT AGGADEEN WITH ME.
I THOUGHT YOU WOULD LIKE TO HEAR HIM YOURSELF.

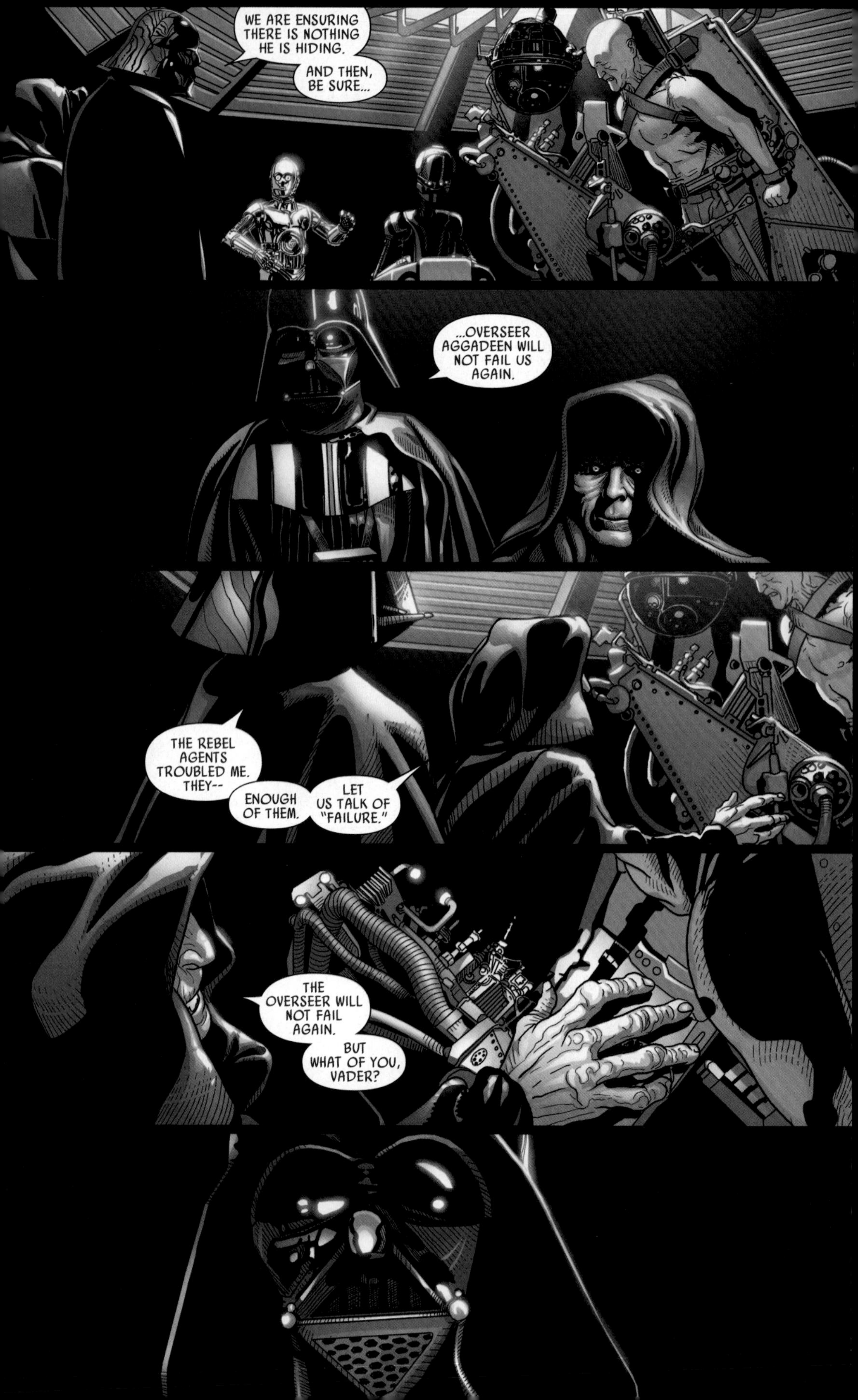
WE ARE ENSURING THERE IS NOTHING HE IS HIDING.
AND THEN, BE SURE...
...OVERSEER AGGADEEN WILL NOT FAIL US AGAIN.
THE REBEL AGENTS TROUBLED ME. THEY--
ENOUGH OF THEM.
LET US TALK OF "FAILURE."
THE OVERSEER WILL NOT FAIL AGAIN.
BUT WHAT OF YOU, VADER?

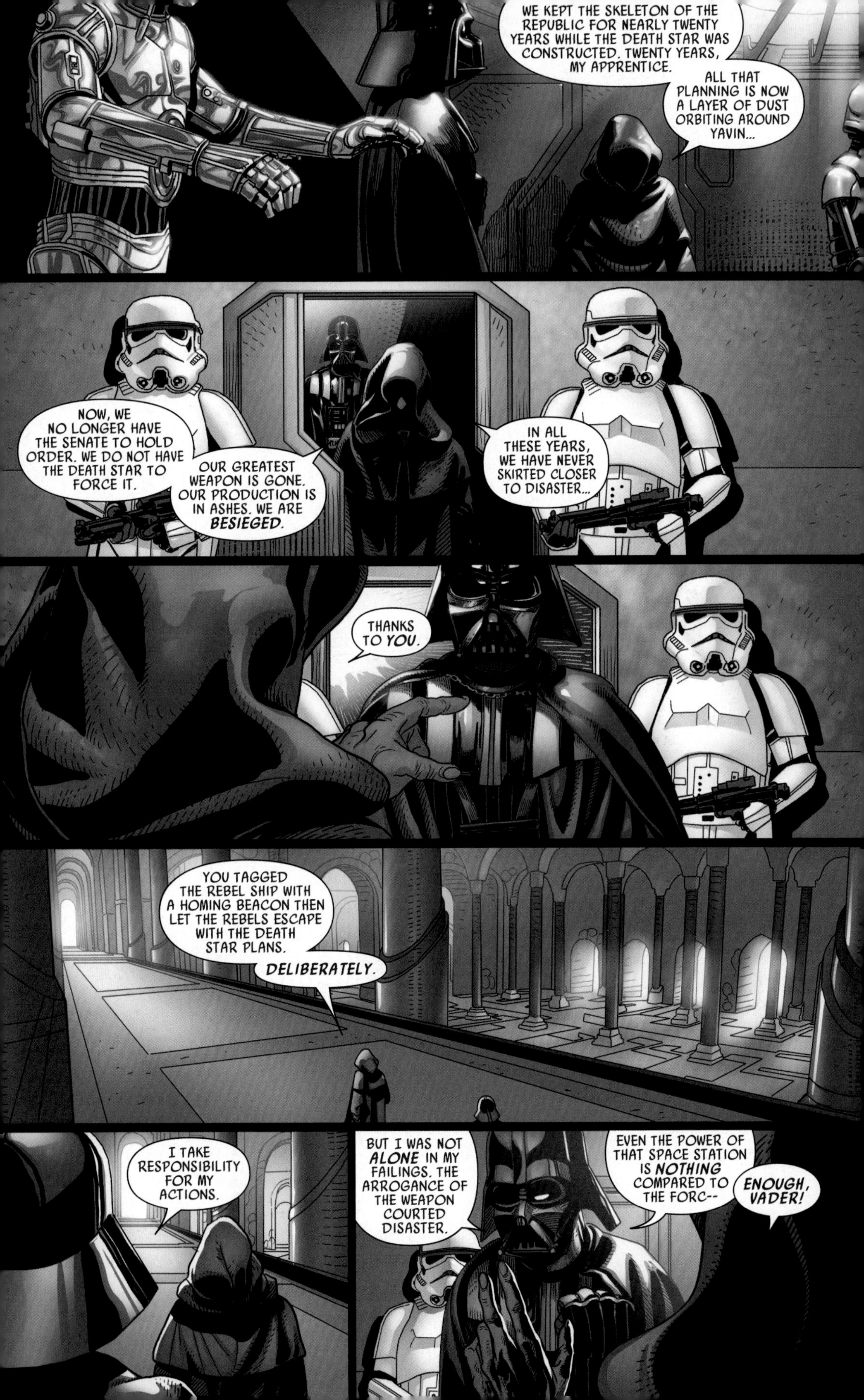
WE KEPT THE SKELETON OF THE REPUBLIC FOR NEARLY TWENTY YEARS WHILE THE DEATH STAR WAS CONSTRUCTED. TWENTY YEARS, MY APPRENTICE.
ALL THAT PLANNING IS NOW A LAYER OF DUST ORBITING AROUND YAVIN...
NOW, WE NO LONGER HAVE THE SENATE TO HOLD ORDER. WE DO NOT HAVE THE DEATH STAR TO FORCE IT.
OUR GREATEST WEAPON IS GONE. OUR PRODUCTION IS IN ASHES. WE ARE *BESIEGED*.
IN ALL THESE YEARS, WE HAVE NEVER SKIRTED CLOSER TO DISASTER...
THANKS TO *YOU*.
YOU TAGGED THE REBEL SHIP WITH A HOMING BEACON THEN LET THE REBELS ESCAPE WITH THE DEATH STAR PLANS.
DELIBERATELY.
I TAKE RESPONSIBILITY FOR MY ACTIONS.
BUT I WAS NOT *ALONE* IN MY FAILINGS. THE ARROGANCE OF THE WEAPON COURTED DISASTER.
EVEN THE POWER OF THAT SPACE STATION IS *NOTHING* COMPARED TO THE FORC--
ENOUGH, VADER!

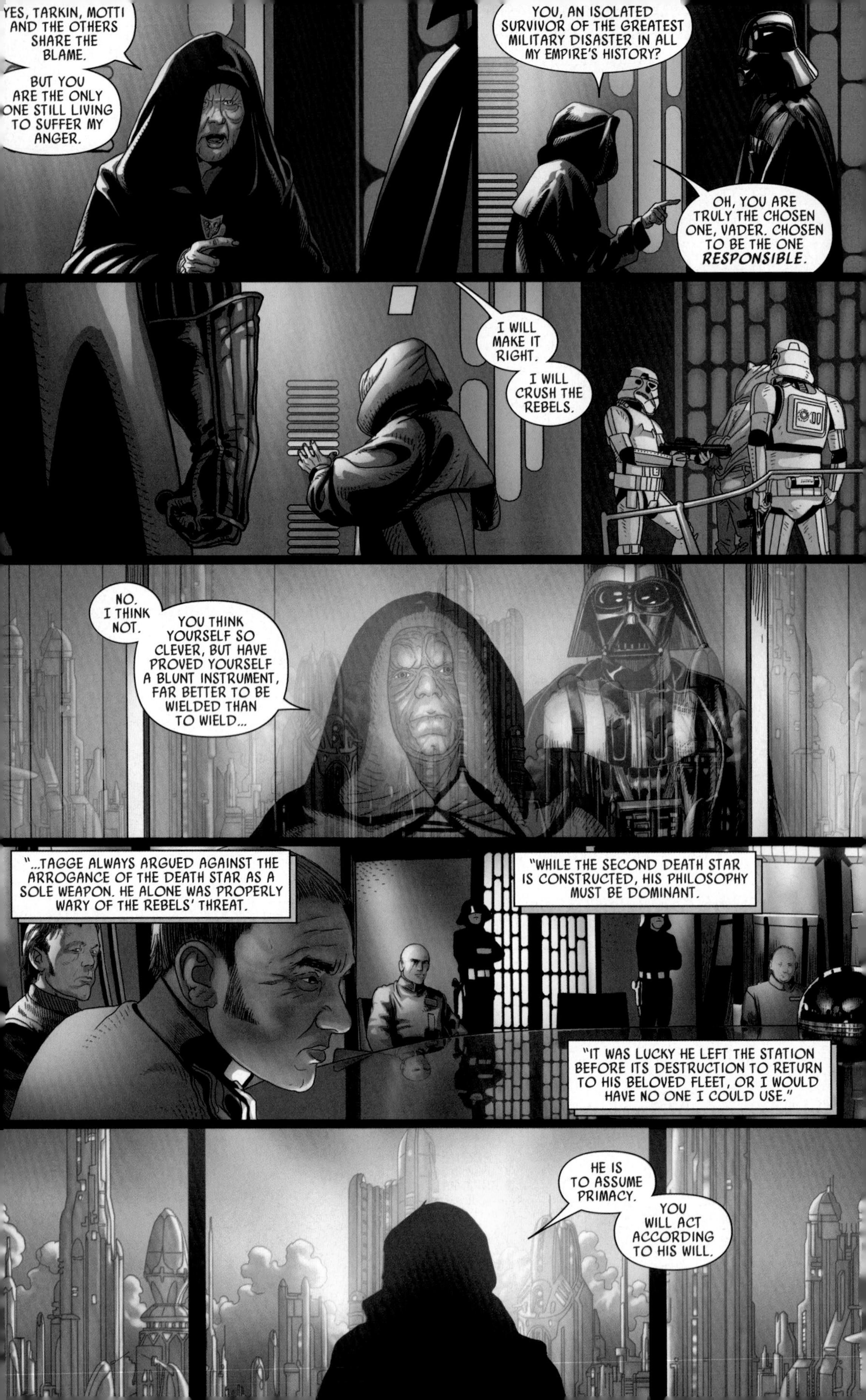

YES, TARKIN, MOTTI AND THE OTHERS SHARE THE BLAME.
BUT YOU ARE THE ONLY ONE STILL LIVING TO SUFFER MY ANGER.
YOU, AN ISOLATED SURVIVOR OF THE GREATEST MILITARY DISASTER IN ALL MY EMPIRE'S HISTORY?
OH, YOU ARE TRULY THE CHOSEN ONE, VADER. CHOSEN TO BE THE ONE *RESPONSIBLE*.
I WILL MAKE IT RIGHT.
I WILL CRUSH THE REBELS.
NO. I THINK NOT.
YOU THINK YOURSELF SO CLEVER, BUT HAVE PROVED YOURSELF A BLUNT INSTRUMENT, FAR BETTER TO BE WIELDED THAN TO WIELD...
"...TAGGE ALWAYS ARGUED AGAINST THE ARROGANCE OF THE DEATH STAR AS A SOLE WEAPON. HE ALONE WAS PROPERLY WARY OF THE REBELS' THREAT.
"WHILE THE SECOND DEATH STAR IS CONSTRUCTED, HIS PHILOSOPHY MUST BE DOMINANT.
"IT WAS LUCKY HE LEFT THE STATION BEFORE ITS DESTRUCTION TO RETURN TO HIS BELOVED FLEET, OR I WOULD HAVE NO ONE I COULD USE."
HE IS TO ASSUME PRIMACY.
YOU WILL ACT ACCORDING TO HIS WILL.

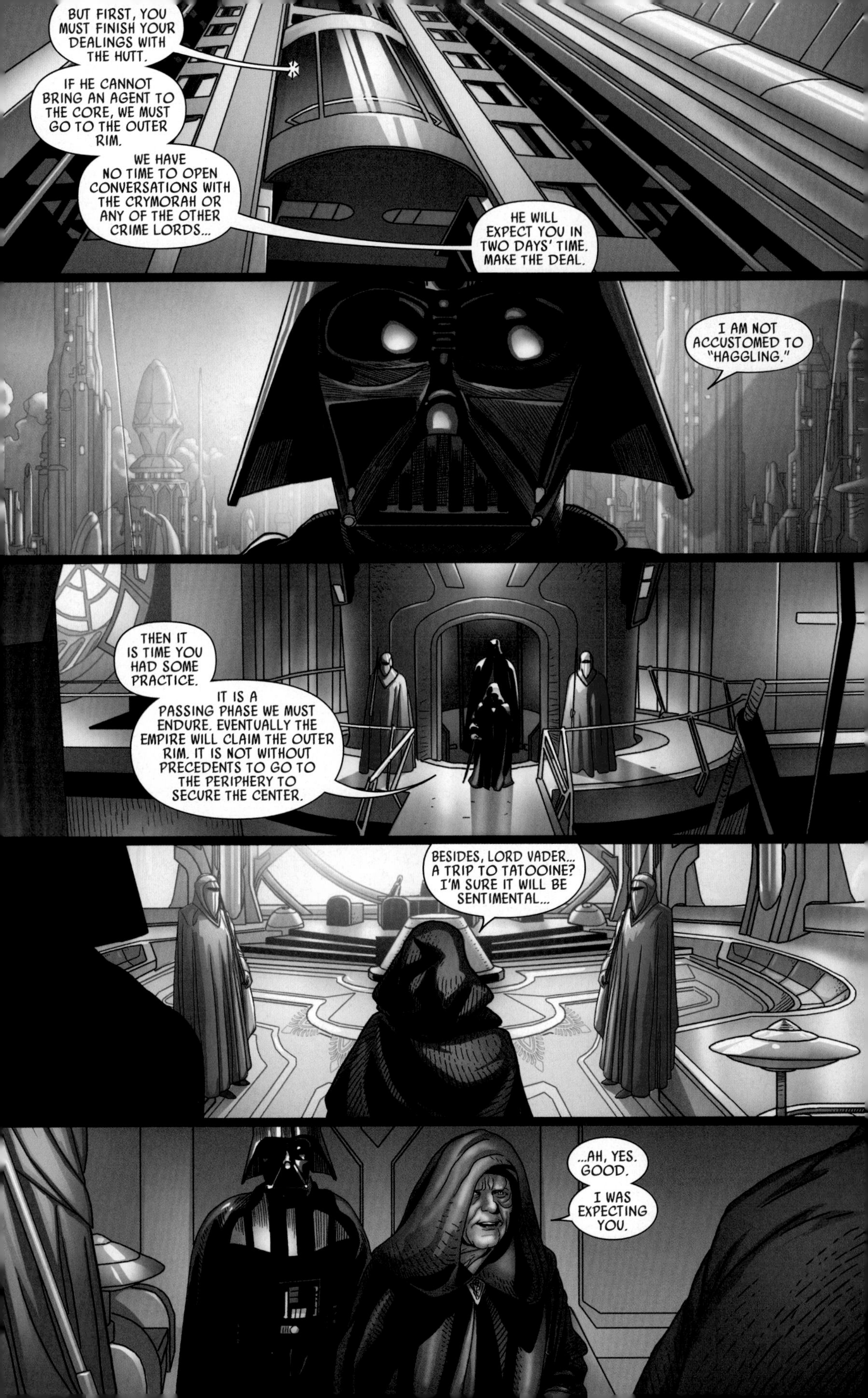
BUT FIRST, YOU MUST FINISH YOUR DEALINGS WITH THE HUTT.
IF HE CANNOT BRING AN AGENT TO THE CORE, WE MUST GO TO THE OUTER RIM.
WE HAVE NO TIME TO OPEN CONVERSATIONS WITH THE CRYMORAH OR ANY OF THE OTHER CRIME LORDS...
HE WILL EXPECT YOU IN TWO DAYS' TIME. MAKE THE DEAL.
I AM NOT ACCUSTOMED TO "HAGGLING."
THEN IT IS TIME YOU HAD SOME PRACTICE.
IT IS A PASSING PHASE WE MUST ENDURE. EVENTUALLY THE EMPIRE WILL CLAIM THE OUTER RIM. IT IS NOT WITHOUT PRECEDENTS TO GO TO THE PERIPHERY TO SECURE THE CENTER.
BESIDES, LORD VADER... A TRIP TO TATOOINE? I'M SURE IT WILL BE SENTIMENTAL...
...AH, YES. GOOD.
I WAS EXPECTING YOU.

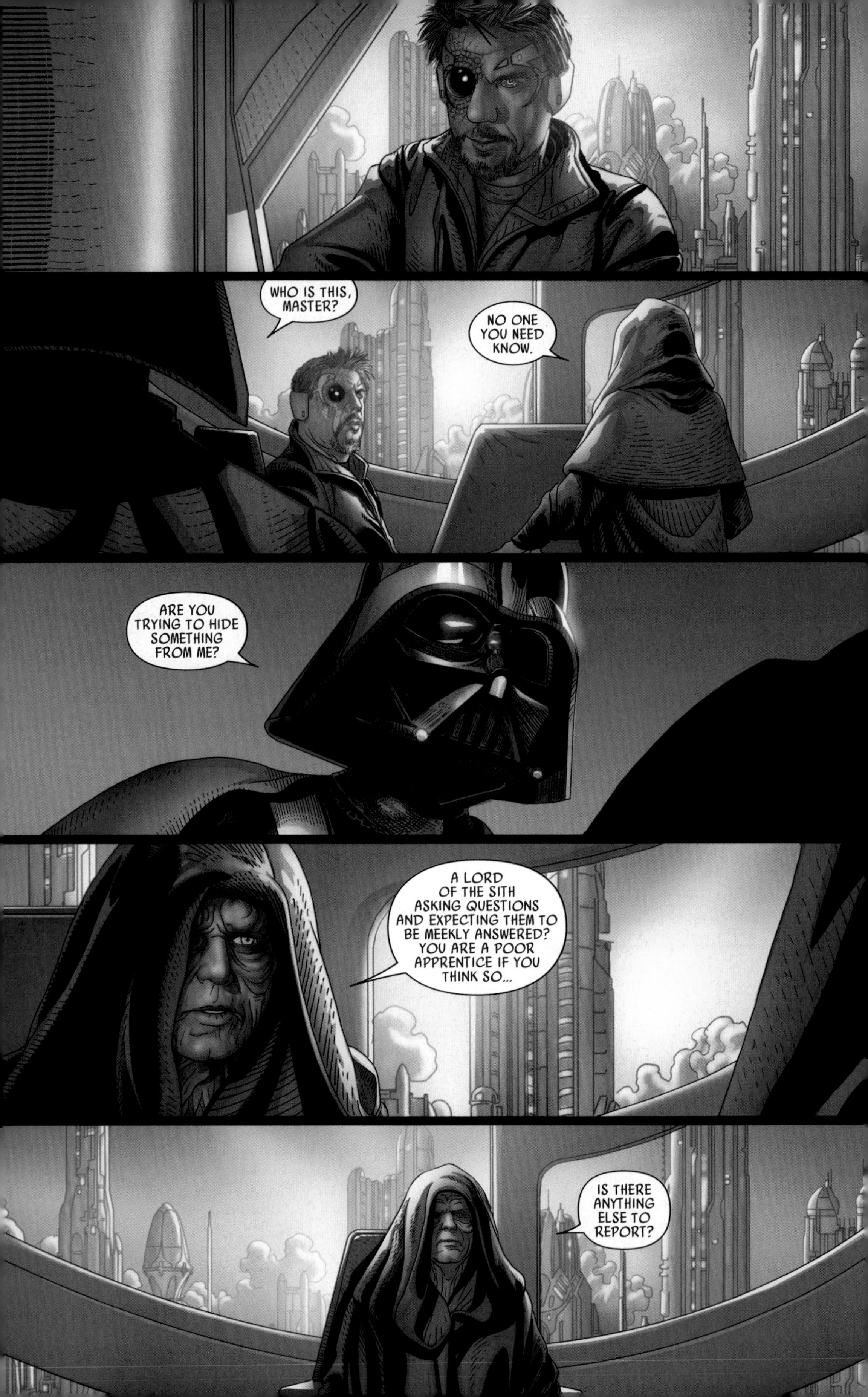
WHO IS THIS, MASTER?
NO ONE YOU NEED KNOW.
ARE YOU TRYING TO HIDE SOMETHING FROM ME?
A LORD OF THE SITH ASKING QUESTIONS AND EXPECTING THEM TO BE MEEKLY ANSWERED? YOU ARE A POOR APPRENTICE IF YOU THINK SO...
IS THERE ANYTHING ELSE TO REPORT?

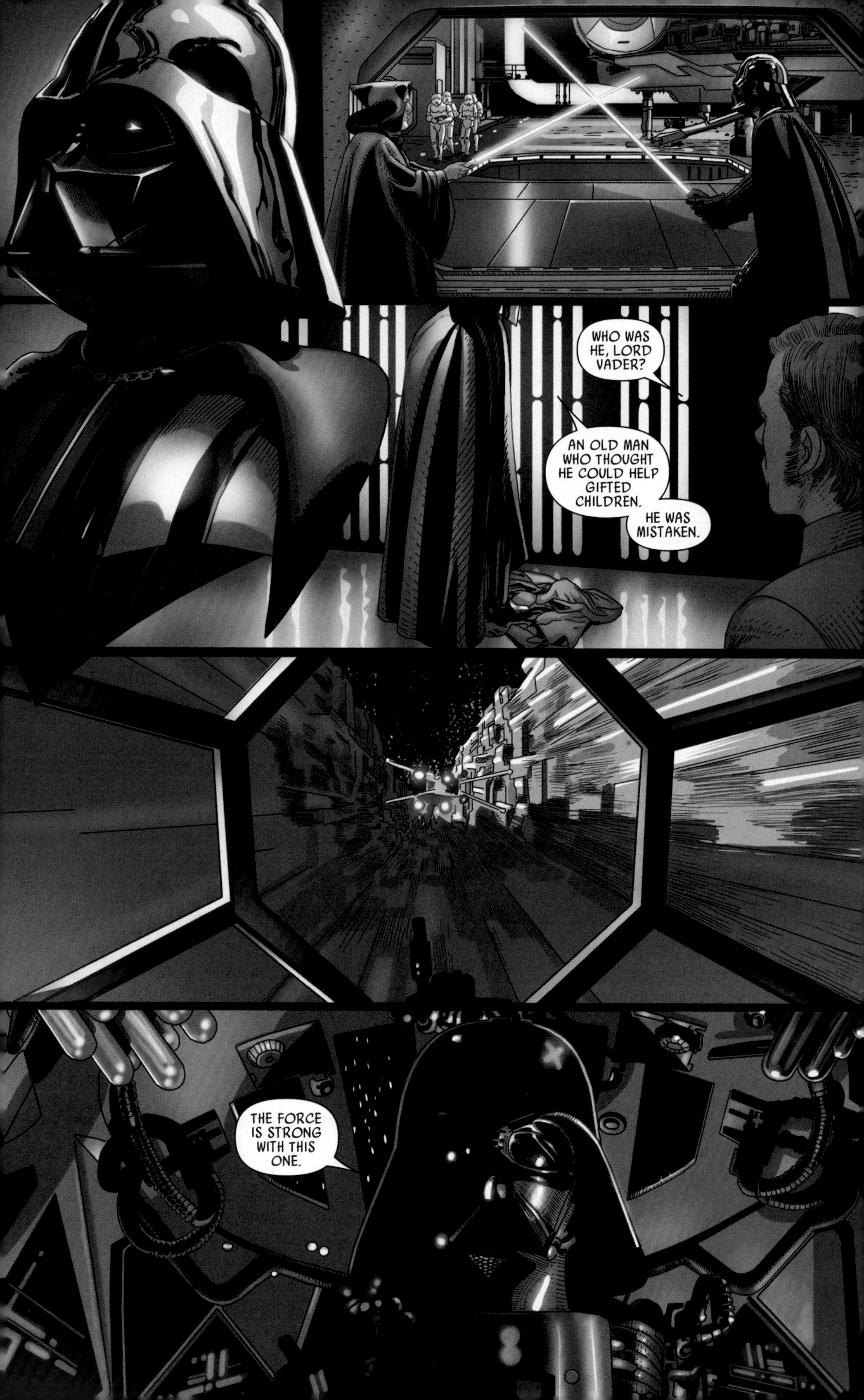
WHO WAS HE, LORD VADER?
AN OLD MAN WHO THOUGHT HE COULD HELP GIFTED CHILDREN.
HE WAS MISTAKEN.
THE FORCE IS STRONG WITH THIS ONE.

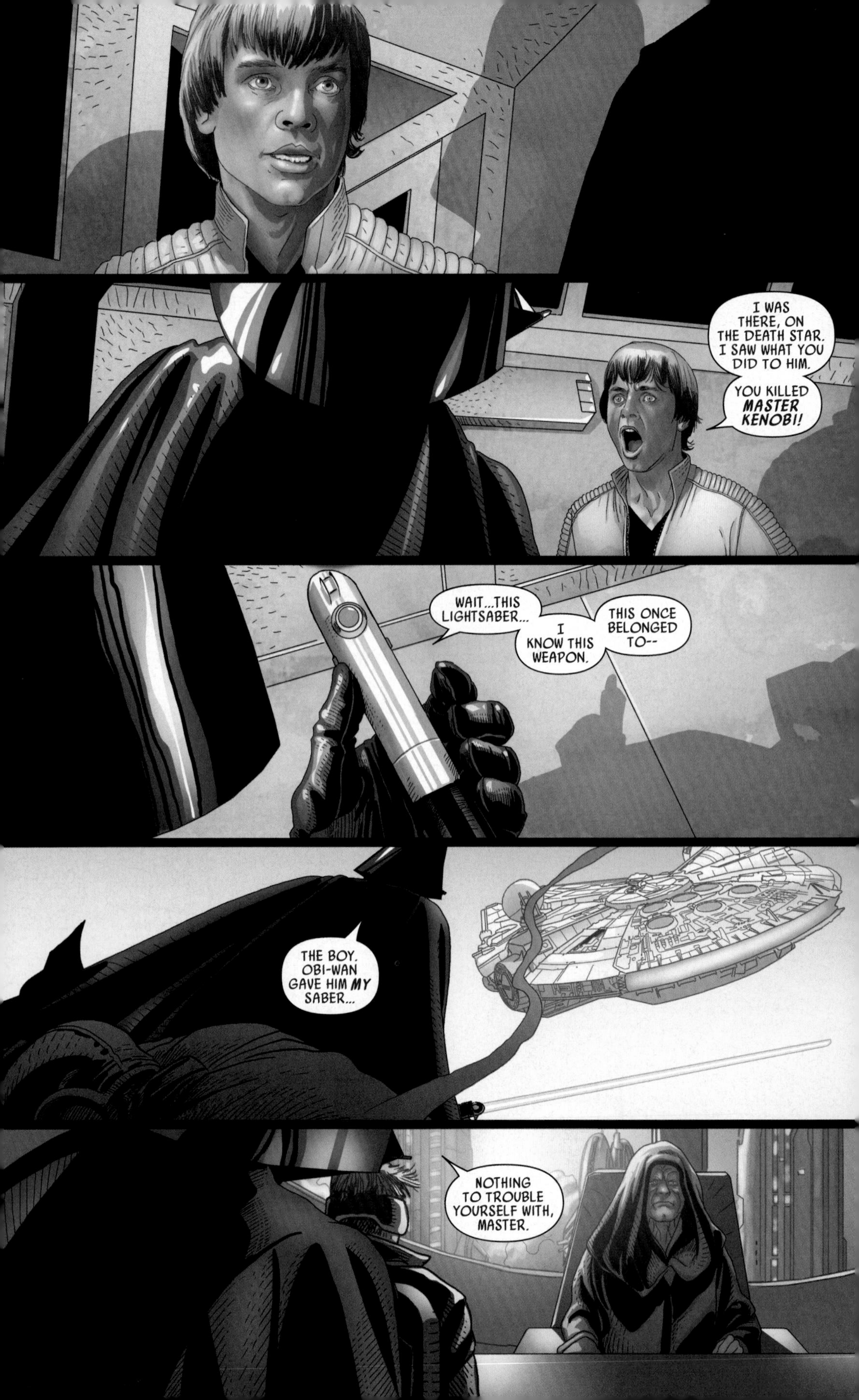
I WAS THERE, ON THE DEATH STAR. I SAW WHAT YOU DID TO HIM.
YOU KILLED MASTER KENOBI!
WAIT...THIS LIGHTSABER...
I KNOW THIS WEAPON.
THIS ONCE BELONGED TO--
THE BOY. OBI-WAN GAVE HIM MY SABER...
NOTHING TO TROUBLE YOURSELF WITH, MASTER.

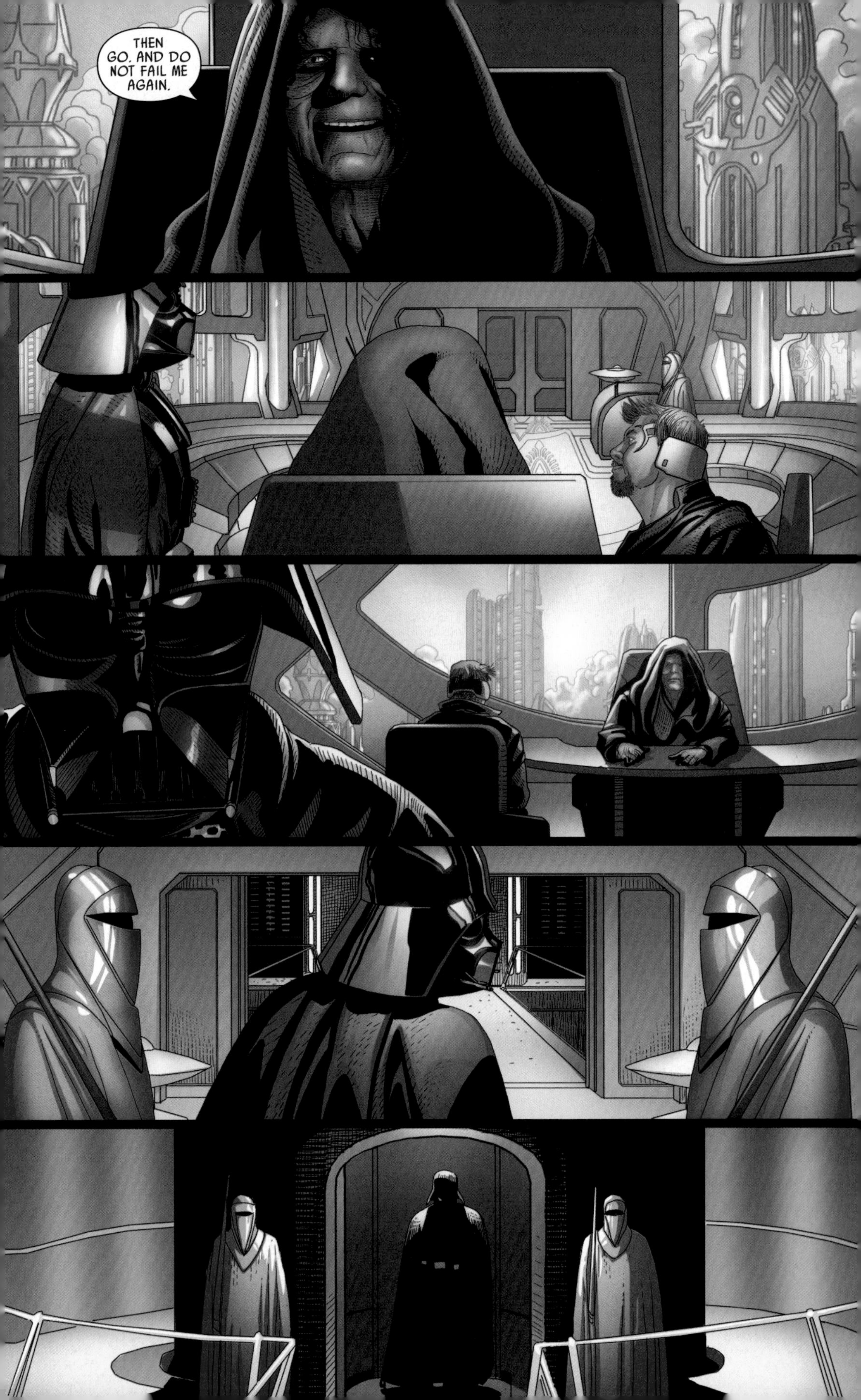
THEN GO. AND DO NOT FAIL ME AGAIN.

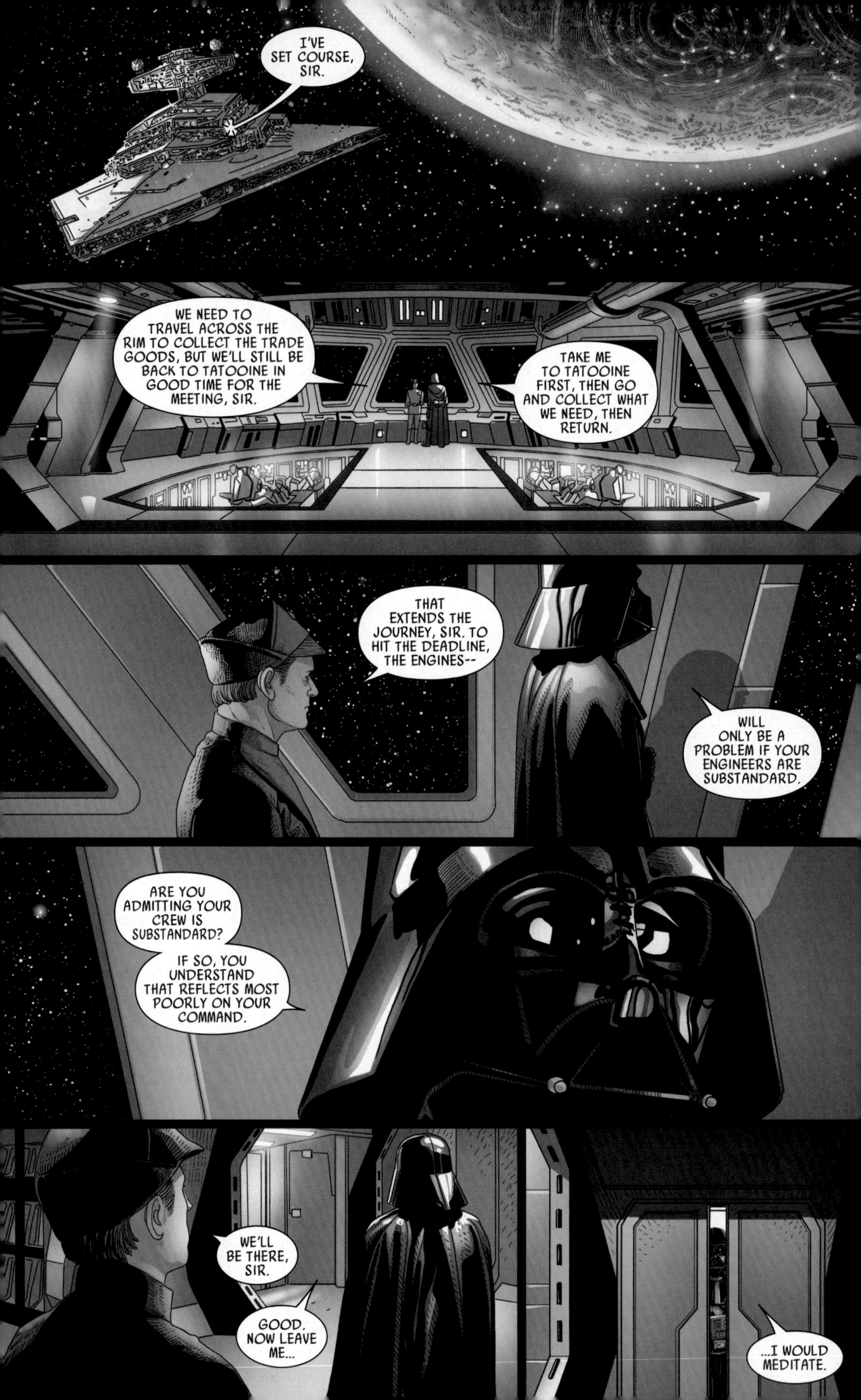
I'VE SET COURSE, SIR.
WE NEED TO TRAVEL ACROSS THE RIM TO COLLECT THE TRADE GOODS, BUT WE'LL STILL BE BACK TO TATOOINE IN GOOD TIME FOR THE MEETING, SIR.
TAKE ME TO TATOOINE FIRST, THEN GO AND COLLECT WHAT WE NEED, THEN RETURN.
THAT EXTENDS THE JOURNEY, SIR. TO HIT THE DEADLINE, THE ENGINES--
WILL ONLY BE A PROBLEM IF YOUR ENGINEERS ARE SUBSTANDARD.
ARE YOU ADMITTING YOUR CREW IS SUBSTANDARD?
IF SO, YOU UNDERSTAND THAT REFLECTS MOST POORLY ON YOUR COMMAND.
WE'LL BE THERE, SIR.
GOOD. NOW LEAVE ME...
...I WOULD MEDITATE.

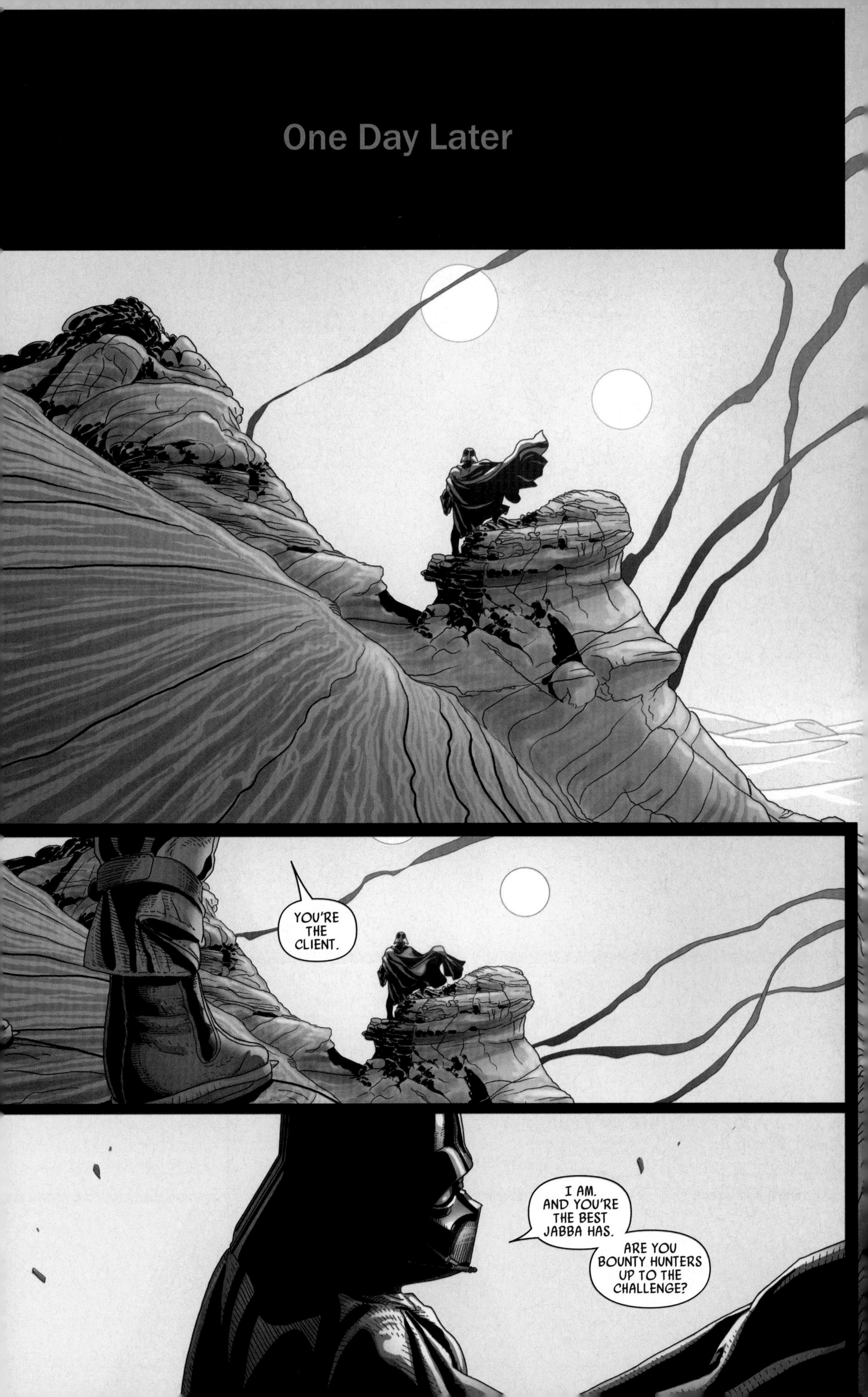
One Day Later
YOU'RE THE CLIENT.
I AM. AND YOU'RE THE BEST JABBA HAS.
ARE YOU BOUNTY HUNTERS UP TO THE CHALLENGE?

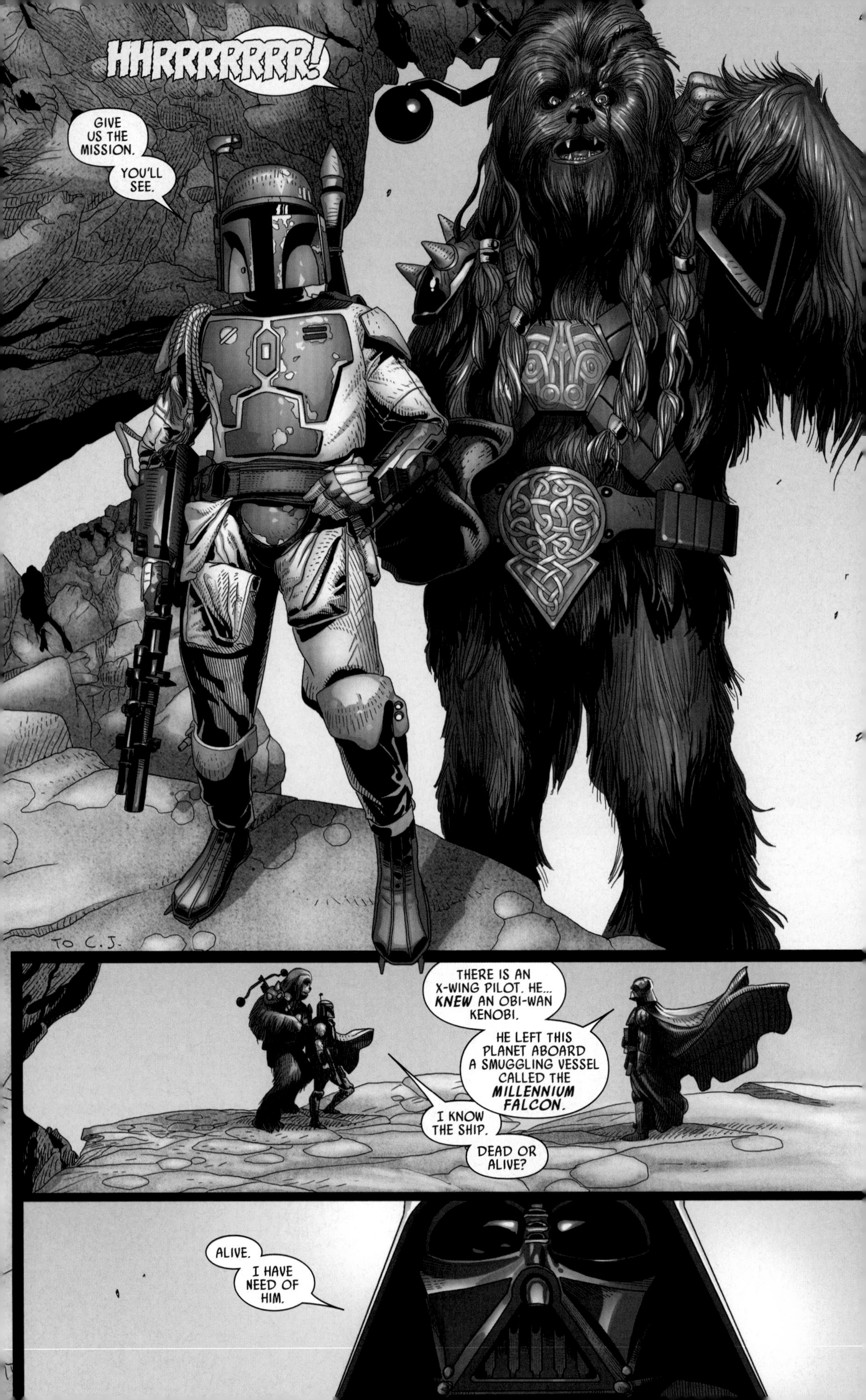
HHRRRRRRR!
GIVE US THE MISSION.
YOU'LL SEE.
TO C.J.
THERE IS AN X-WING PILOT. HE... KNEW AN OBI-WAN KENOBI.
HE LEFT THIS PLANET ABOARD A SMUGGLING VESSEL CALLED THE MILLENNIUM FALCON.
I KNOW THE SHIP.
DEAD OR ALIVE?
ALIVE.
I HAVE NEED OF HIM.

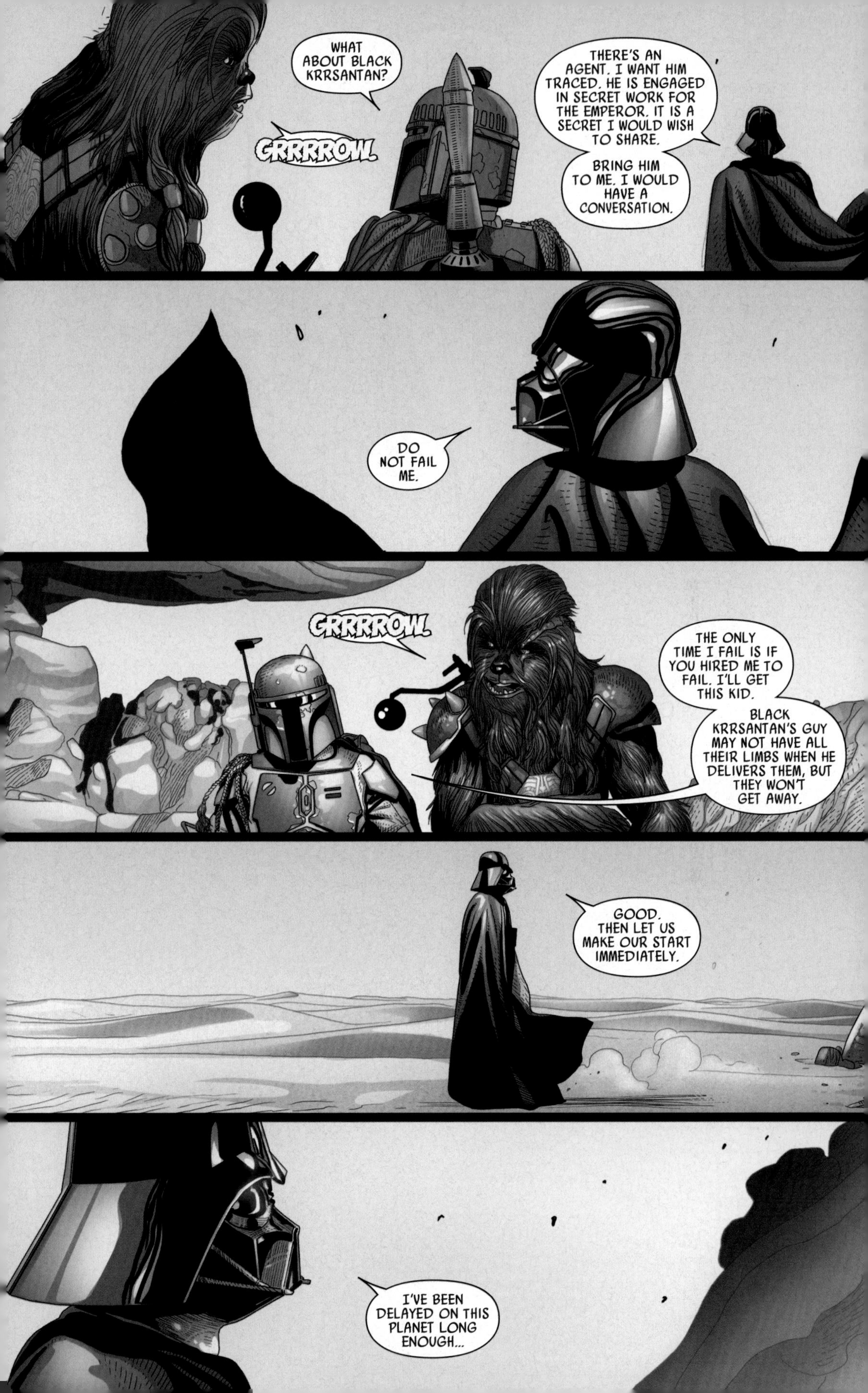
WHAT ABOUT BLACK KRRSANTAN?
GRRRROW!
THERE'S AN AGENT. I WANT HIM TRACED. HE IS ENGAGED IN SECRET WORK FOR THE EMPEROR. IT IS A SECRET I WOULD WISH TO SHARE.
BRING HIM TO ME. I WOULD HAVE A CONVERSATION.
DO NOT FAIL ME.
GRRRROW!
THE ONLY TIME I FAIL IS IF YOU HIRED ME TO FAIL. I'LL GET THIS KID.
BLACK KRRSANTAN'S GUY MAY NOT HAVE ALL THEIR LIMBS WHEN HE DELIVERS THEM, BUT THEY WON'T GET AWAY.
GOOD. THEN LET US MAKE OUR START IMMEDIATELY.
I'VE BEEN DELAYED ON THIS PLANET LONG ENOUGH...

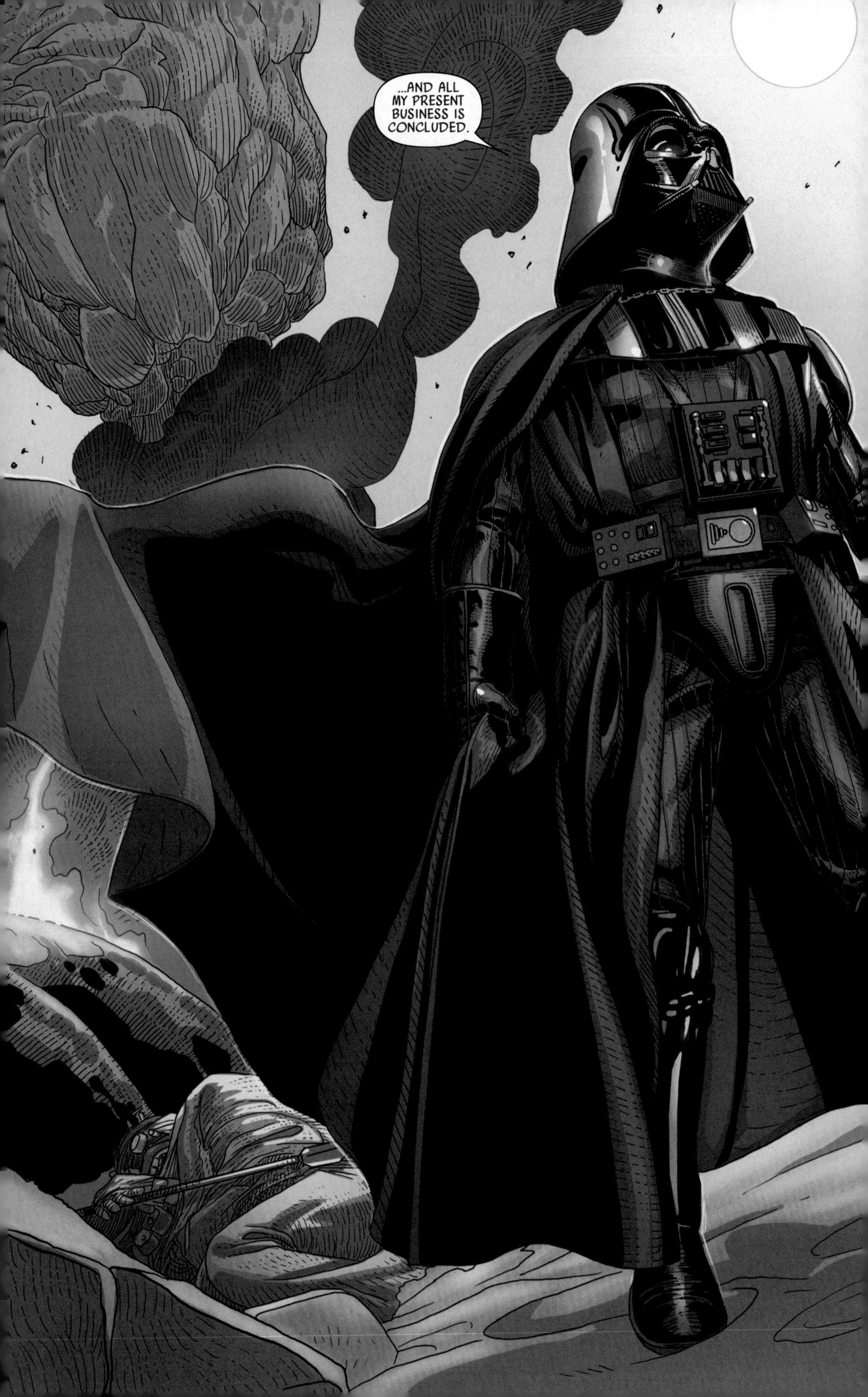
...AND ALL MY PRESENT BUSINESS IS CONCLUDED.

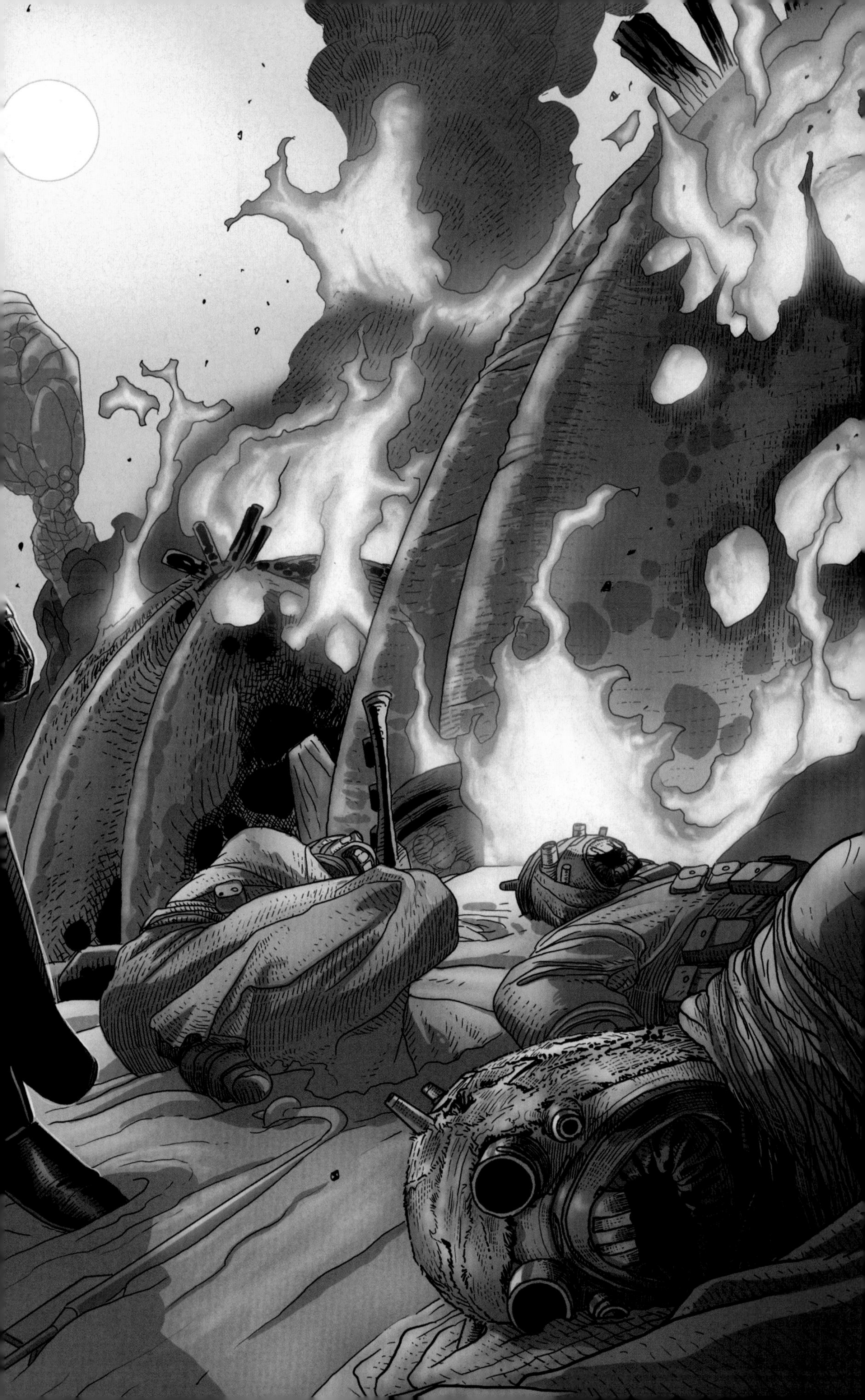

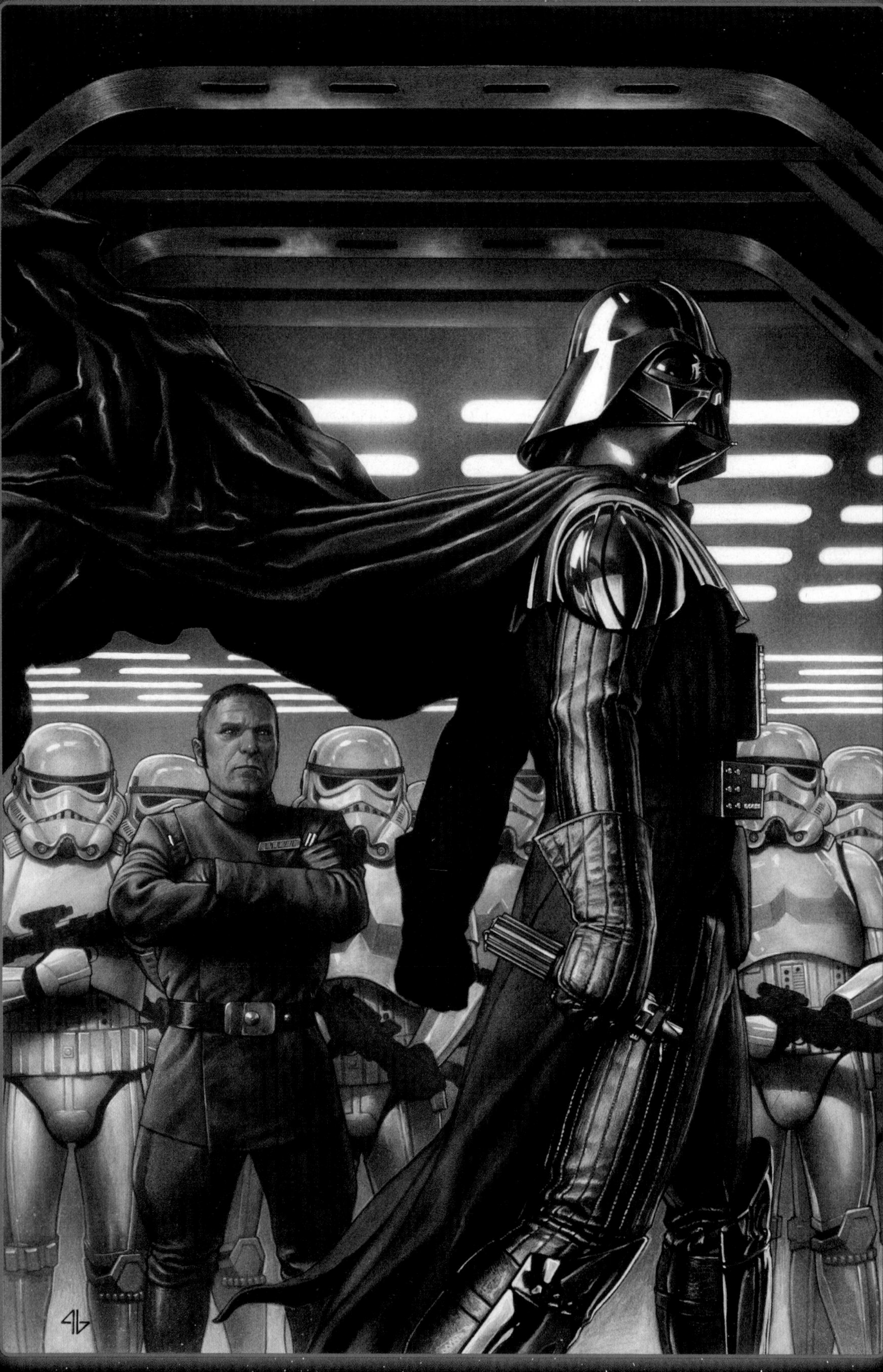

2

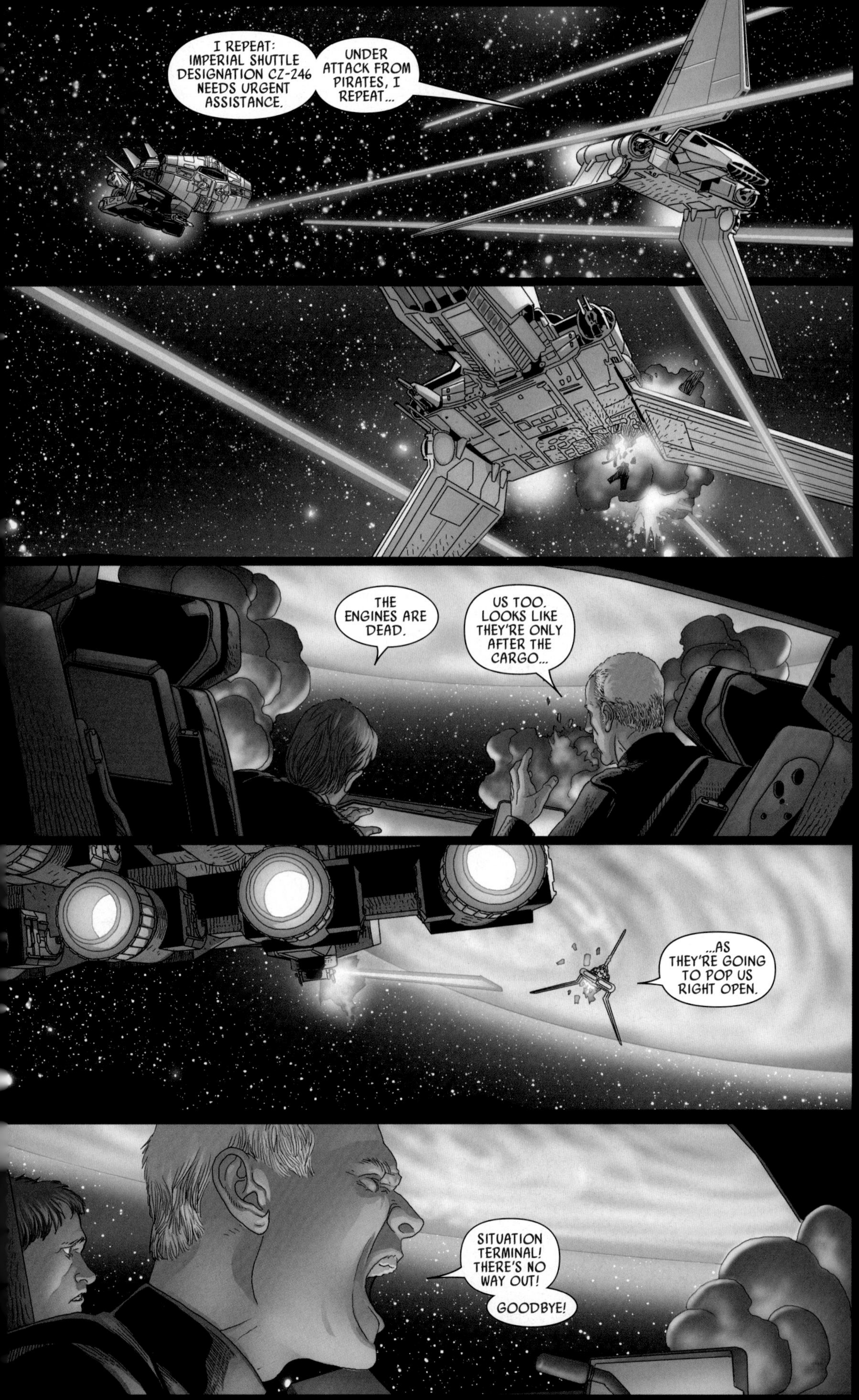
I REPEAT: IMPERIAL SHUTTLE DESIGNATION CZ-246 NEEDS URGENT ASSISTANCE.
UNDER ATTACK FROM PIRATES, I REPEAT...
THE ENGINES ARE DEAD.
US TOO. LOOKS LIKE THEY'RE ONLY AFTER THE CARGO...
...AS THEY'RE GOING TO POP US RIGHT OPEN.
SITUATION TERMINAL! THERE'S NO WAY OUT!
GOODBYE!

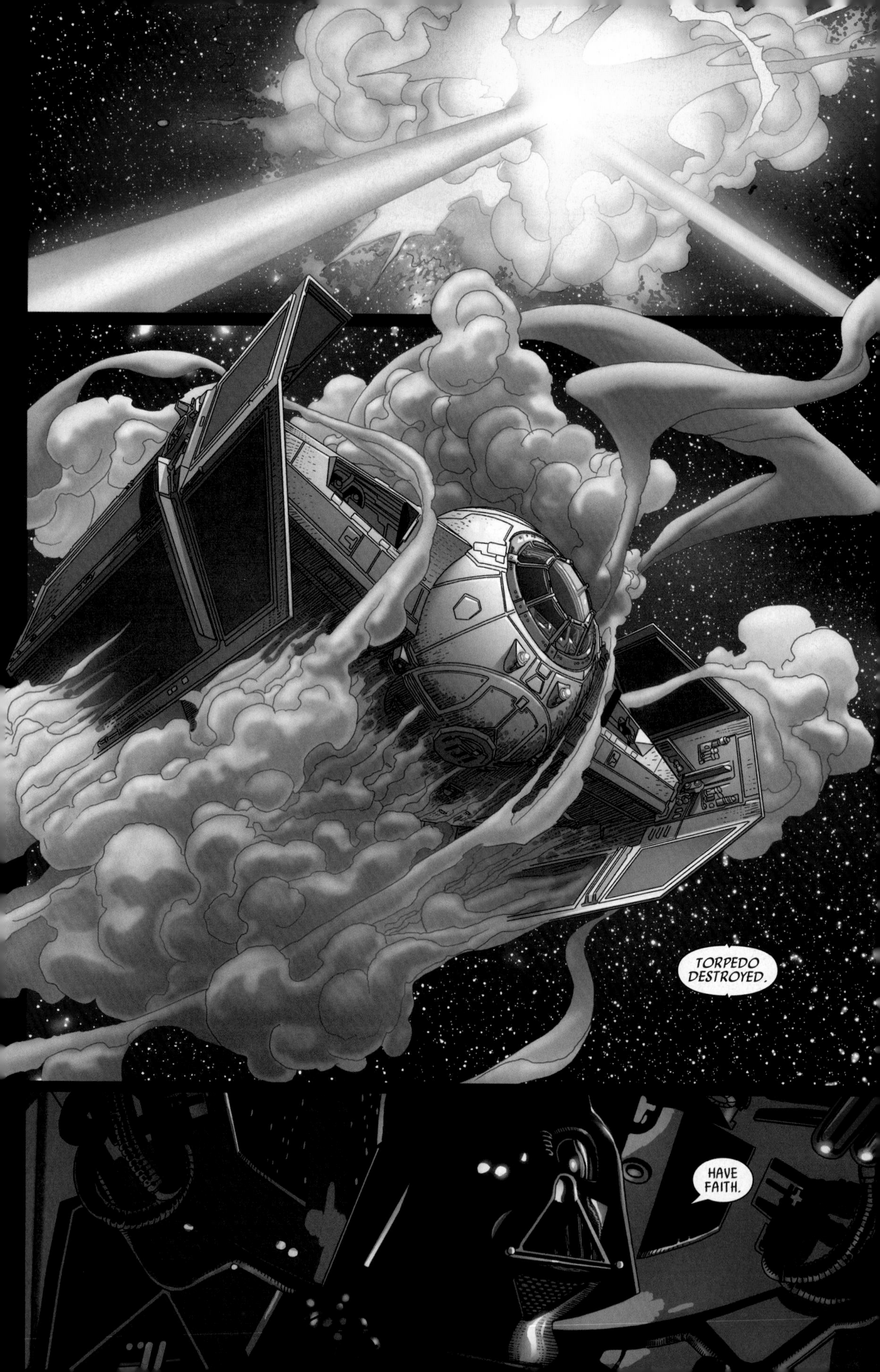
TORPEDO DESTROYED.
HAVE FAITH.

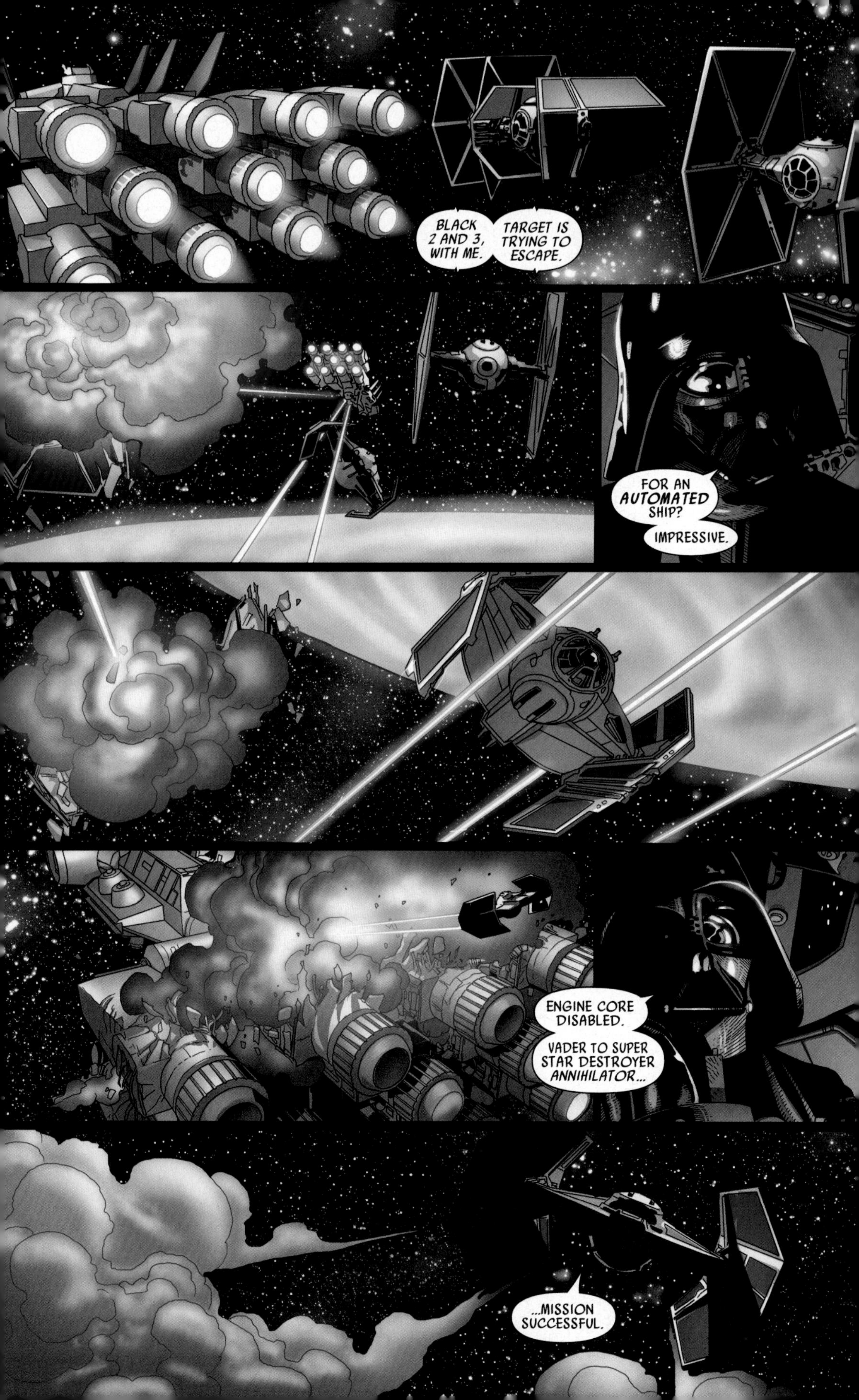
BLACK 2 AND 3, WITH ME.
TARGET IS TRYING TO ESCAPE.
FOR AN AUTOMATED SHIP?
IMPRESSIVE.
ENGINE CORE DISABLED.
VADER TO SUPER STAR DESTROYER ANNIHILATOR...
...MISSION SUCCESSFUL.

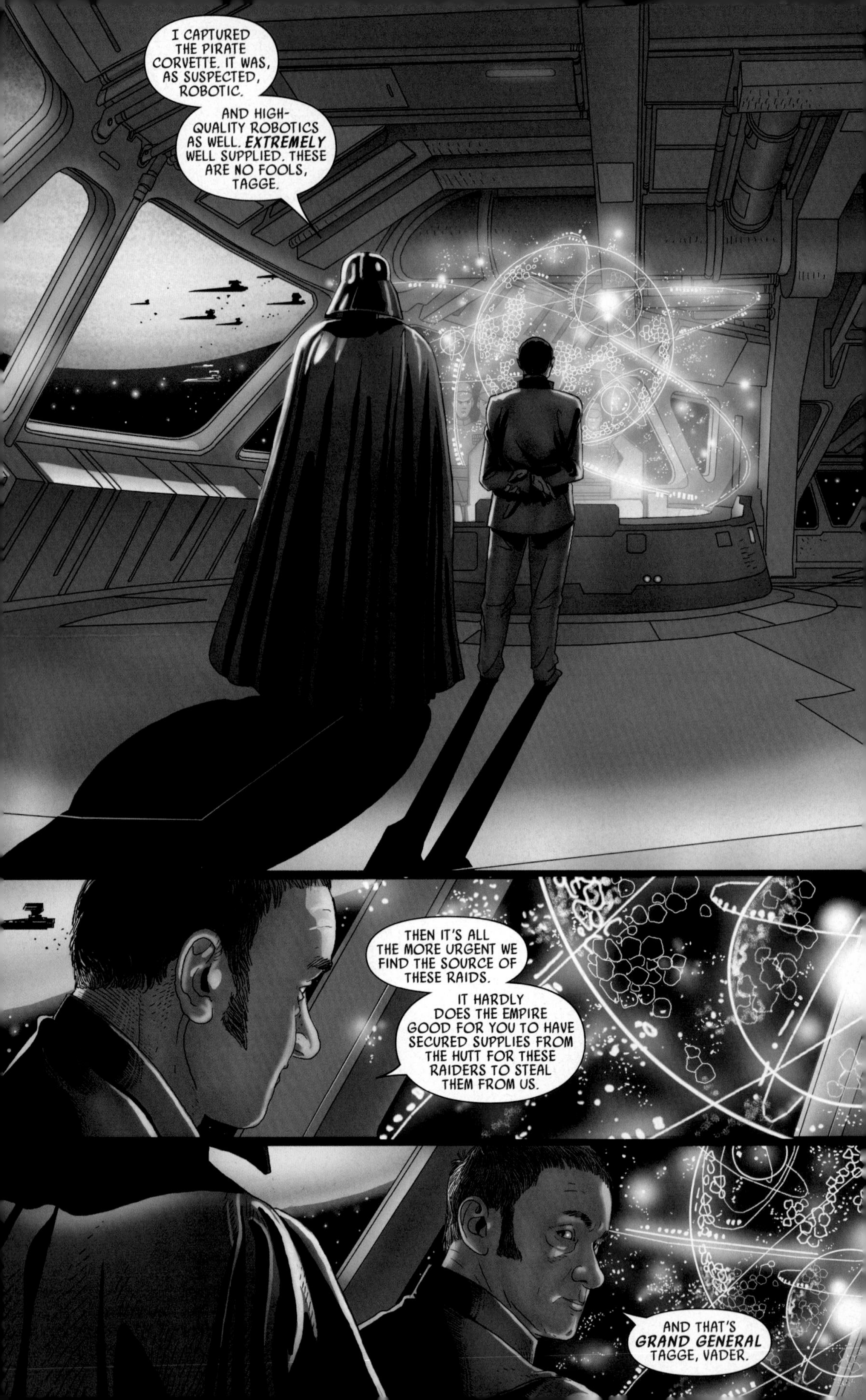
I CAPTURED THE PIRATE CORVETTE. IT WAS, AS SUSPECTED, ROBOTIC.
AND HIGH-QUALITY ROBOTICS AS WELL. *EXTREMELY* WELL SUPPLIED. THESE ARE NO FOOLS, TAGGE.
THEN IT'S ALL THE MORE URGENT WE FIND THE SOURCE OF THESE RAIDS.
IT HARDLY DOES THE EMPIRE GOOD FOR YOU TO HAVE SECURED SUPPLIES FROM THE HUTT FOR THESE RAIDERS TO STEAL THEM FROM US.
AND THAT'S ***GRAND GENERAL*** TAGGE, VADER.

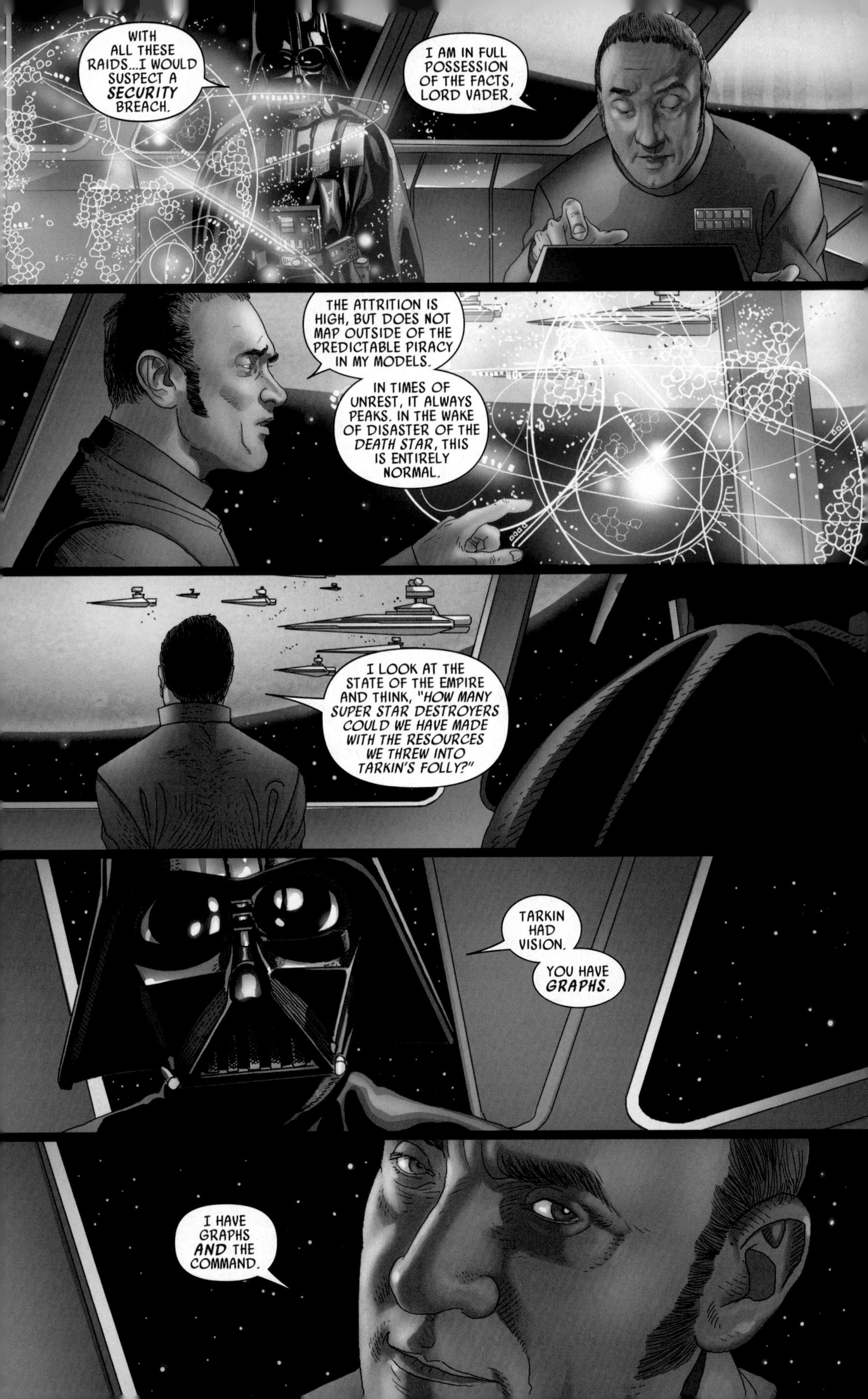
WITH ALL THESE RAIDS...I WOULD SUSPECT A **SECURITY** BREACH.
I AM IN FULL POSSESSION OF THE FACTS, LORD VADER.
THE ATTRITION IS HIGH, BUT DOES NOT MAP OUTSIDE OF THE PREDICTABLE PIRACY IN MY MODELS.
IN TIMES OF UNREST, IT ALWAYS PEAKS. IN THE WAKE OF DISASTER OF THE *DEATH STAR*, THIS IS ENTIRELY NORMAL.
I LOOK AT THE STATE OF THE EMPIRE AND THINK, *"HOW MANY SUPER STAR DESTROYERS COULD WE HAVE MADE WITH THE RESOURCES WE THREW INTO TARKIN'S FOLLY?"*
TARKIN HAD VISION.
YOU HAVE **GRAPHS**.
I HAVE GRAPHS **AND** THE COMMAND.

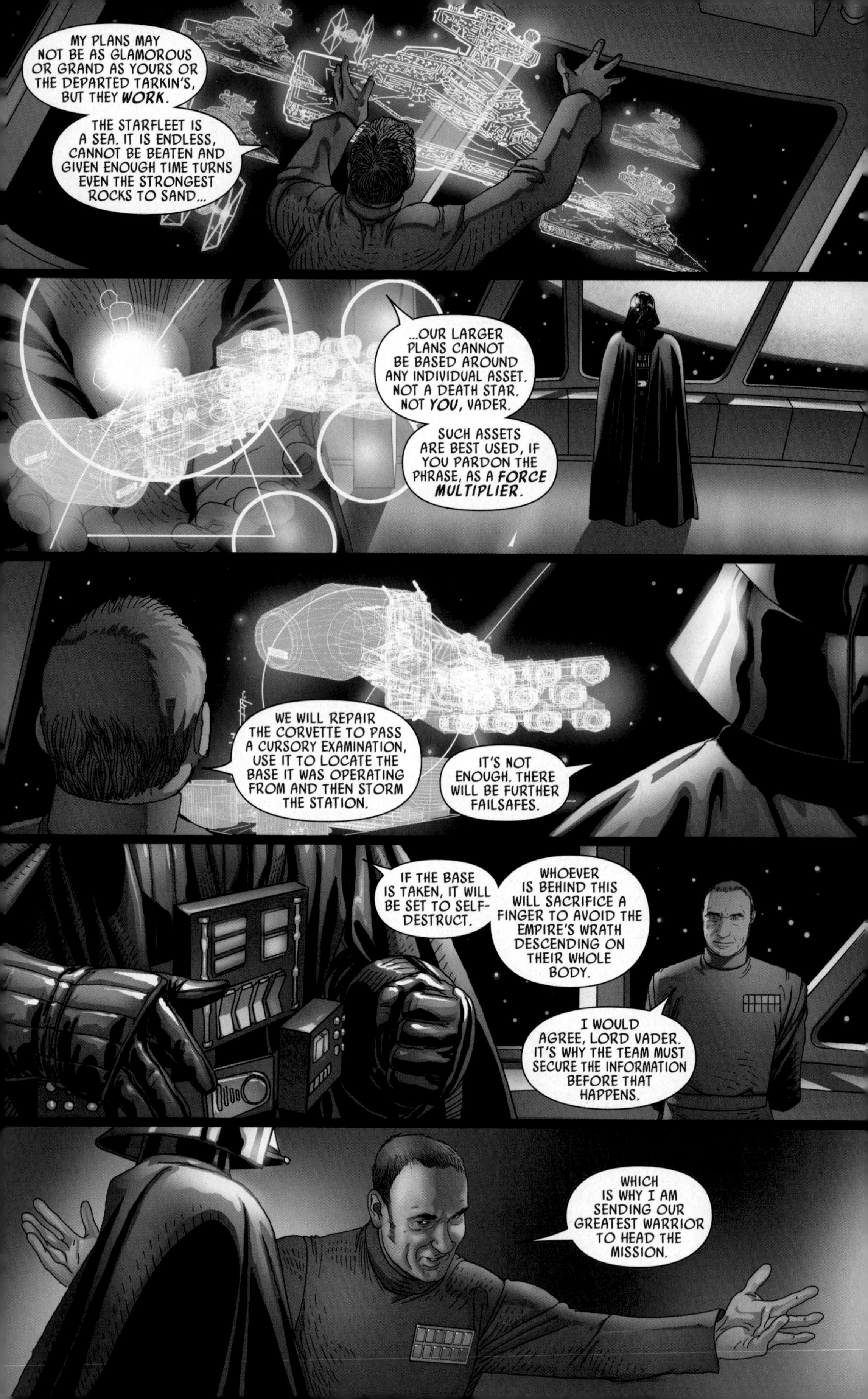
MY PLANS MAY NOT BE AS GLAMOROUS OR GRAND AS YOURS OR THE DEPARTED TARKIN'S, BUT THEY WORK.
THE STARFLEET IS A SEA. IT IS ENDLESS, CANNOT BE BEATEN AND GIVEN ENOUGH TIME TURNS EVEN THE STRONGEST ROCKS TO SAND...
...OUR LARGER PLANS CANNOT BE BASED AROUND ANY INDIVIDUAL ASSET. NOT A DEATH STAR. NOT YOU, VADER.
SUCH ASSETS ARE BEST USED, IF YOU PARDON THE PHRASE, AS A FORCE MULTIPLIER.
WE WILL REPAIR THE CORVETTE TO PASS A CURSORY EXAMINATION, USE IT TO LOCATE THE BASE IT WAS OPERATING FROM AND THEN STORM THE STATION.
IT'S NOT ENOUGH. THERE WILL BE FURTHER FAILSAFES.
IF THE BASE IS TAKEN, IT WILL BE SET TO SELF-DESTRUCT.
WHOEVER IS BEHIND THIS WILL SACRIFICE A FINGER TO AVOID THE EMPIRE'S WRATH DESCENDING ON THEIR WHOLE BODY.
I WOULD AGREE, LORD VADER. IT'S WHY THE TEAM MUST SECURE THE INFORMATION BEFORE THAT HAPPENS.
WHICH IS WHY I AM SENDING OUR GREATEST WARRIOR TO HEAD THE MISSION.

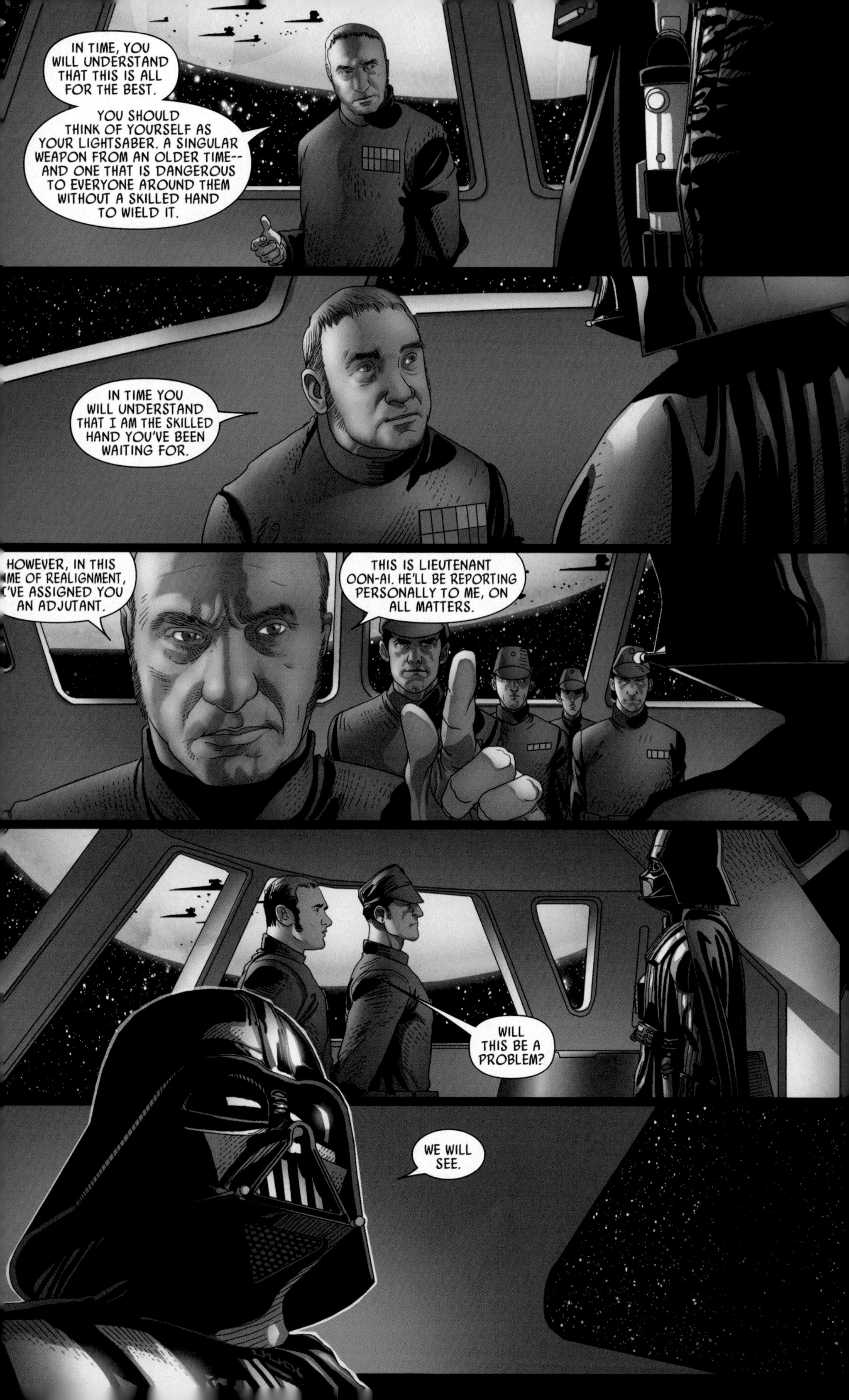
IN TIME, YOU WILL UNDERSTAND THAT THIS IS ALL FOR THE BEST.
YOU SHOULD THINK OF YOURSELF AS YOUR LIGHTSABER. A SINGULAR WEAPON FROM AN OLDER TIME-- AND ONE THAT IS DANGEROUS TO EVERYONE AROUND THEM WITHOUT A SKILLED HAND TO WIELD IT.
IN TIME YOU WILL UNDERSTAND THAT I AM THE SKILLED HAND YOU'VE BEEN WAITING FOR.
HOWEVER, IN THIS ME OF REALIGNMENT, 'VE ASSIGNED YOU AN ADJUTANT.
THIS IS LIEUTENANT OON-AI. HE'LL BE REPORTING PERSONALLY TO ME, ON ALL MATTERS.
WILL THIS BE A PROBLEM?
WE WILL SEE.

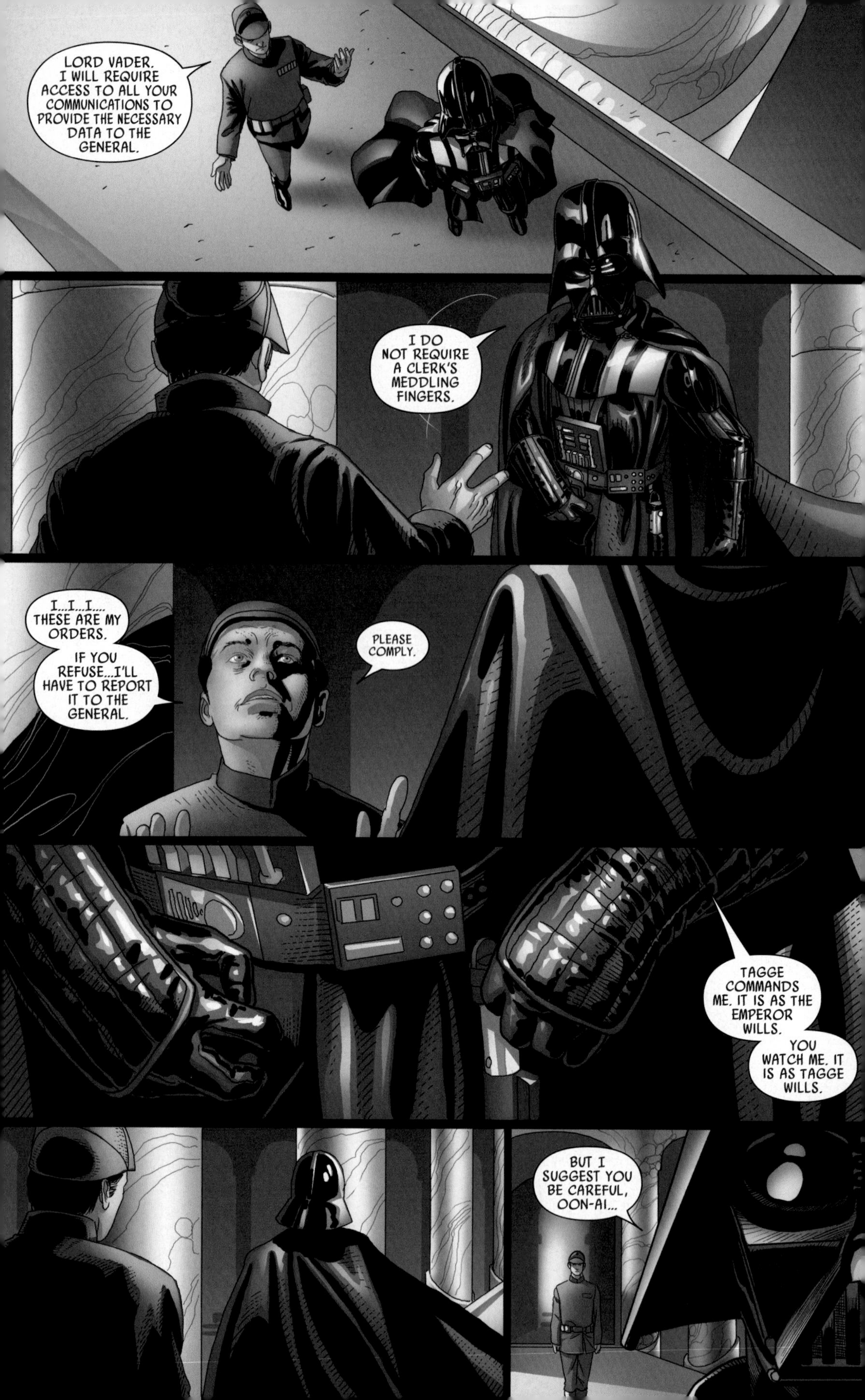
LORD VADER. I WILL REQUIRE ACCESS TO ALL YOUR COMMUNICATIONS TO PROVIDE THE NECESSARY DATA TO THE GENERAL.
I DO NOT REQUIRE A CLERK'S MEDDLING FINGERS.
I...I...I.... THESE ARE MY ORDERS.
IF YOU REFUSE...I'LL HAVE TO REPORT IT TO THE GENERAL.
PLEASE COMPLY.
TAGGE COMMANDS ME. IT IS AS THE EMPEROR WILLS.
YOU WATCH ME. IT IS AS TAGGE WILLS.
BUT I SUGGEST YOU BE CAREFUL, OON-AI...

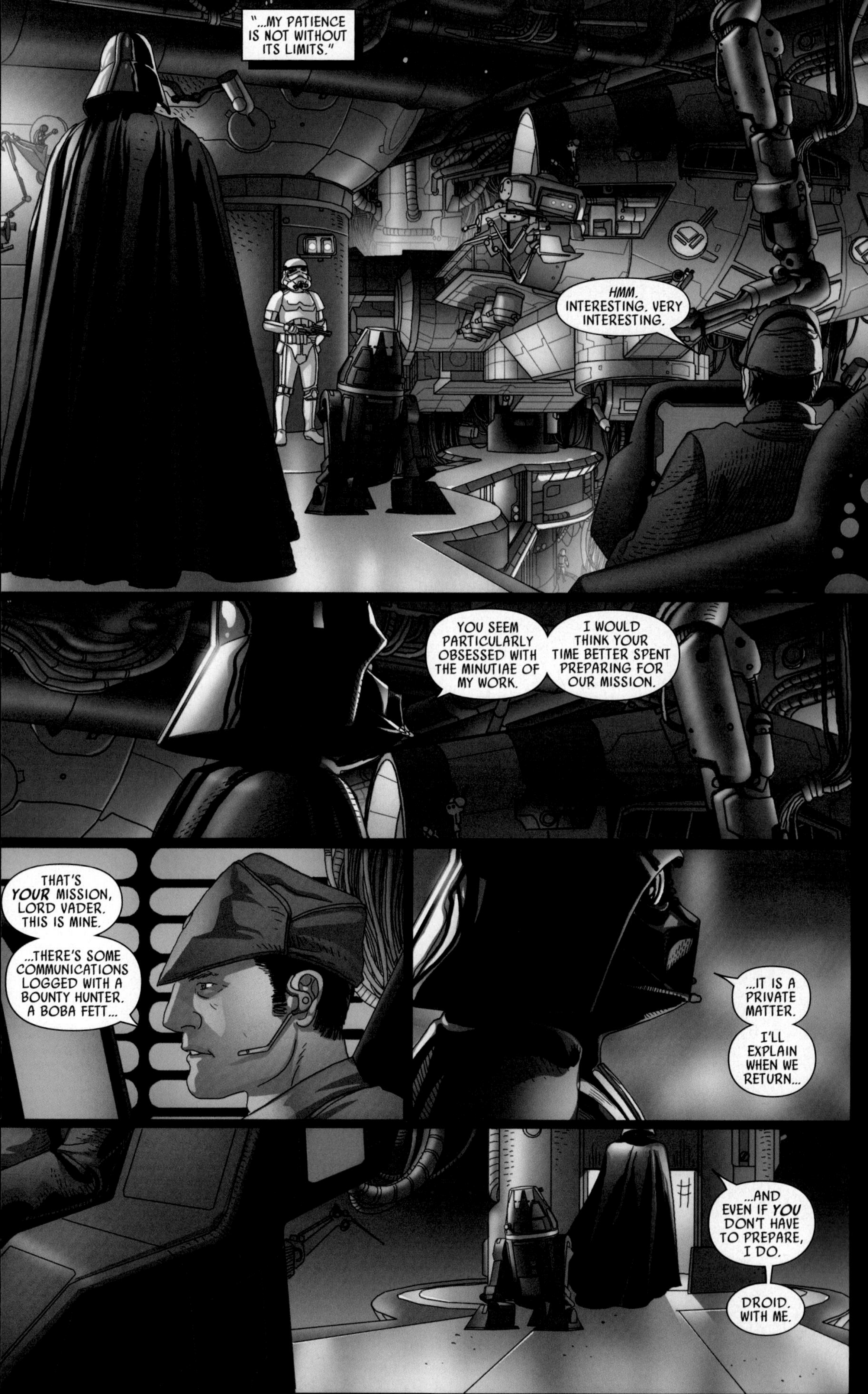
"...MY PATIENCE IS NOT WITHOUT ITS LIMITS."
HMM. INTERESTING. VERY INTERESTING.
YOU SEEM PARTICULARLY OBSESSED WITH THE MINUTIAE OF MY WORK.
I WOULD THINK YOUR TIME BETTER SPENT PREPARING FOR OUR MISSION.
THAT'S ***YOUR*** MISSION, LORD VADER. THIS IS MINE.
...THERE'S SOME COMMUNICATIONS LOGGED WITH A BOUNTY HUNTER. A BOBA FETT...
...IT IS A PRIVATE MATTER.
I'LL EXPLAIN WHEN WE RETURN...
...AND EVEN IF ***YOU*** DON'T HAVE TO PREPARE, I DO.
DROID. WITH ME.

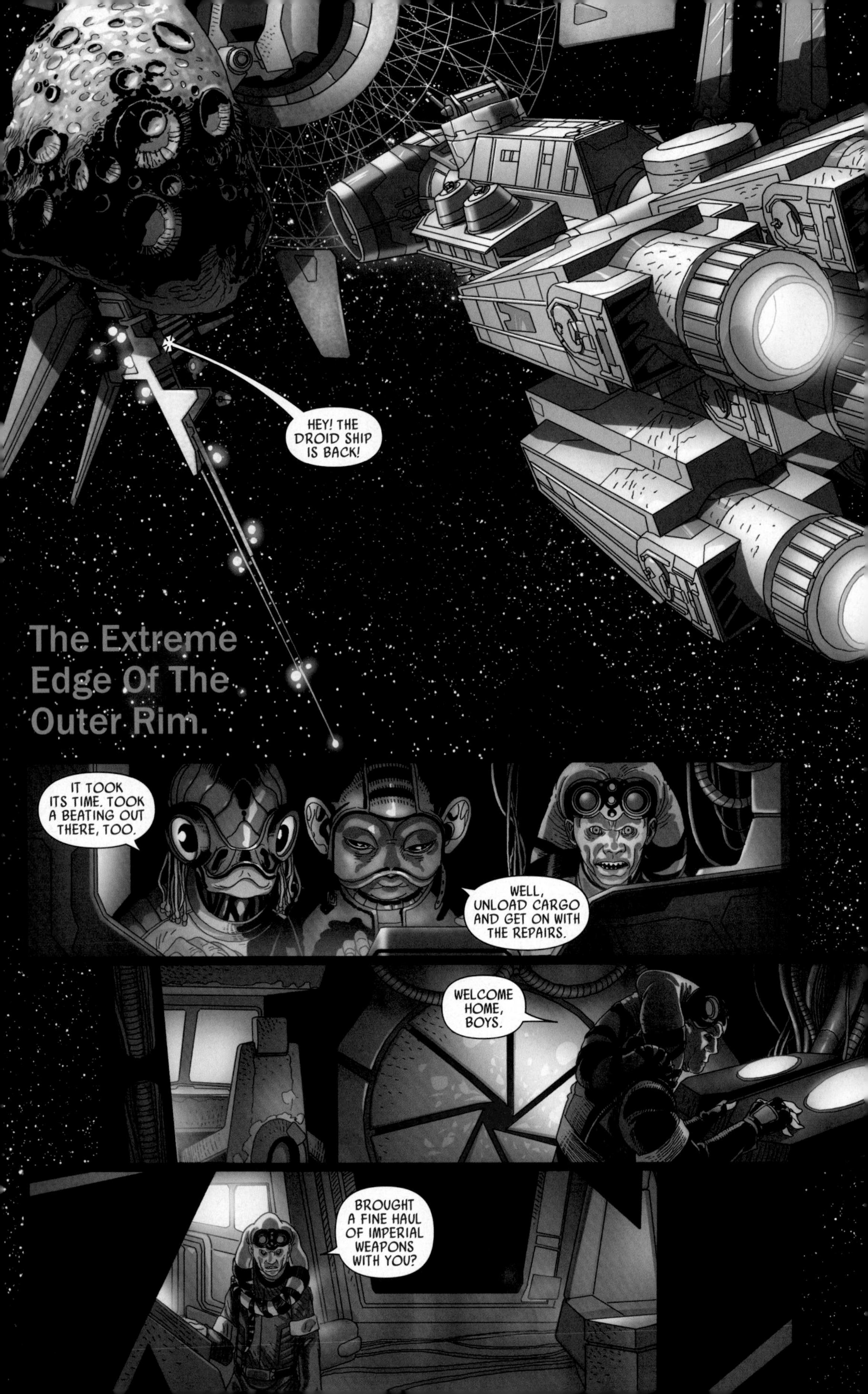
HEY! THE DROID SHIP IS BACK!
The Extreme Edge Of The Outer Rim.
IT TOOK ITS TIME. TOOK A BEATING OUT THERE, TOO.
WELL, UNLOAD CARGO AND GET ON WITH THE REPAIRS.
WELCOME HOME, BOYS.
BROUGHT A FINE HAUL OF IMPERIAL WEAPONS WITH YOU?

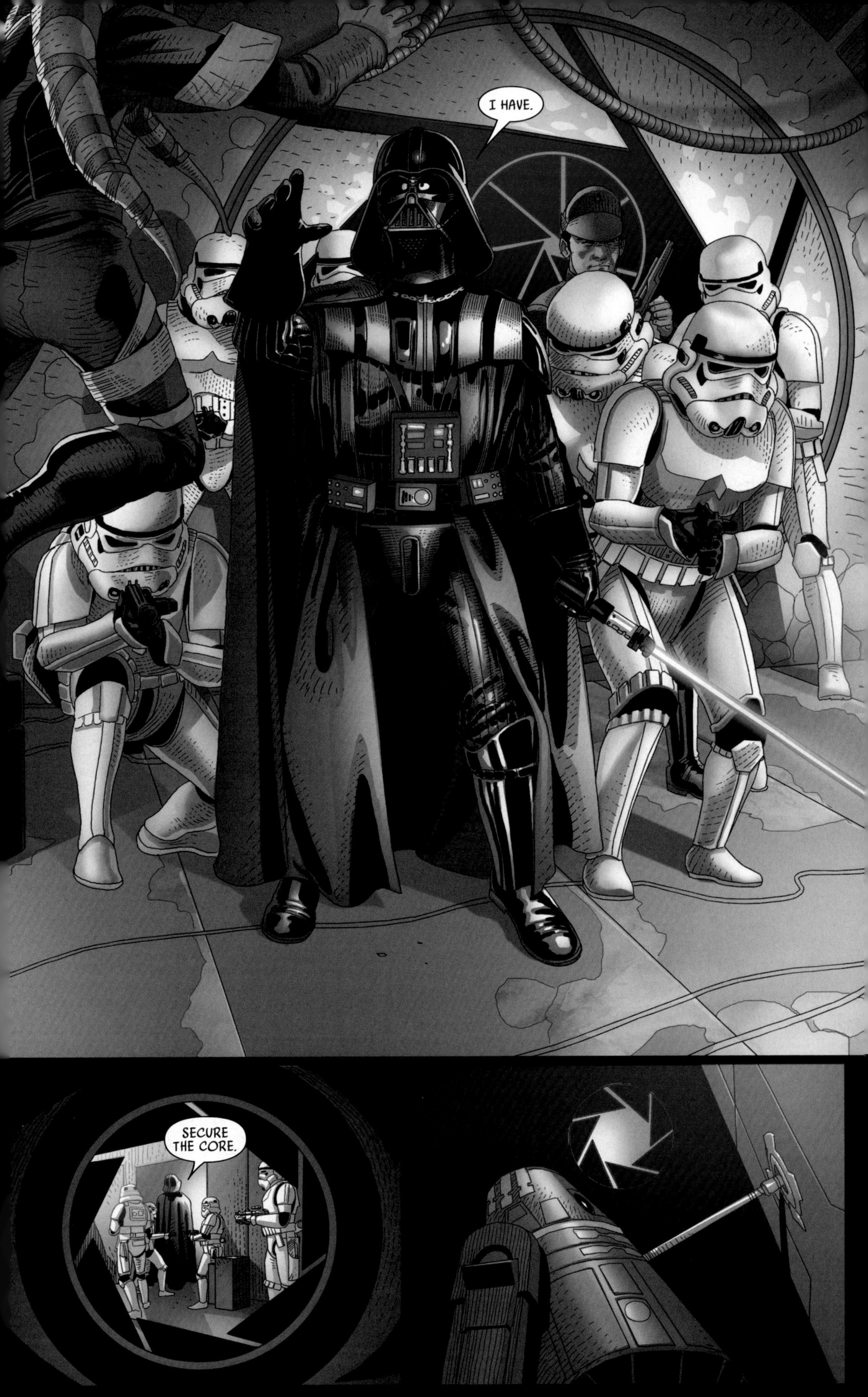
I HAVE.
SECURE THE CORE.

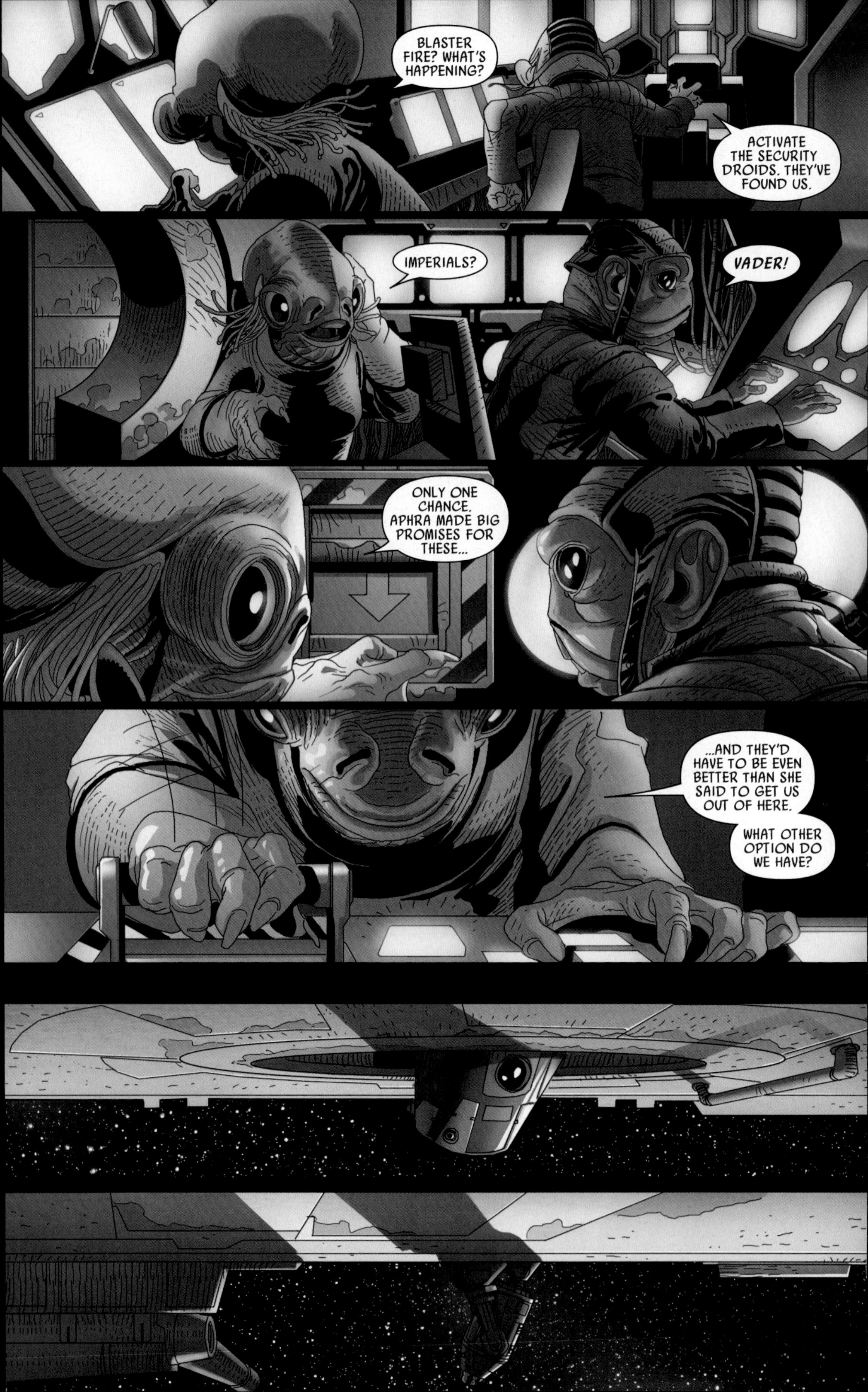
BLASTER FIRE? WHAT'S HAPPENING?
ACTIVATE THE SECURITY DROIDS. THEY'VE FOUND US.
IMPERIALS?
VADER!
ONLY ONE CHANCE. APHRA MADE BIG PROMISES FOR THESE...
...AND THEY'D HAVE TO BE EVEN BETTER THAN SHE SAID TO GET US OUT OF HERE.
WHAT OTHER OPTION DO WE HAVE?

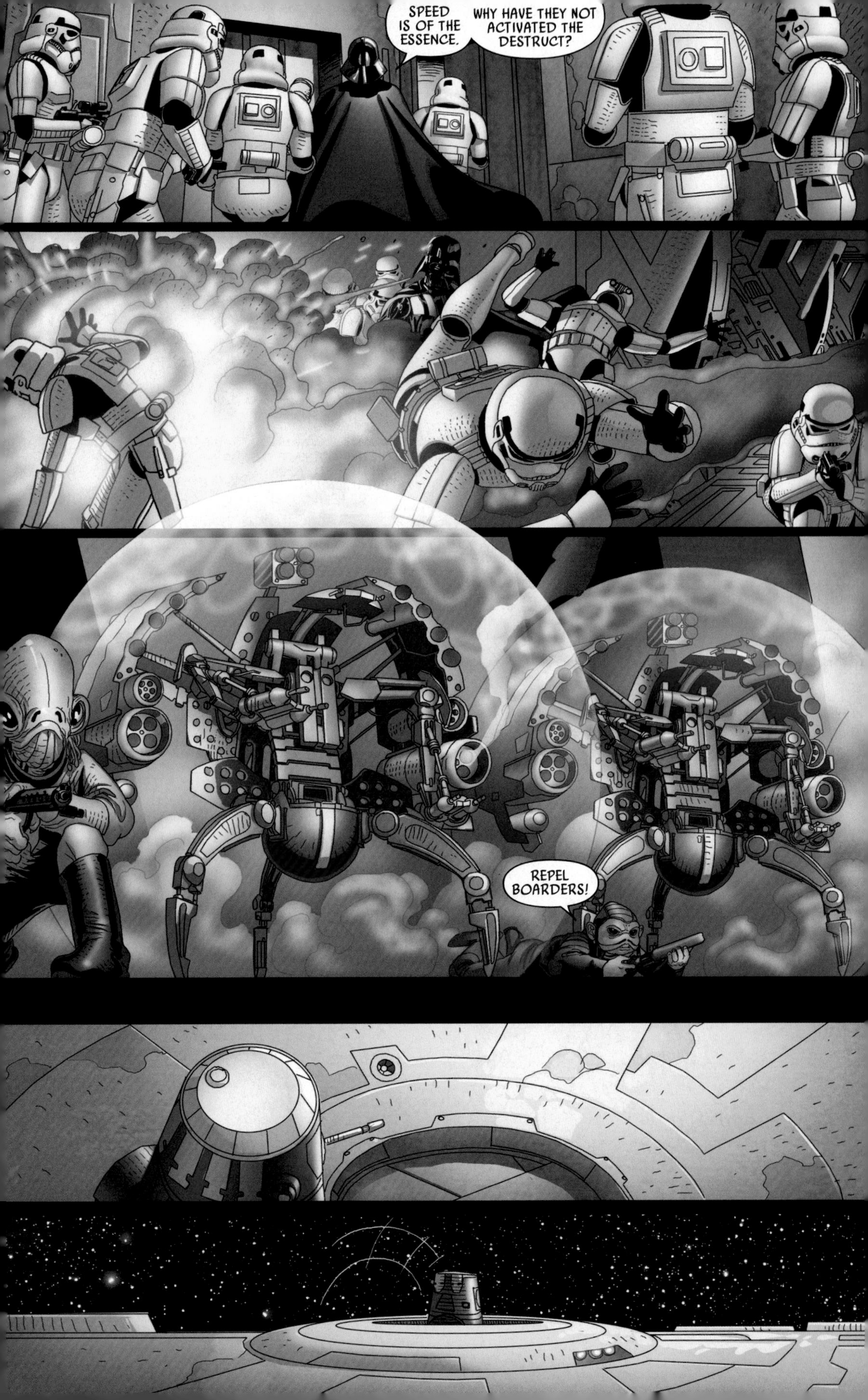
SPEED IS OF THE ESSENCE.
WHY HAVE THEY NOT ACTIVATED THE DESTRUCT?
REPEL BOARDERS!

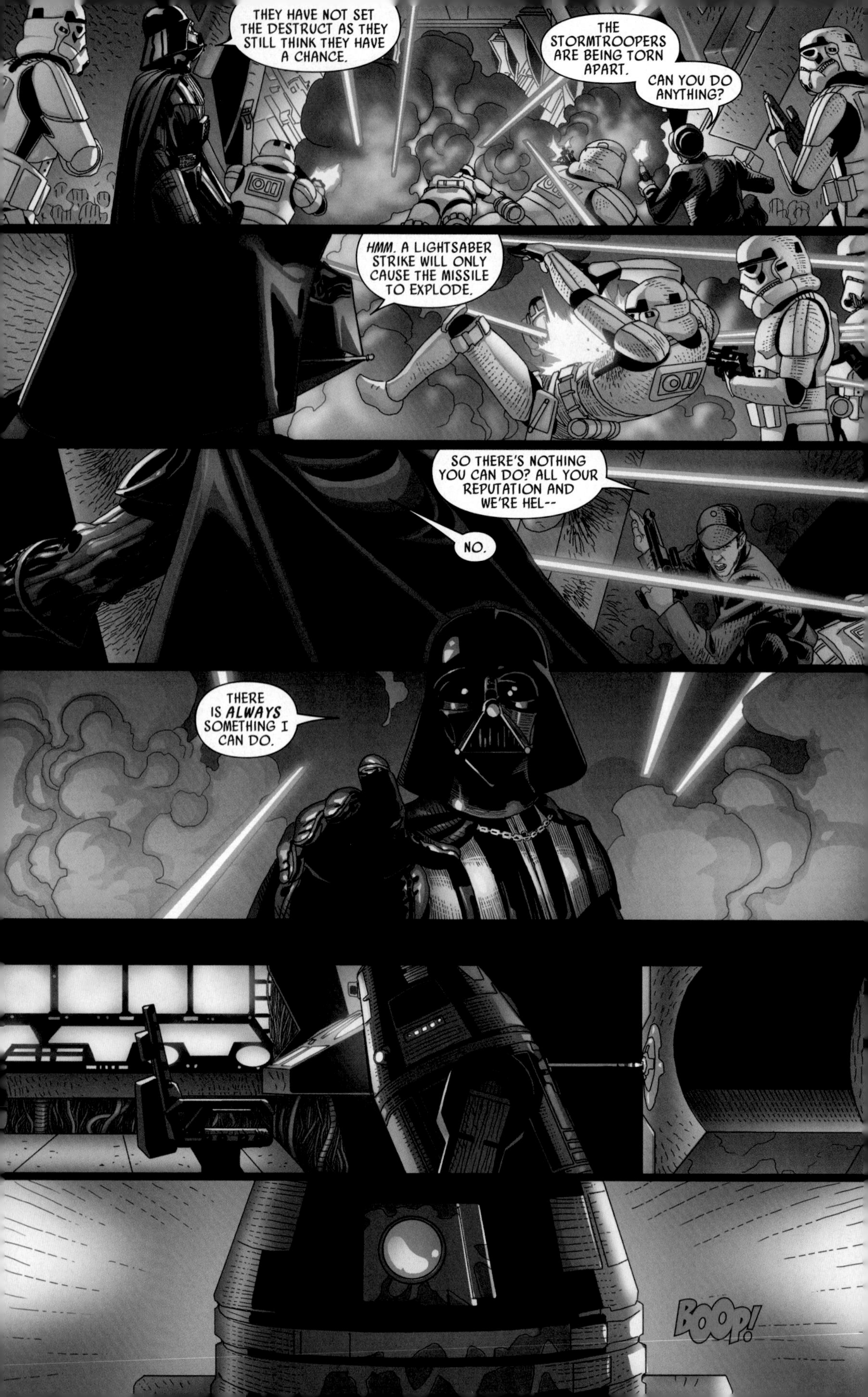
THEY HAVE NOT SET THE DESTRUCT AS THEY STILL THINK THEY HAVE A CHANCE.
THE STORMTROOPERS ARE BEING TORN APART.
CAN YOU DO ANYTHING?
HMM. A LIGHTSABER STRIKE WILL ONLY CAUSE THE MISSILE TO EXPLODE.
SO THERE'S NOTHING YOU CAN DO? ALL YOUR REPUTATION AND WE'RE HEL--
NO.
THERE IS *ALWAYS* SOMETHING I CAN DO.
BOOP!

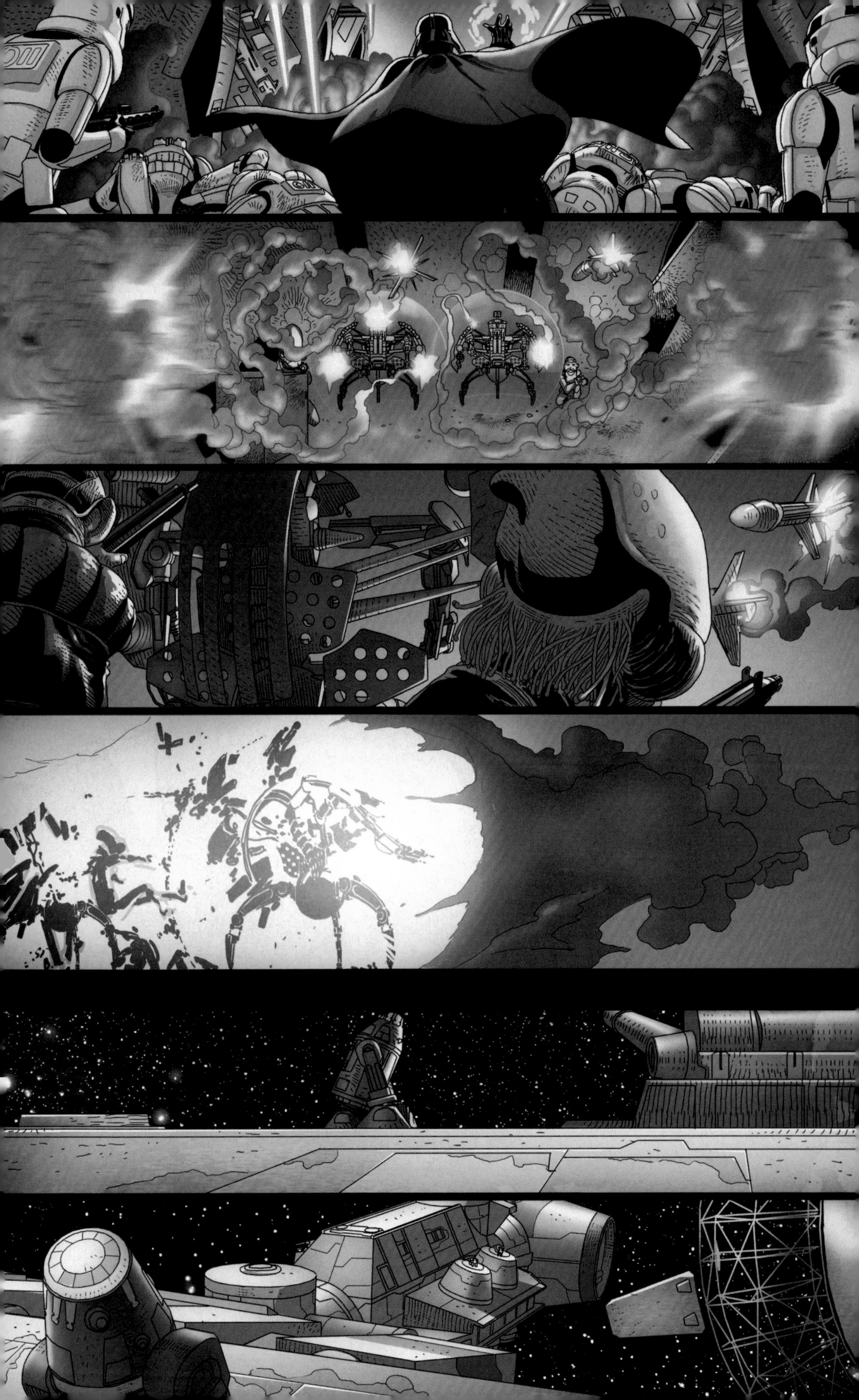

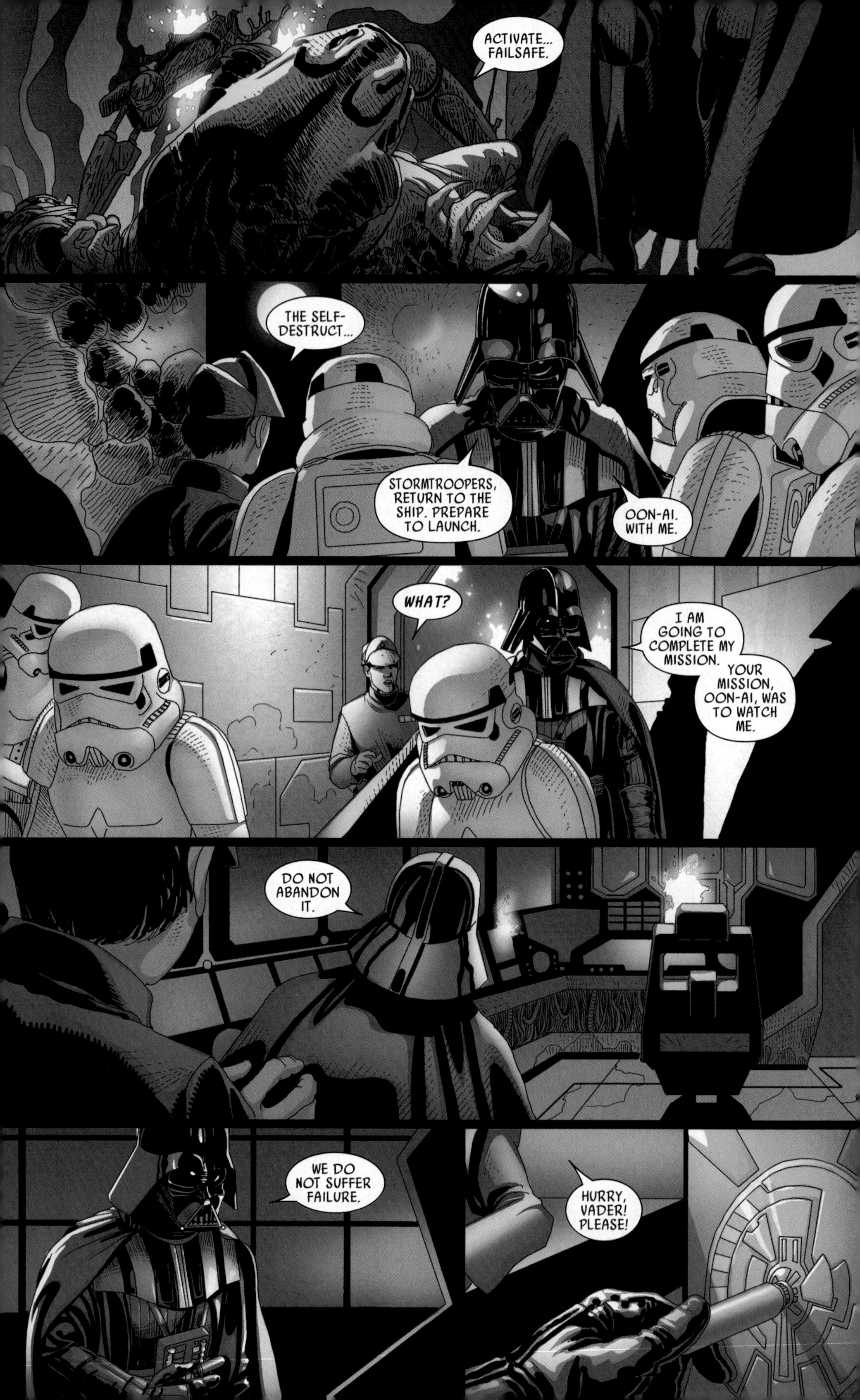
ACTIVATE... FAILSAFE.
THE SELF-DESTRUCT...
STORMTROOPERS, RETURN TO THE SHIP. PREPARE TO LAUNCH.
OON-AI. WITH ME.
WHAT?
I AM GOING TO COMPLETE MY MISSION.
YOUR MISSION, OON-AI, WAS TO WATCH ME.
DO NOT ABANDON IT.
WE DO NOT SUFFER FAILURE.
HURRY, VADER! PLEASE!

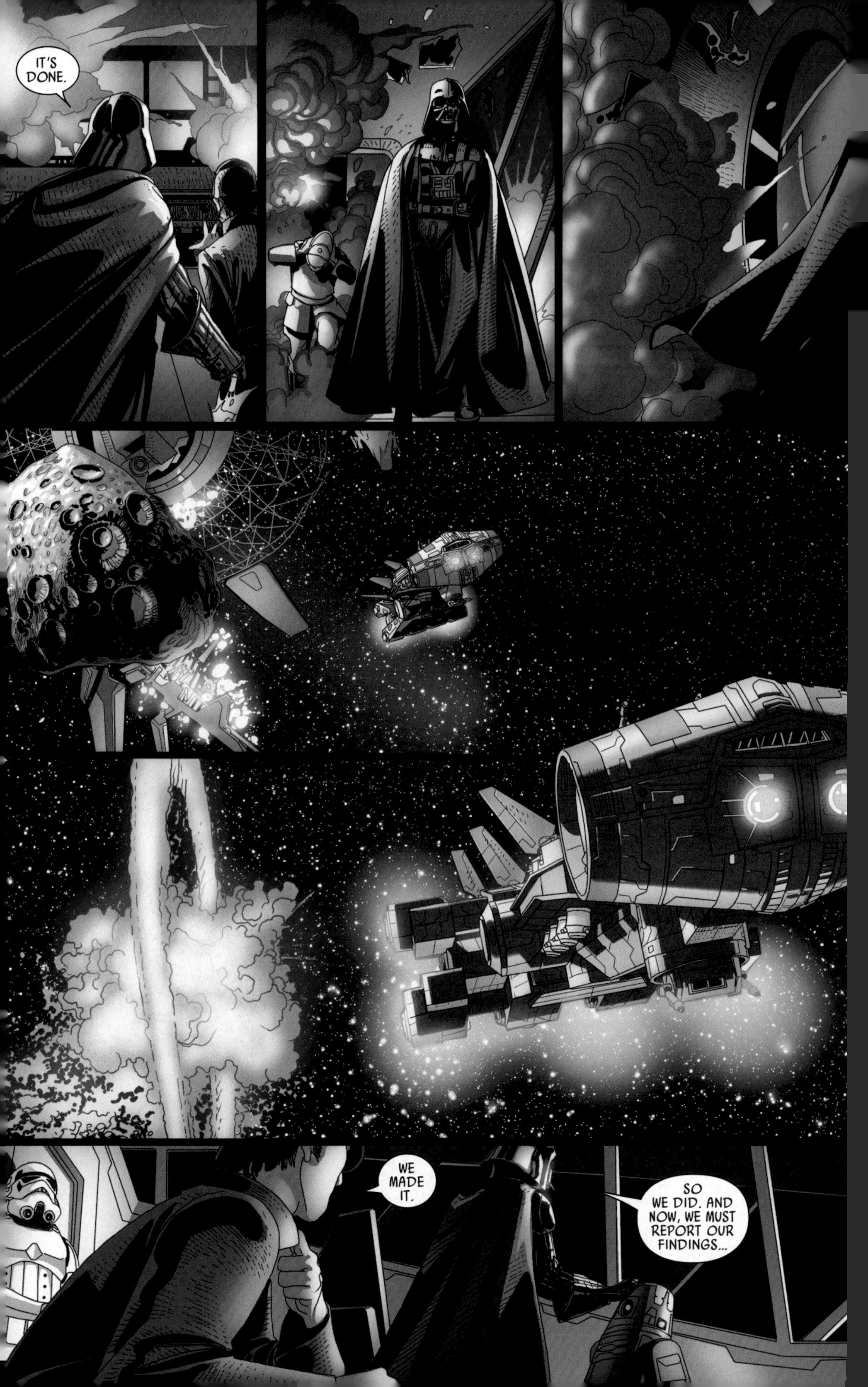
IT'S DONE.
WE MADE IT.
SO WE DID. AND NOW, WE MUST REPORT OUR FINDINGS...

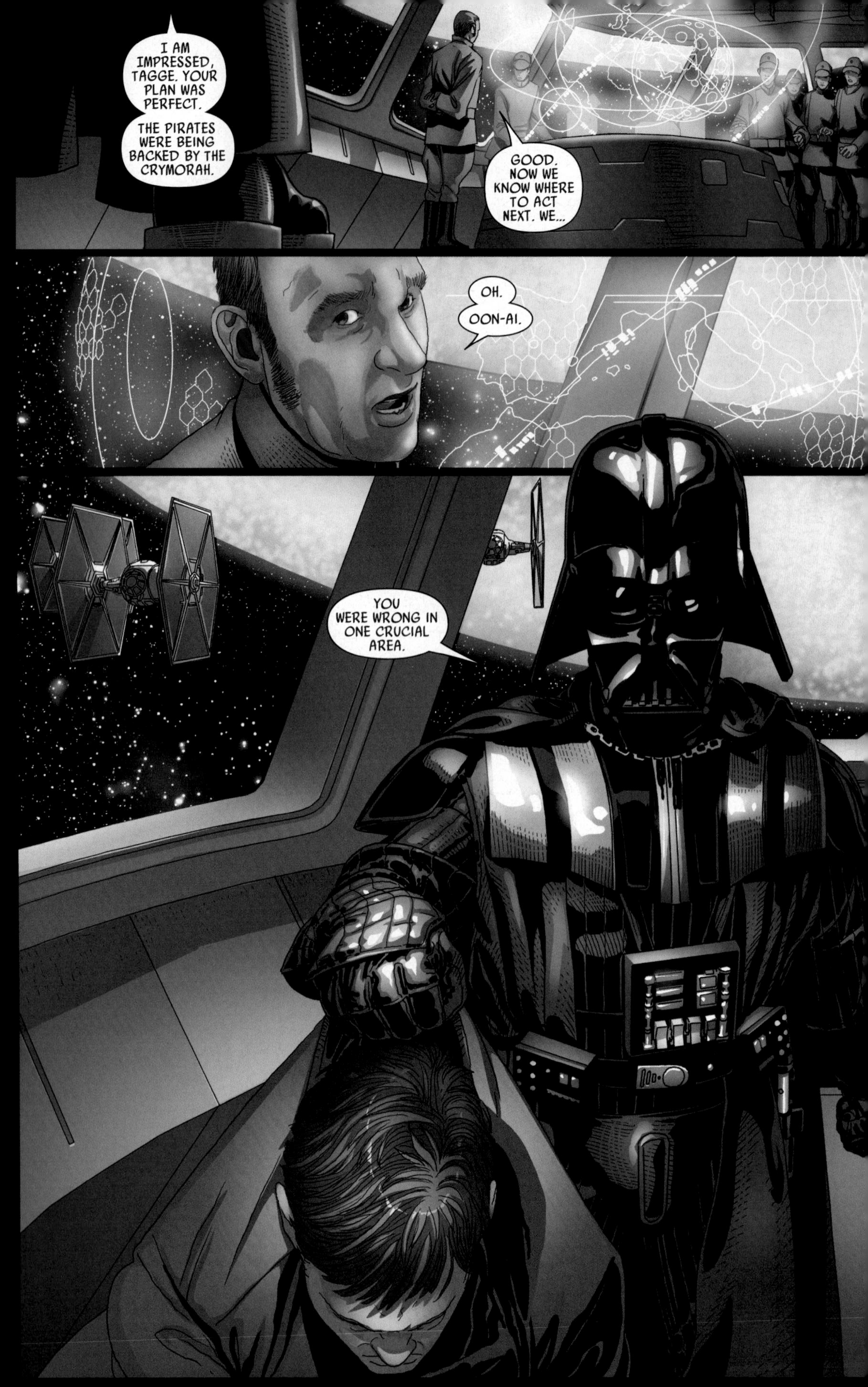
I AM IMPRESSED, TAGGE. YOUR PLAN WAS PERFECT.
THE PIRATES WERE BEING BACKED BY THE CRYMORAH.
GOOD. NOW WE KNOW WHERE TO ACT NEXT. WE...
OH.
OON-AI.
YOU WERE WRONG IN ONE CRUCIAL AREA.

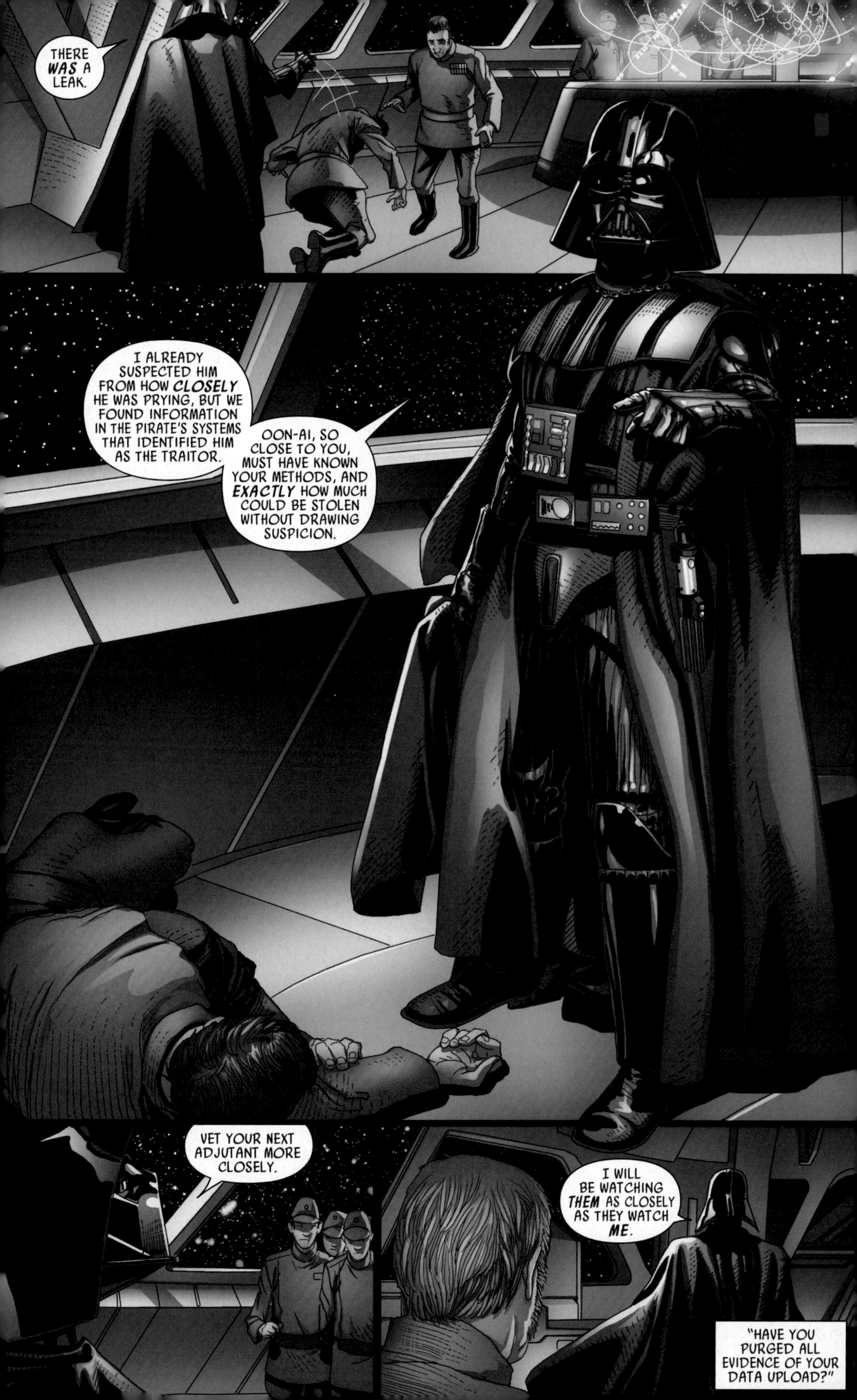
THERE WAS A LEAK.
I ALREADY SUSPECTED HIM FROM HOW CLOSELY HE WAS PRYING, BUT WE FOUND INFORMATION IN THE PIRATE'S SYSTEMS THAT IDENTIFIED HIM AS THE TRAITOR.
OON-AI, SO CLOSE TO YOU, MUST HAVE KNOWN YOUR METHODS, AND EXACTLY HOW MUCH COULD BE STOLEN WITHOUT DRAWING SUSPICION.
VET YOUR NEXT ADJUTANT MORE CLOSELY.
I WILL BE WATCHING THEM AS CLOSELY AS THEY WATCH ME.
"HAVE YOU PURGED ALL EVIDENCE OF YOUR DATA UPLOAD?"

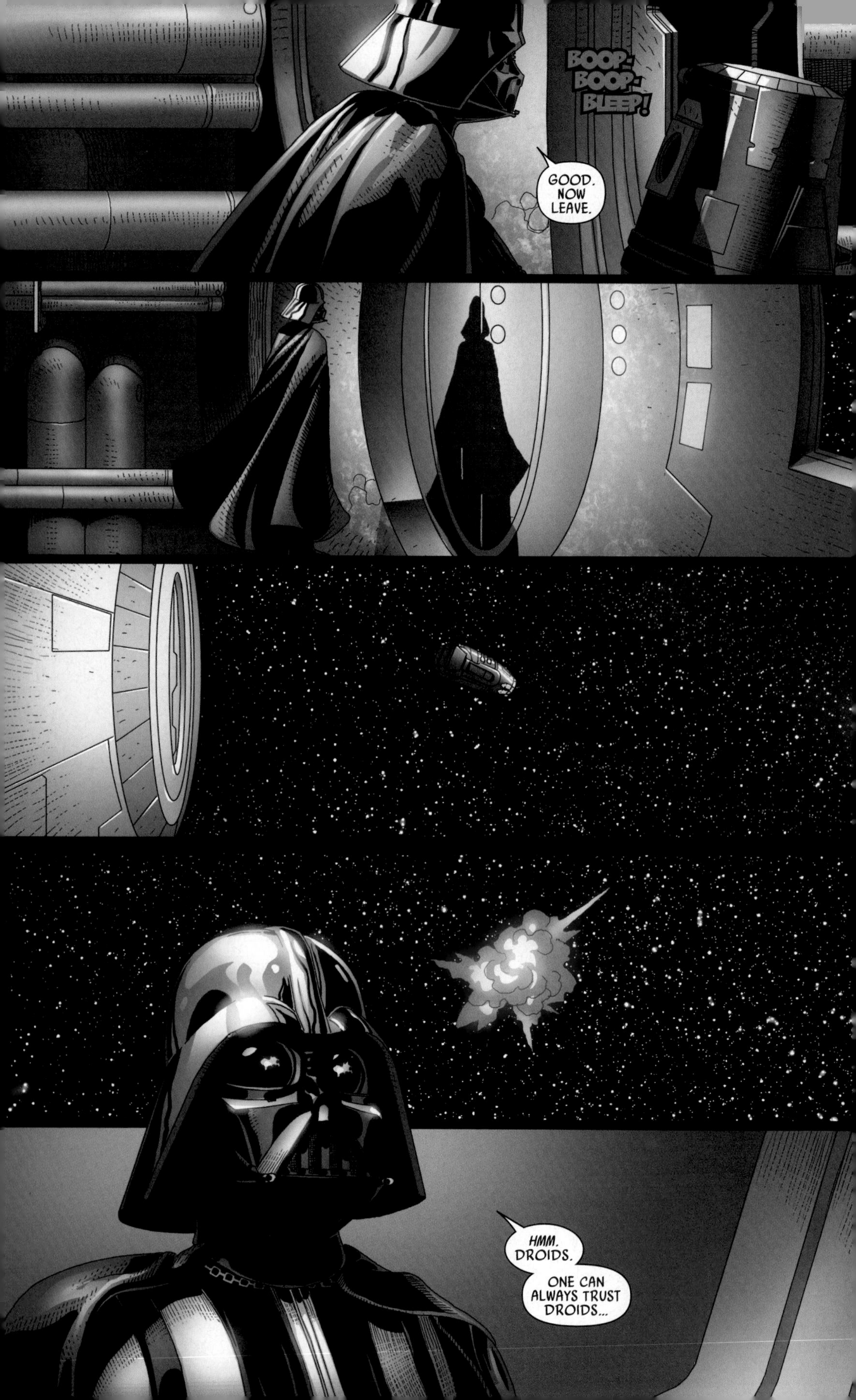
BOOP-BOOP-BLEEP!
GOOD. NOW LEAVE.
HMM. DROIDS.
ONE CAN ALWAYS TRUST DROIDS...

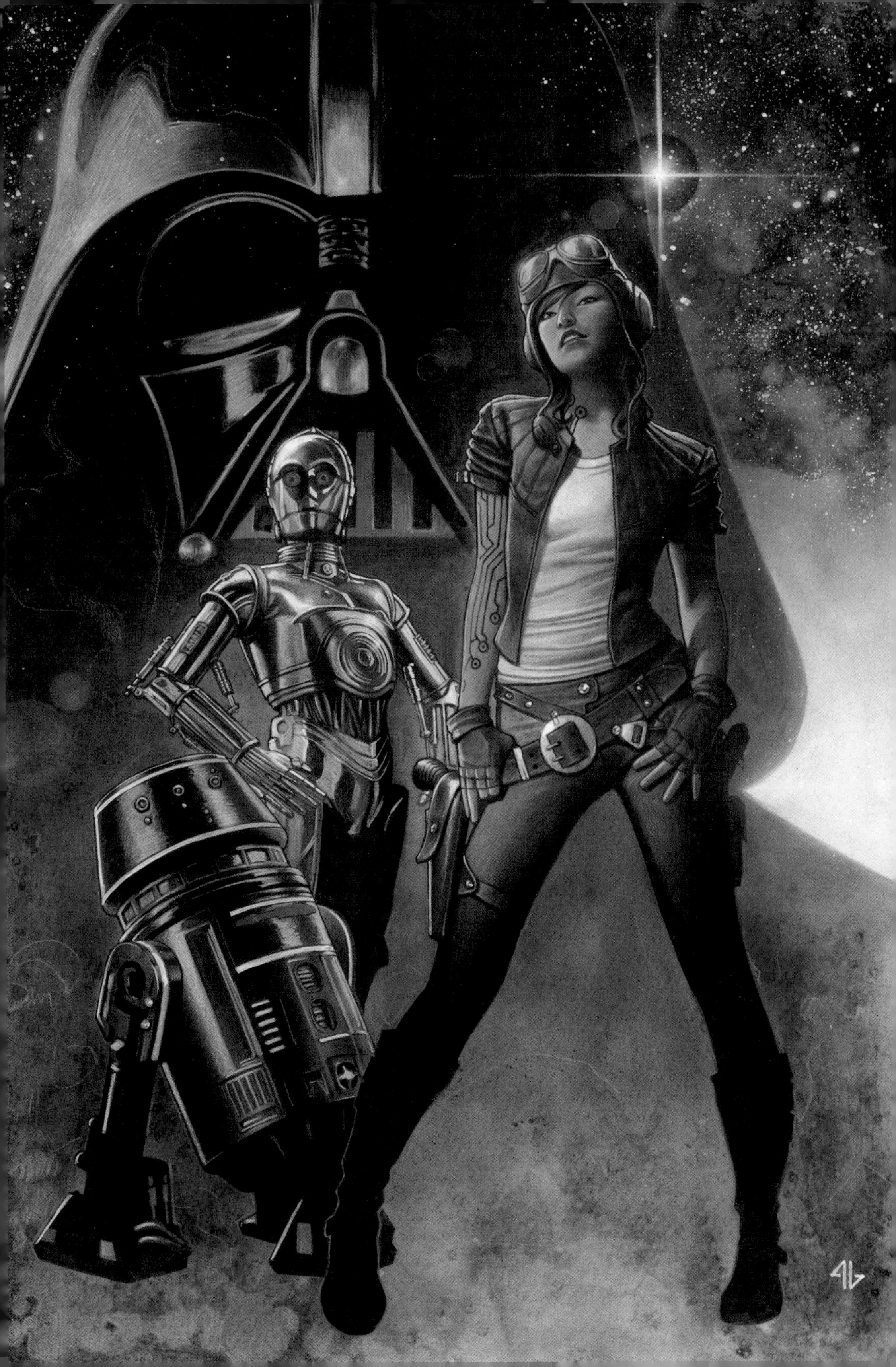

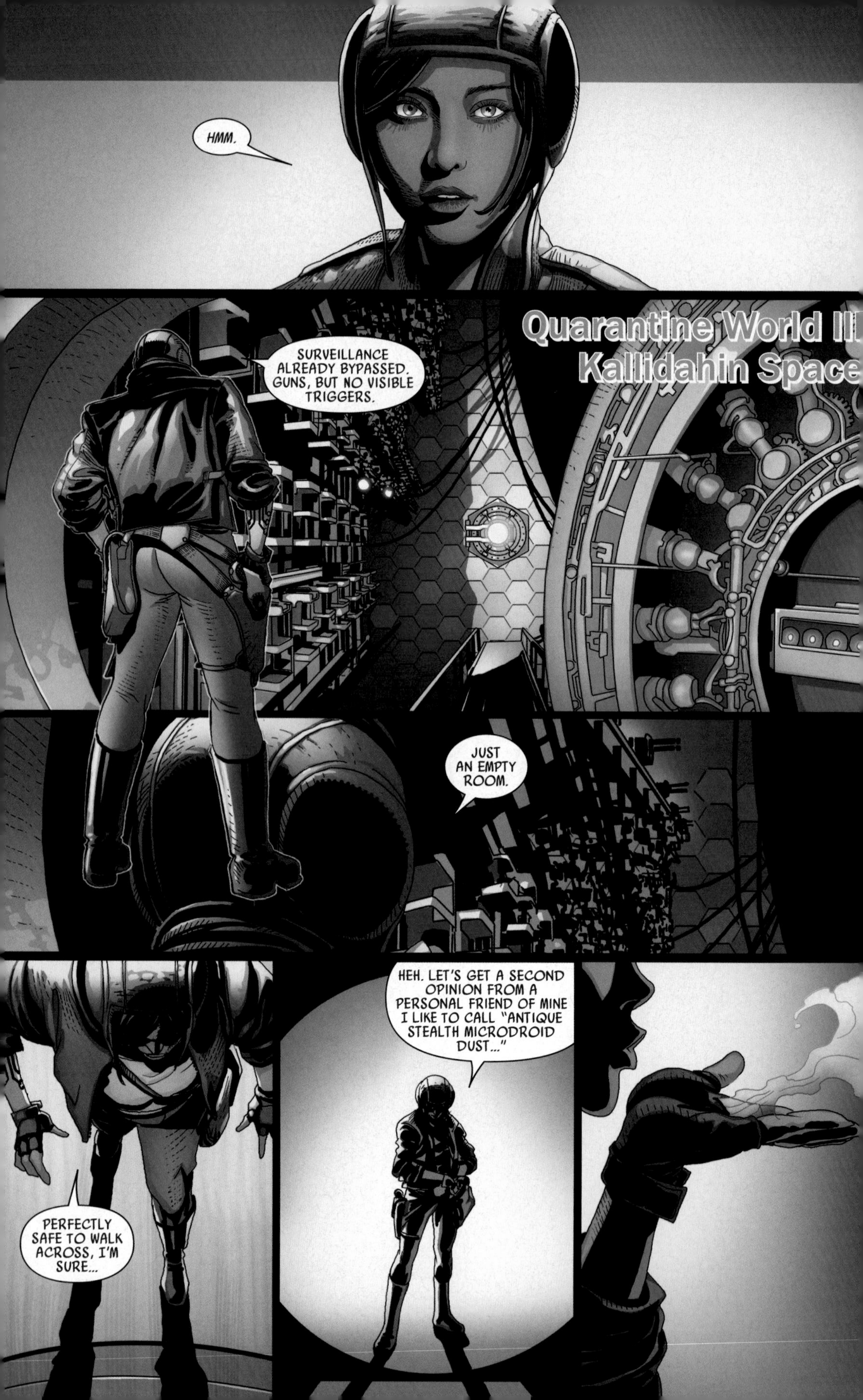
HMM.
Quarantine World III
Kallidahin Space
SURVEILLANCE ALREADY BYPASSED. GUNS, BUT NO VISIBLE TRIGGERS.
JUST AN EMPTY ROOM.
PERFECTLY SAFE TO WALK ACROSS, I'M SURE...
HEH. LET'S GET A SECOND OPINION FROM A PERSONAL FRIEND OF MINE I LIKE TO CALL "ANTIQUE STEALTH MICRODROID DUST..."

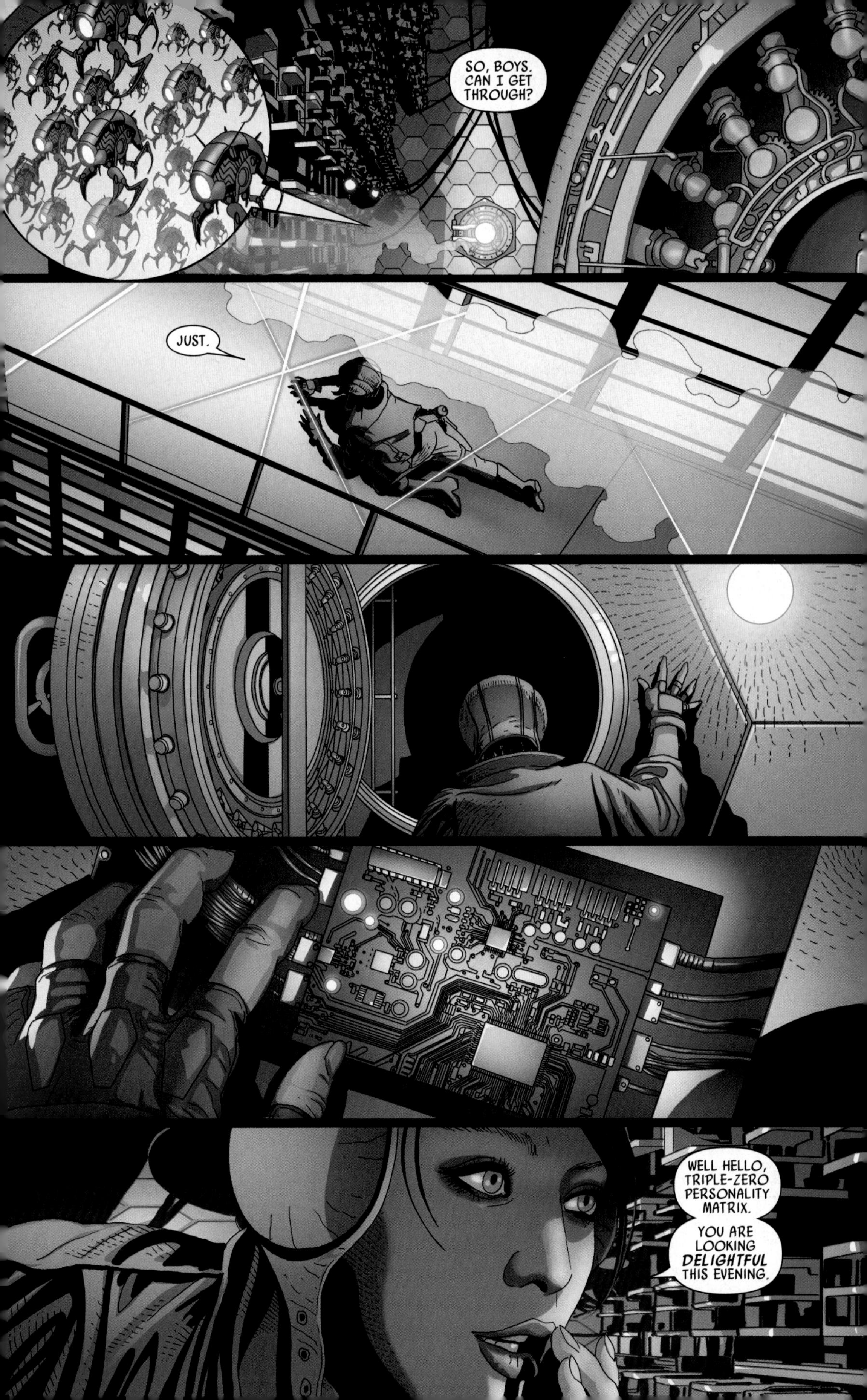
SO, BOYS. CAN I GET THROUGH?
JUST.
WELL HELLO, TRIPLE-ZERO PERSONALITY MATRIX.
YOU ARE LOOKING *DELIGHTFUL* THIS EVENING.

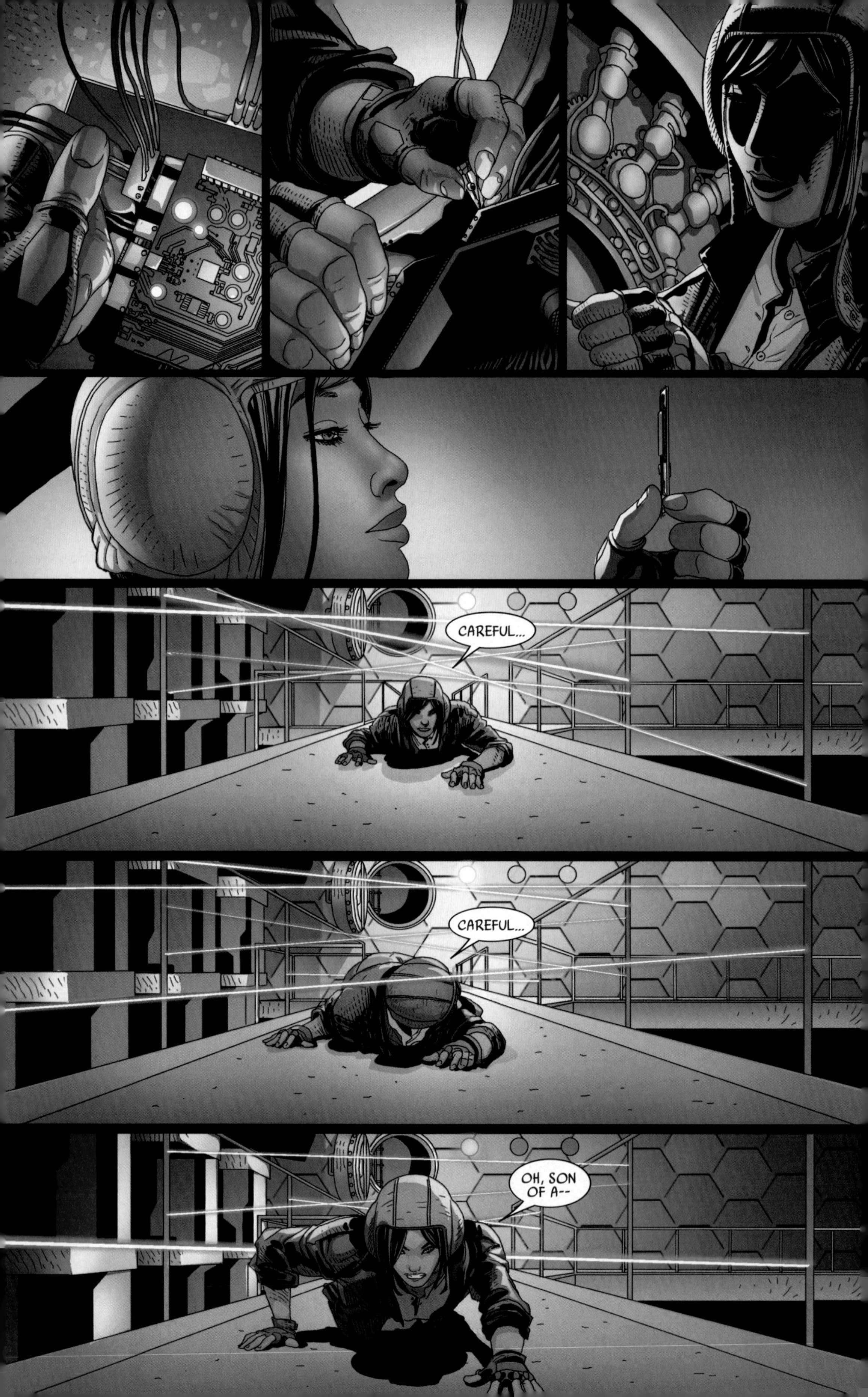
CAREFUL...
CAREFUL...
OH, SON OF A--

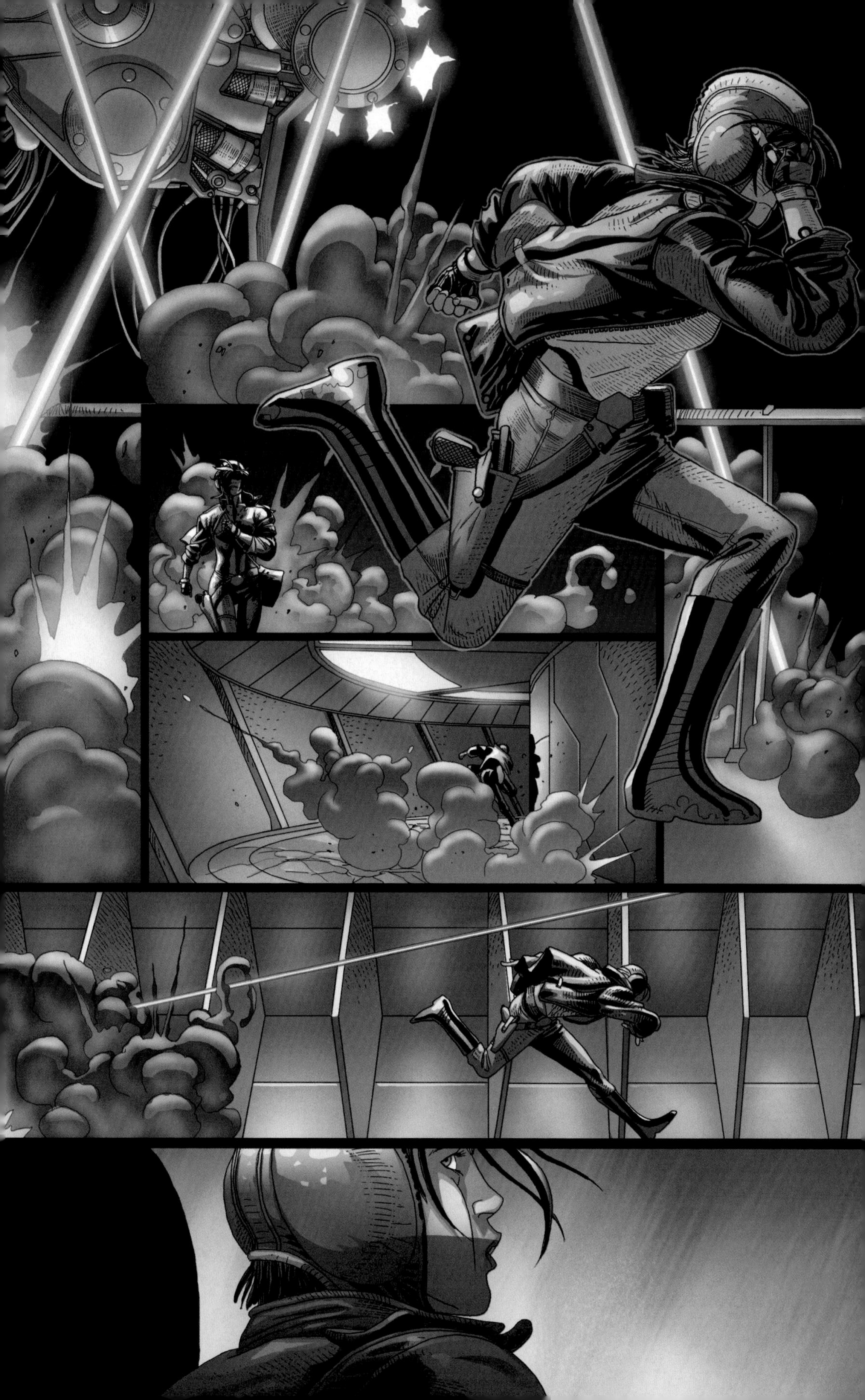

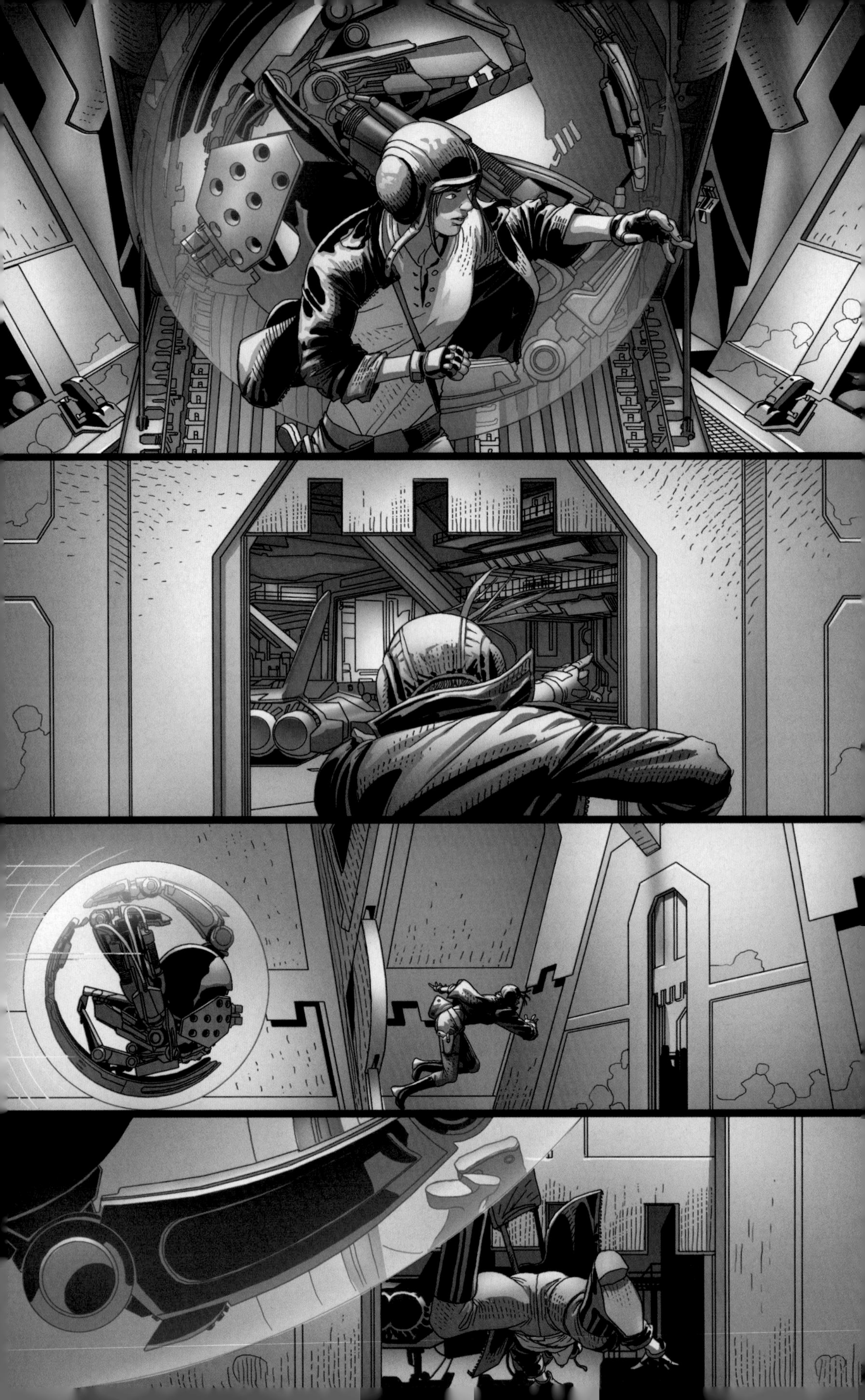

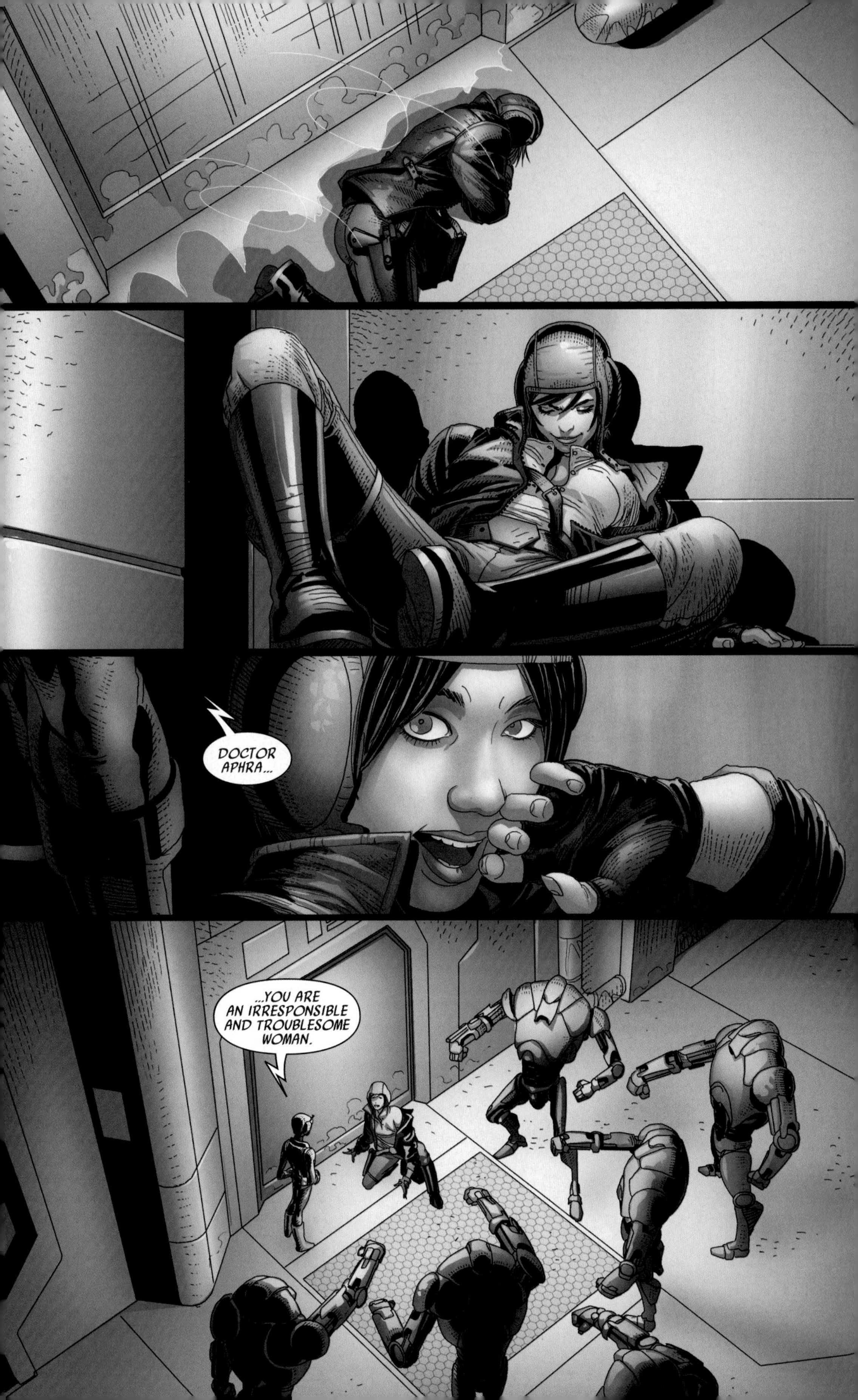
DOCTOR APHRA...
...YOU ARE AN IRRESPONSIBLE AND TROUBLESOME WOMAN.

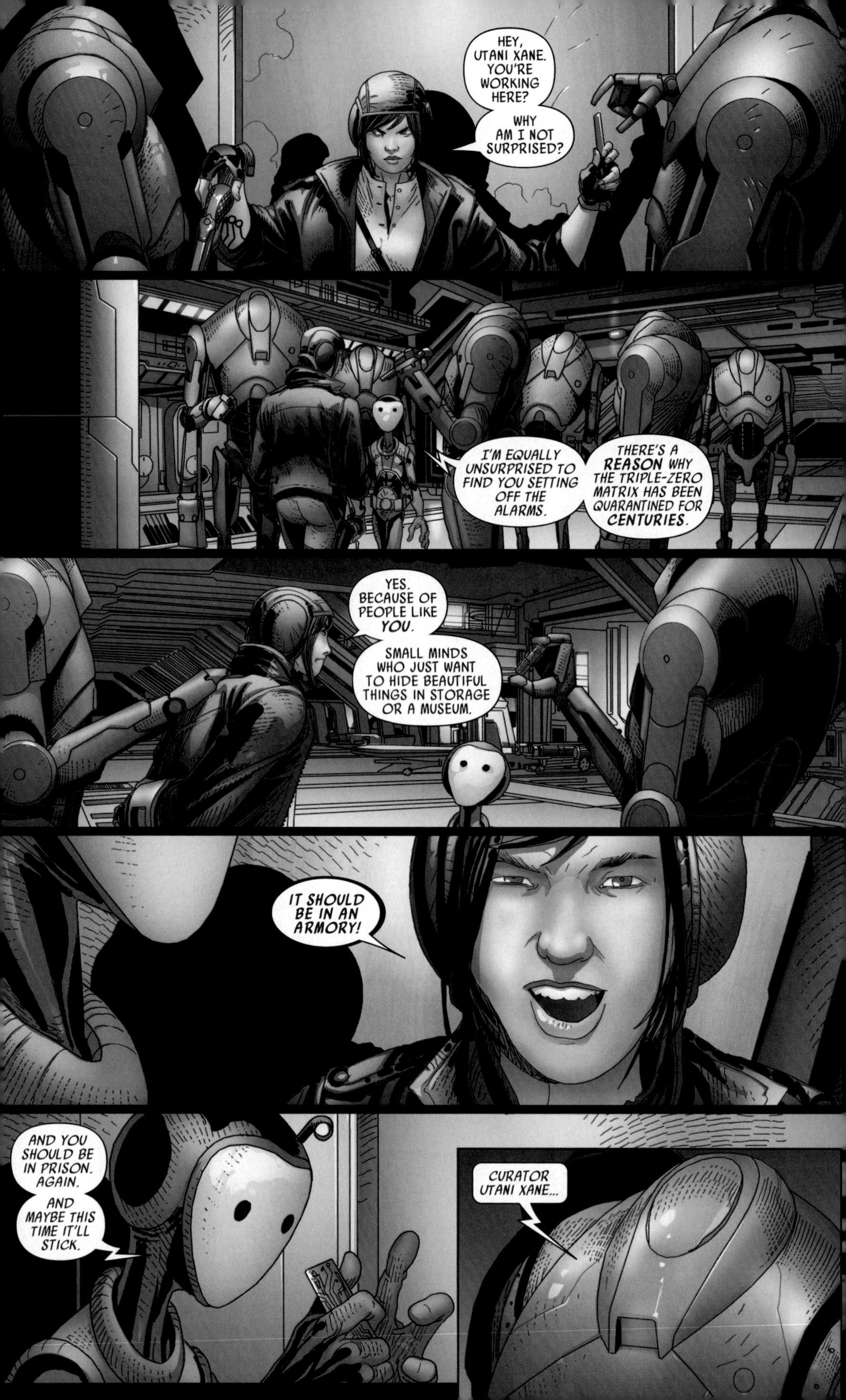

HEY, UTANI XANE. YOU'RE WORKING HERE?
WHY AM I NOT SURPRISED?
I'M EQUALLY UNSURPRISED TO FIND YOU SETTING OFF THE ALARMS.
THERE'S A REASON WHY THE TRIPLE-ZERO MATRIX HAS BEEN QUARANTINED FOR CENTURIES.
YES. BECAUSE OF PEOPLE LIKE YOU.
SMALL MINDS WHO JUST WANT TO HIDE BEAUTIFUL THINGS IN STORAGE OR A MUSEUM.
IT SHOULD BE IN AN ARMORY!
AND YOU SHOULD BE IN PRISON. AGAIN.
AND MAYBE THIS TIME IT'LL STICK.
CURATOR UTANI XANE...

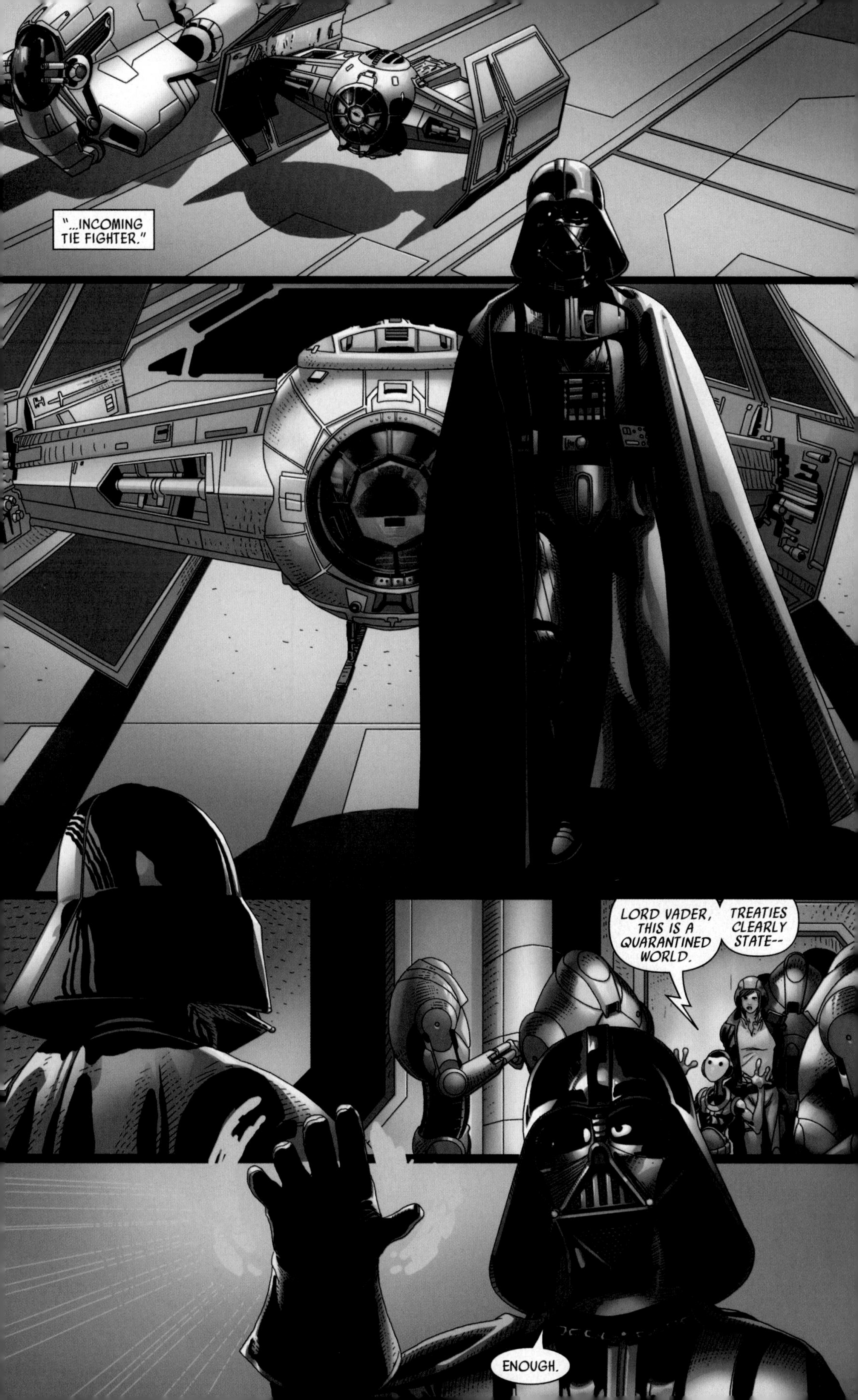
"...INCOMING
TIE FIGHTER."
LORD VADER, THIS IS A QUARANTINED WORLD.
TREATIES CLEARLY STATE--
ENOUGH.

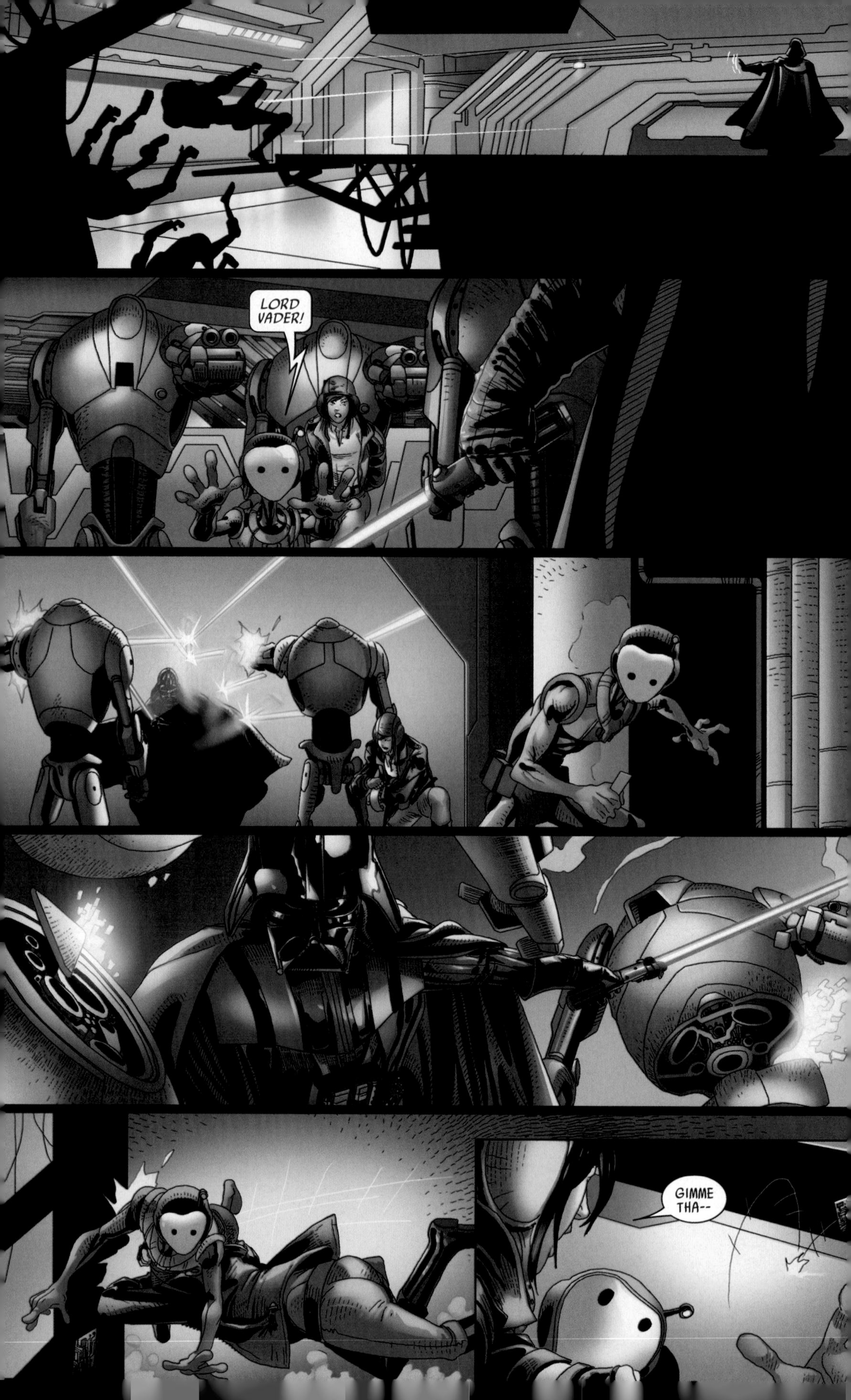
LORD VADER!
GIMME THA--

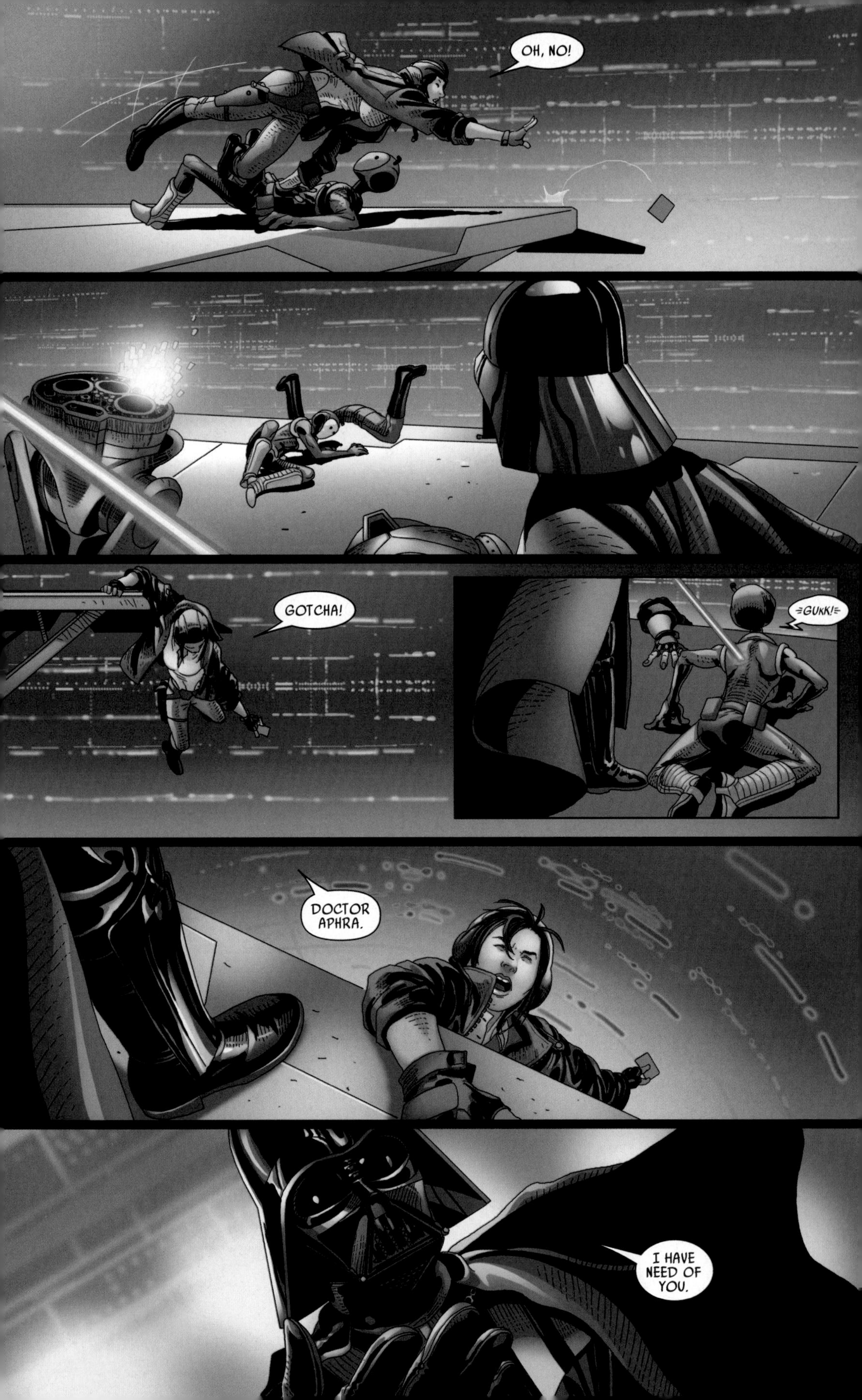
OH, NO!
GOTCHA!
GUKK!
DOCTOR APHRA.
I HAVE NEED OF YOU.

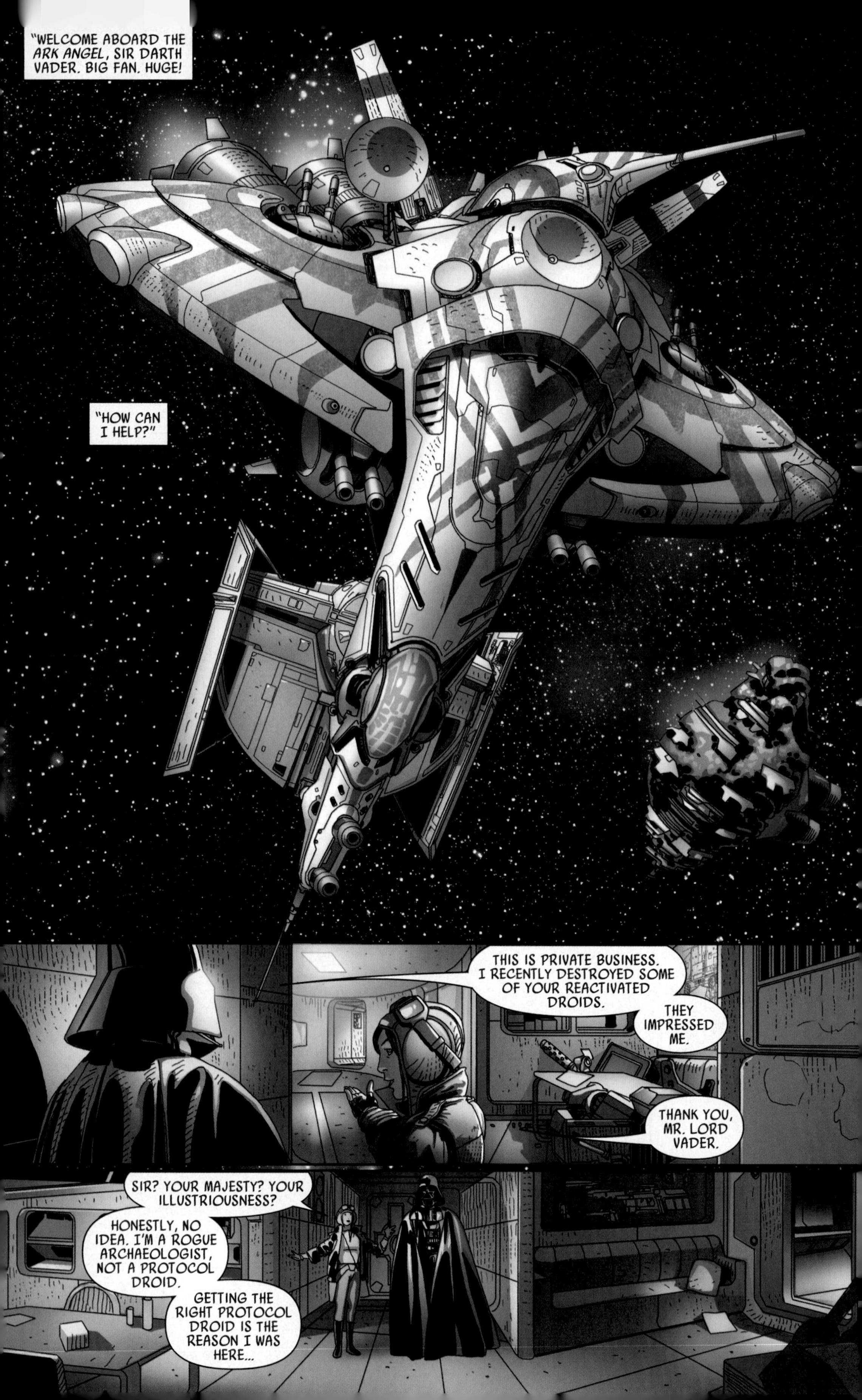
"WELCOME ABOARD THE ARK ANGEL, SIR DARTH VADER. BIG FAN. HUGE!
"HOW CAN I HELP?"
THIS IS PRIVATE BUSINESS. I RECENTLY DESTROYED SOME OF YOUR REACTIVATED DROIDS.
THEY IMPRESSED ME.
THANK YOU, MR. LORD VADER.
SIR? YOUR MAJESTY? YOUR ILLUSTRIOUSNESS?
HONESTLY, NO IDEA. I'M A ROGUE ARCHAEOLOGIST, NOT A PROTOCOL DROID.
GETTING THE RIGHT PROTOCOL DROID IS THE REASON I WAS HERE...

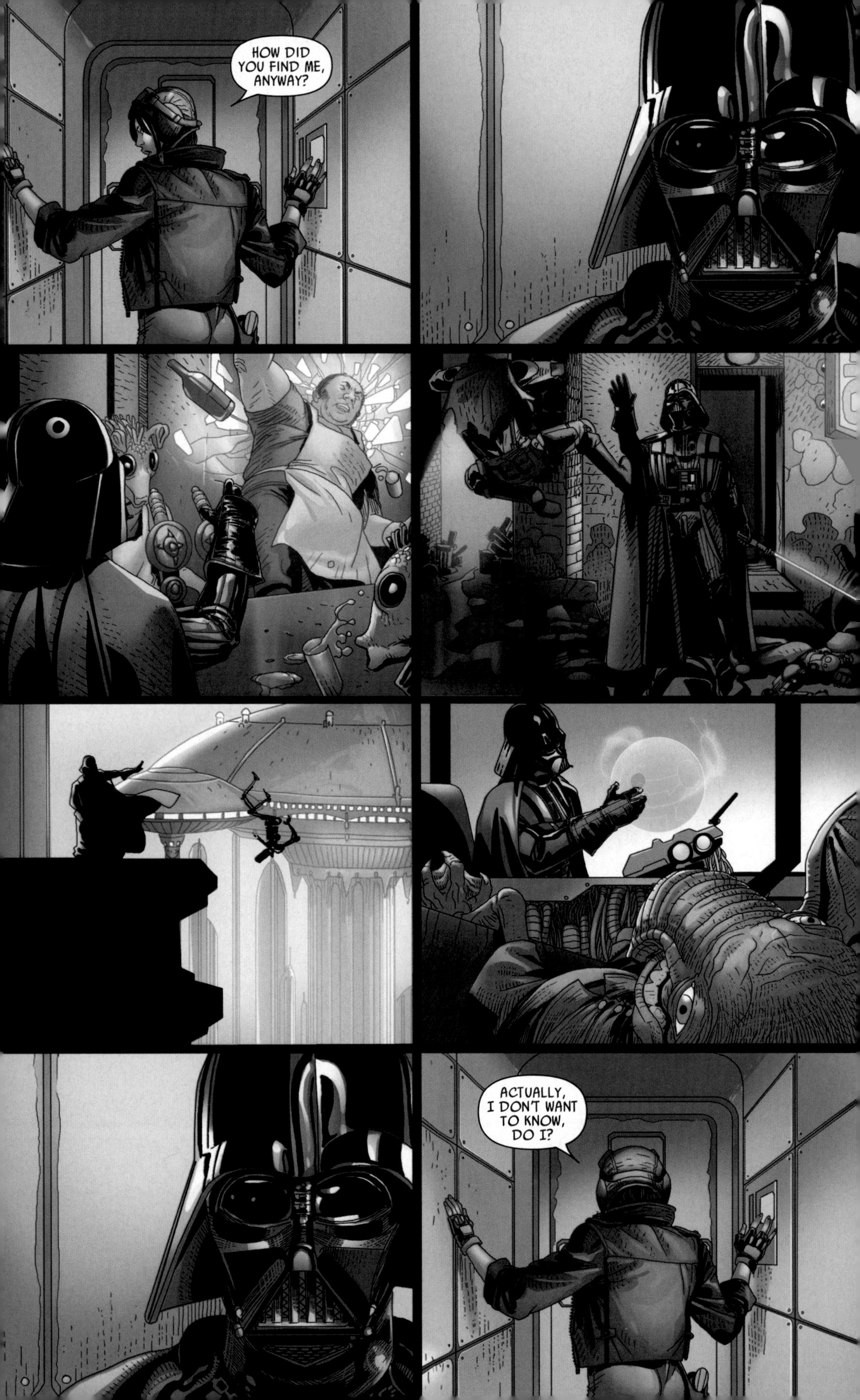
HOW DID YOU FIND ME, ANYWAY?
ACTUALLY, I DON'T WANT TO KNOW, DO I?

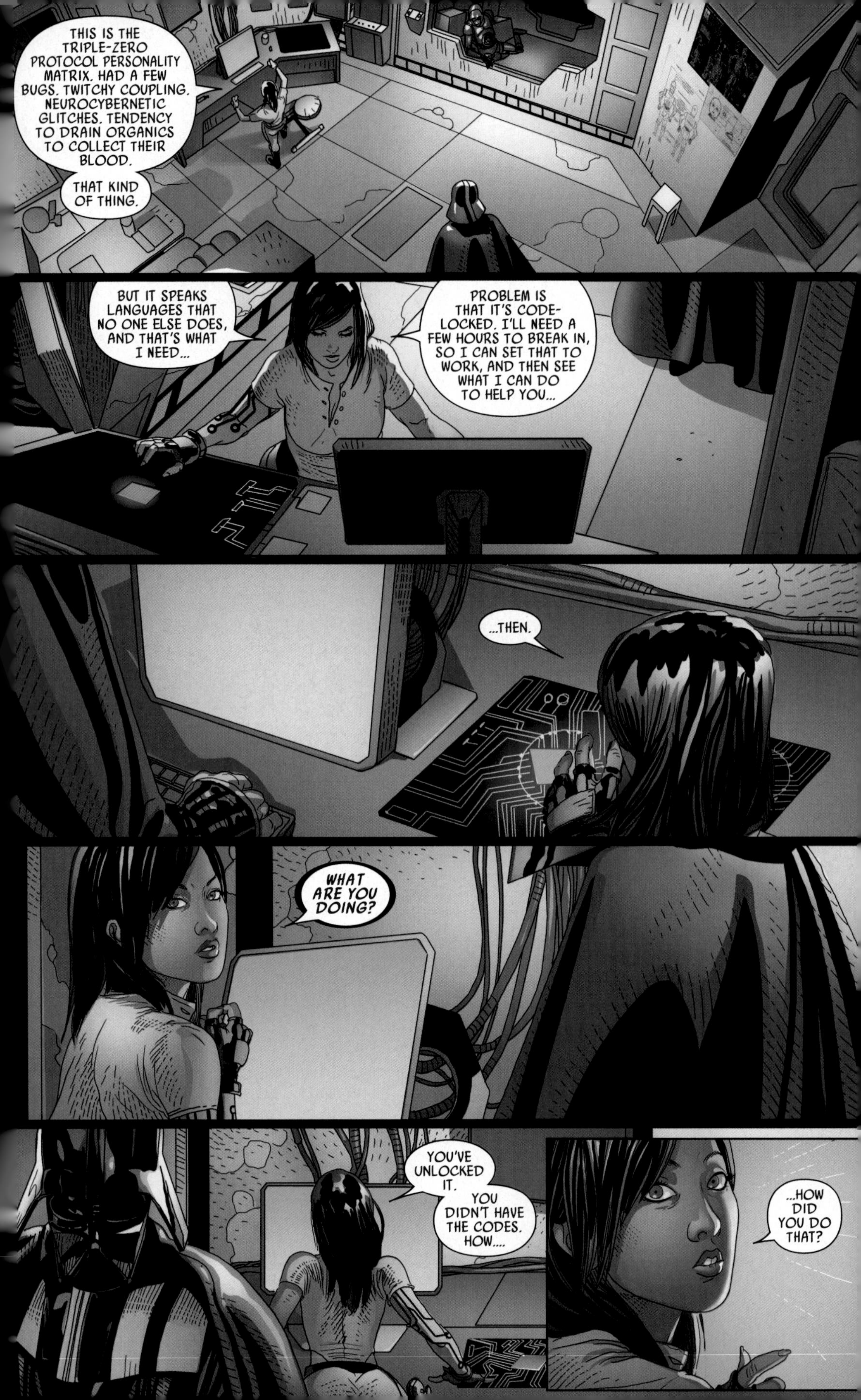
THIS IS THE TRIPLE-ZERO PROTOCOL PERSONALITY MATRIX. HAD A FEW BUGS. TWITCHY COUPLING. NEUROCYBERNETIC GLITCHES. TENDENCY TO DRAIN ORGANICS TO COLLECT THEIR BLOOD.
THAT KIND OF THING.
BUT IT SPEAKS LANGUAGES THAT NO ONE ELSE DOES, AND THAT'S WHAT I NEED...
PROBLEM IS THAT IT'S CODE-LOCKED. I'LL NEED A FEW HOURS TO BREAK IN, SO I CAN SET THAT TO WORK, AND THEN SEE WHAT I CAN DO TO HELP YOU...
...THEN.
WHAT ARE YOU DOING?
YOU'VE UNLOCKED IT.
YOU DIDN'T HAVE THE CODES. HOW....
...HOW DID YOU DO THAT?

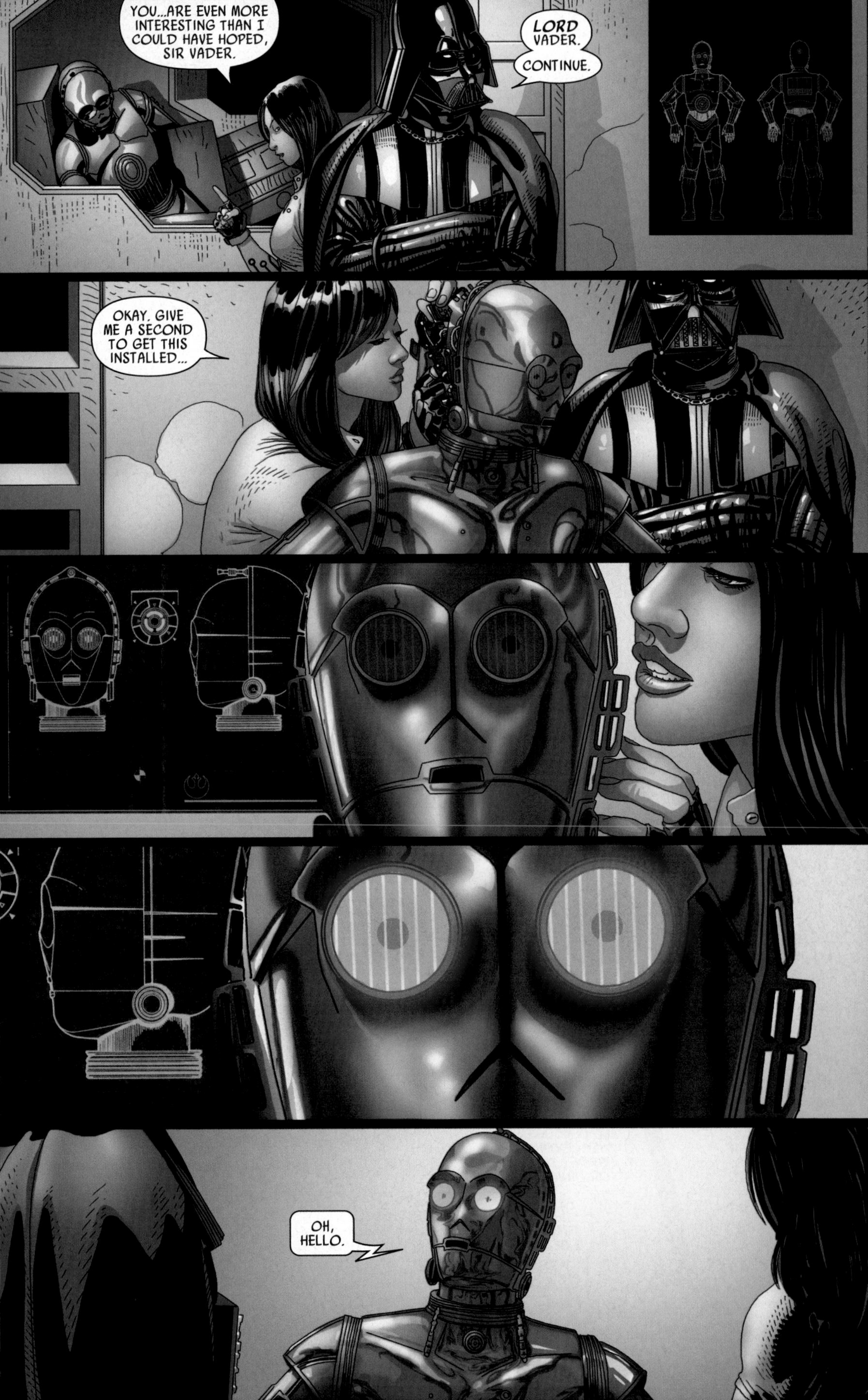
YOU...ARE EVEN MORE INTERESTING THAN I COULD HAVE HOPED, SIR VADER.
LORD VADER.
CONTINUE.
OKAY. GIVE ME A SECOND TO GET THIS INSTALLED...
OH, HELLO.

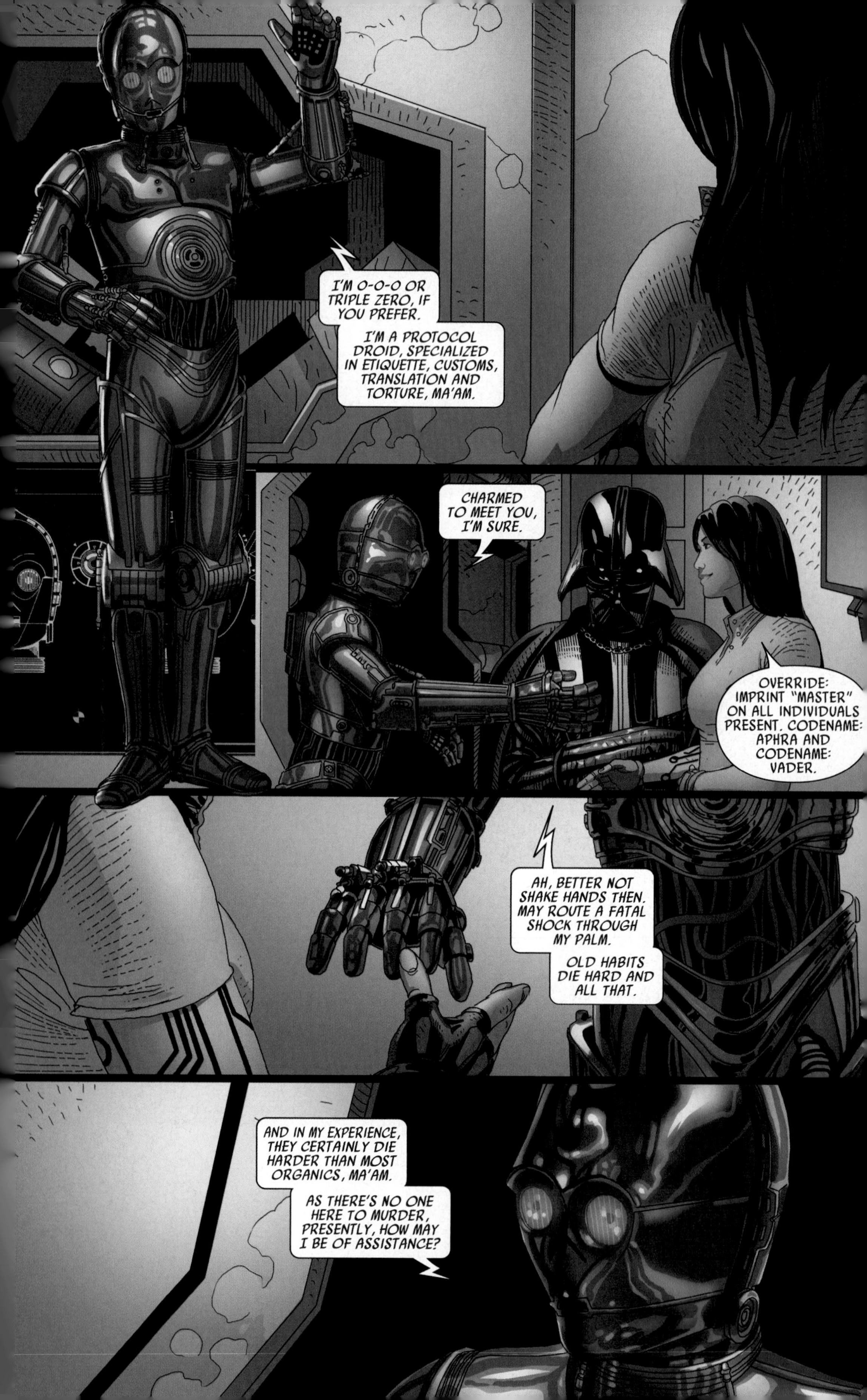
I'M 0-0-0 OR TRIPLE ZERO, IF YOU PREFER.
I'M A PROTOCOL DROID, SPECIALIZED IN ETIQUETTE, CUSTOMS, TRANSLATION AND TORTURE, MA'AM.
CHARMED TO MEET YOU, I'M SURE.
OVERRIDE: IMPRINT "MASTER" ON ALL INDIVIDUALS PRESENT. CODENAME: APHRA AND CODENAME: VADER.
AH, BETTER NOT SHAKE HANDS THEN. MAY ROUTE A FATAL SHOCK THROUGH MY PALM.
OLD HABITS DIE HARD AND ALL THAT.
AND IN MY EXPERIENCE, THEY CERTAINLY DIE HARDER THAN MOST ORGANICS, MA'AM.
AS THERE'S NO ONE HERE TO MURDER, PRESENTLY, HOW MAY I BE OF ASSISTANCE?

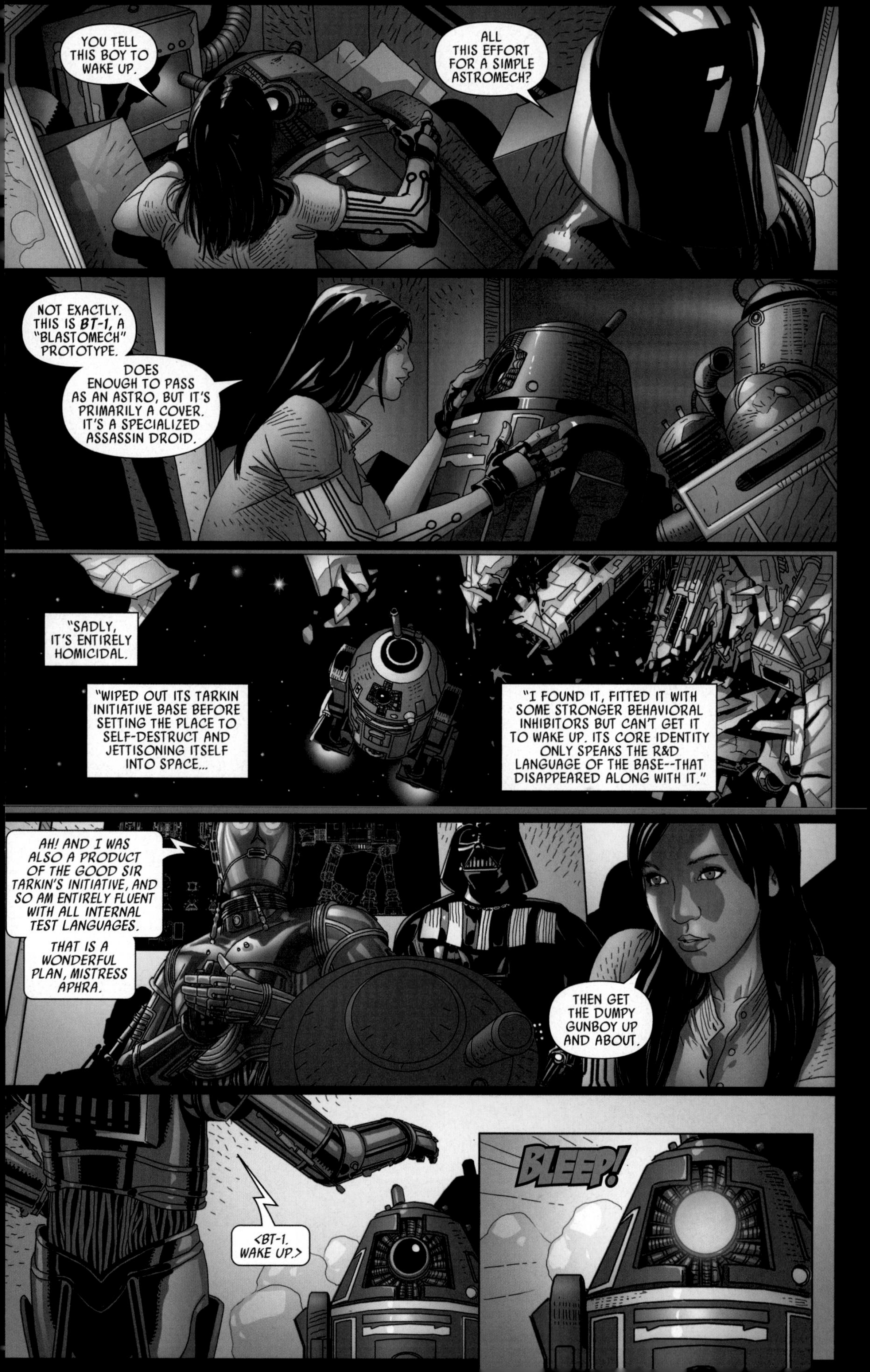
YOU TELL THIS BOY TO WAKE UP.
ALL THIS EFFORT FOR A SIMPLE ASTROMECH?
NOT EXACTLY. THIS IS BT-1, A "BLASTOMECH" PROTOTYPE.
DOES ENOUGH TO PASS AS AN ASTRO, BUT IT'S PRIMARILY A COVER. IT'S A SPECIALIZED ASSASSIN DROID.
"SADLY, IT'S ENTIRELY HOMICIDAL.
"WIPED OUT ITS TARKIN INITIATIVE BASE BEFORE SETTING THE PLACE TO SELF-DESTRUCT AND JETTISONING ITSELF INTO SPACE...
"I FOUND IT, FITTED IT WITH SOME STRONGER BEHAVIORAL INHIBITORS BUT CAN'T GET IT TO WAKE UP. ITS CORE IDENTITY ONLY SPEAKS THE R&D LANGUAGE OF THE BASE--THAT DISAPPEARED ALONG WITH IT."
AH! AND I WAS ALSO A PRODUCT OF THE GOOD SIR TARKIN'S INITIATIVE, AND SO AM ENTIRELY FLUENT WITH ALL INTERNAL TEST LANGUAGES.
THAT IS A WONDERFUL PLAN, MISTRESS APHRA.
THEN GET THE DUMPY GUNBOY UP AND ABOUT.
<BT-1. WAKE UP.>
BLEEP!

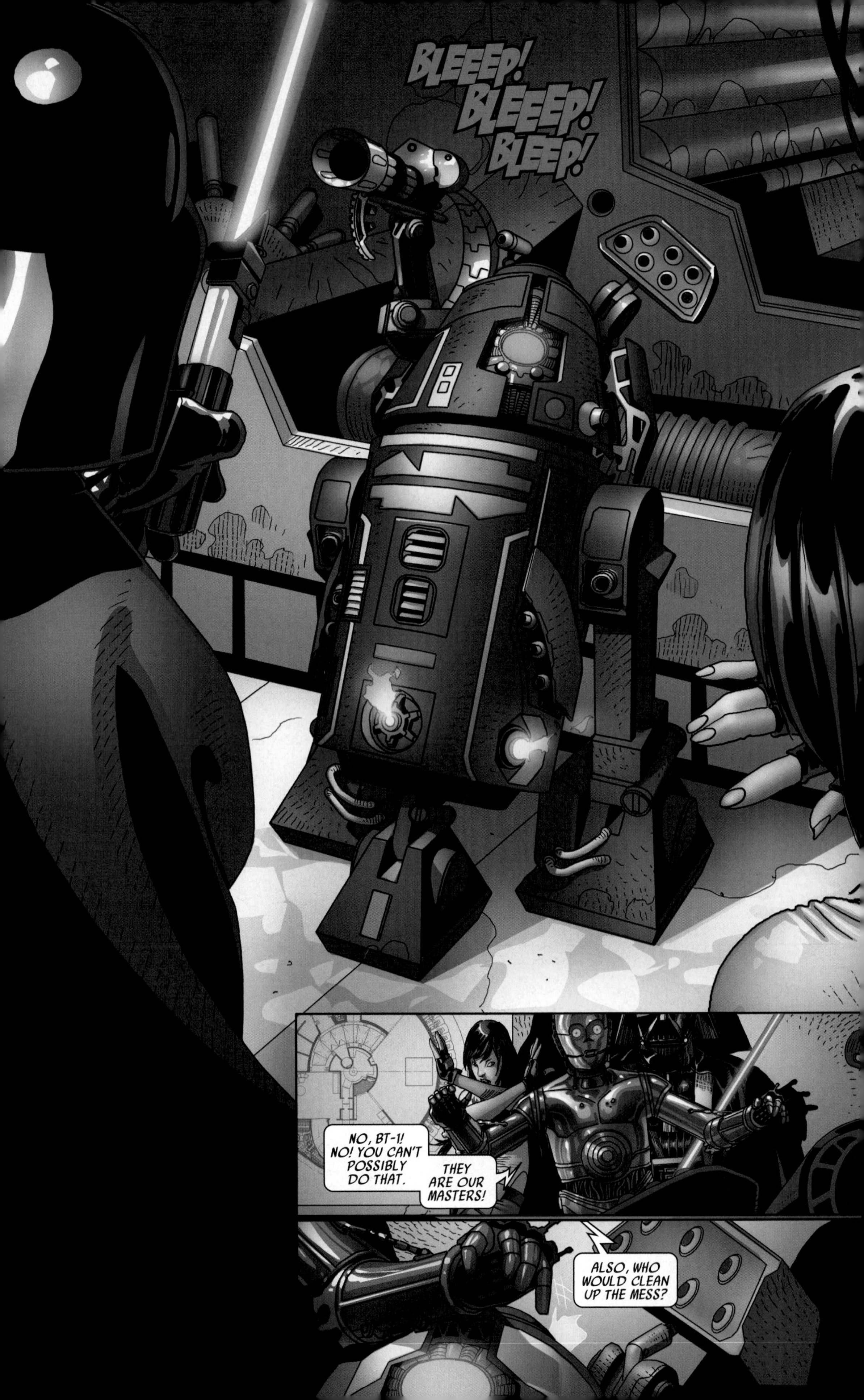
BLEEEP! BLEEEP! BLEEP!
NO, BT-1! NO! YOU CAN'T POSSIBLY DO THAT.
THEY ARE OUR MASTERS!
ALSO, WHO WOULD CLEAN UP THE MESS?

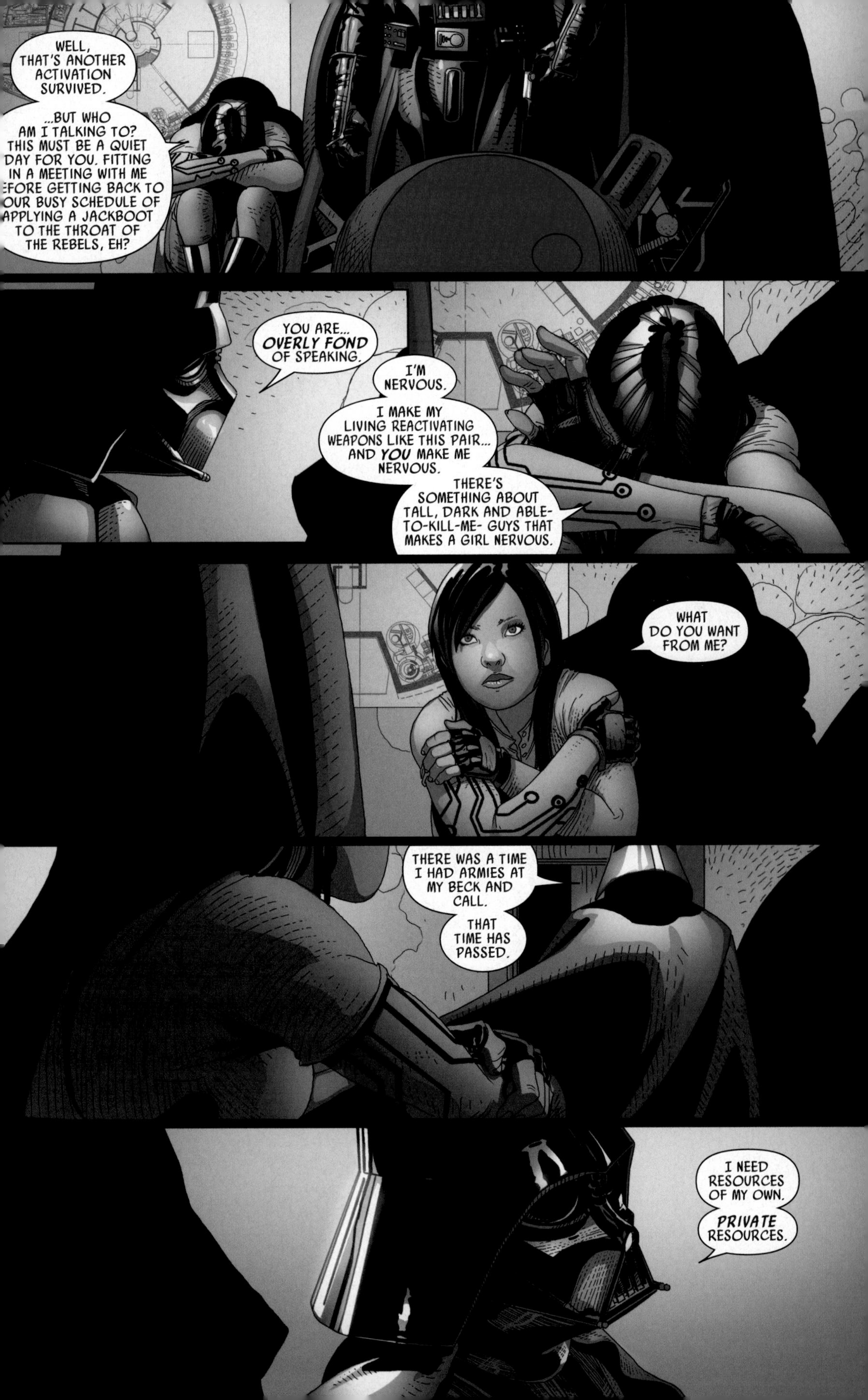
WELL, THAT'S ANOTHER ACTIVATION SURVIVED.
...BUT WHO AM I TALKING TO? THIS MUST BE A QUIET DAY FOR YOU. FITTING IN A MEETING WITH ME EFORE GETTING BACK TO OUR BUSY SCHEDULE OF APPLYING A JACKBOOT TO THE THROAT OF THE REBELS, EH?
YOU ARE... OVERLY FOND OF SPEAKING.
I'M NERVOUS.
I MAKE MY LIVING REACTIVATING WEAPONS LIKE THIS PAIR... AND YOU MAKE ME NERVOUS.
THERE'S SOMETHING ABOUT TALL, DARK AND ABLE-TO-KILL-ME- GUYS THAT MAKES A GIRL NERVOUS.
WHAT DO YOU WANT FROM ME?
THERE WAS A TIME I HAD ARMIES AT MY BECK AND CALL.
THAT TIME HAS PASSED.
I NEED RESOURCES OF MY OWN.
PRIVATE RESOURCES.

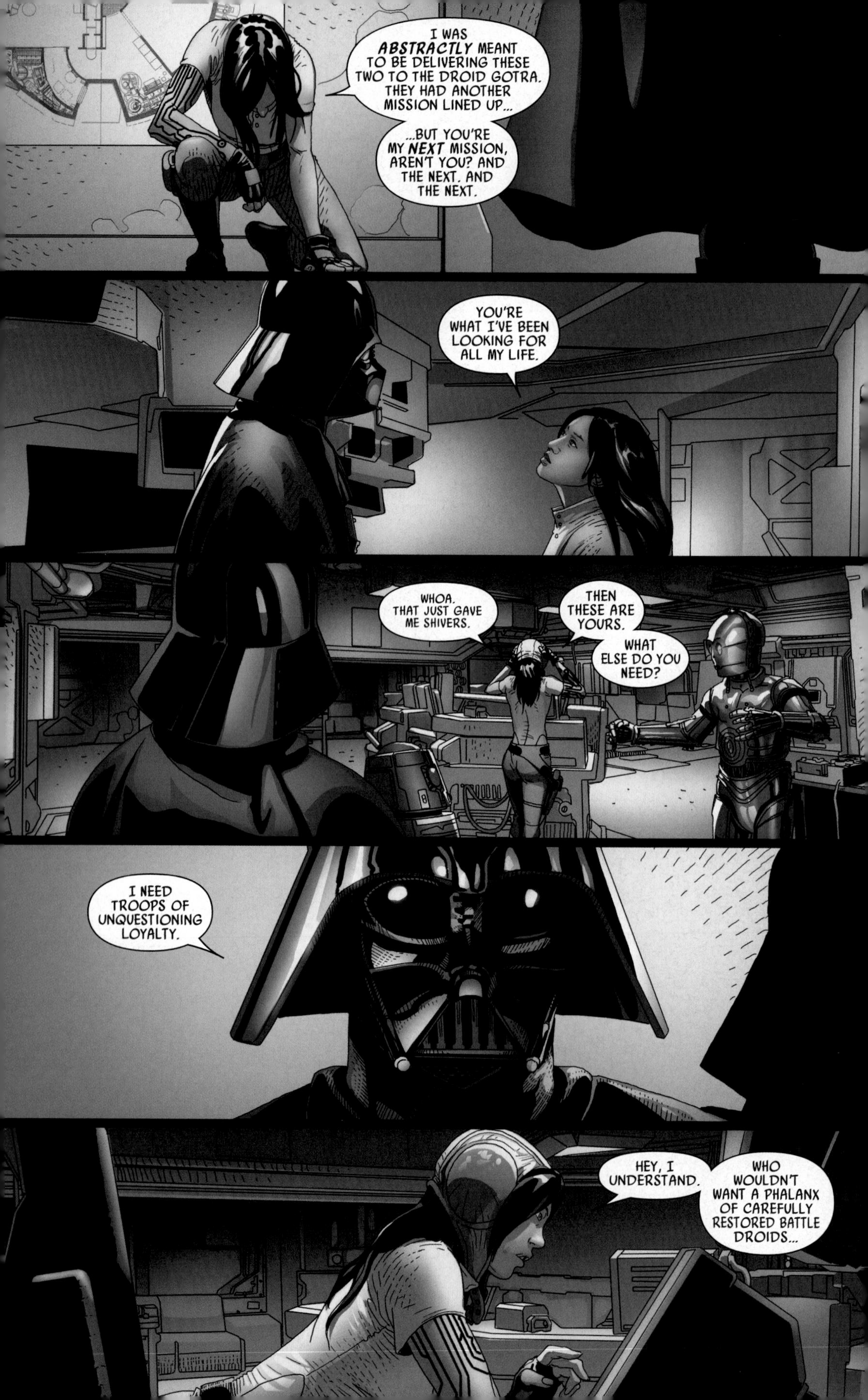
I WAS ABSTRACTLY MEANT TO BE DELIVERING THESE TWO TO THE DROID GOTRA. THEY HAD ANOTHER MISSION LINED UP...
...BUT YOU'RE MY NEXT MISSION, AREN'T YOU? AND THE NEXT. AND THE NEXT.
YOU'RE WHAT I'VE BEEN LOOKING FOR ALL MY LIFE.
WHOA. THAT JUST GAVE ME SHIVERS.
THEN THESE ARE YOURS.
WHAT ELSE DO YOU NEED?
I NEED TROOPS OF UNQUESTIONING LOYALTY.
HEY, I UNDERSTAND.
WHO WOULDN'T WANT A PHALANX OF CAREFULLY RESTORED BATTLE DROIDS...

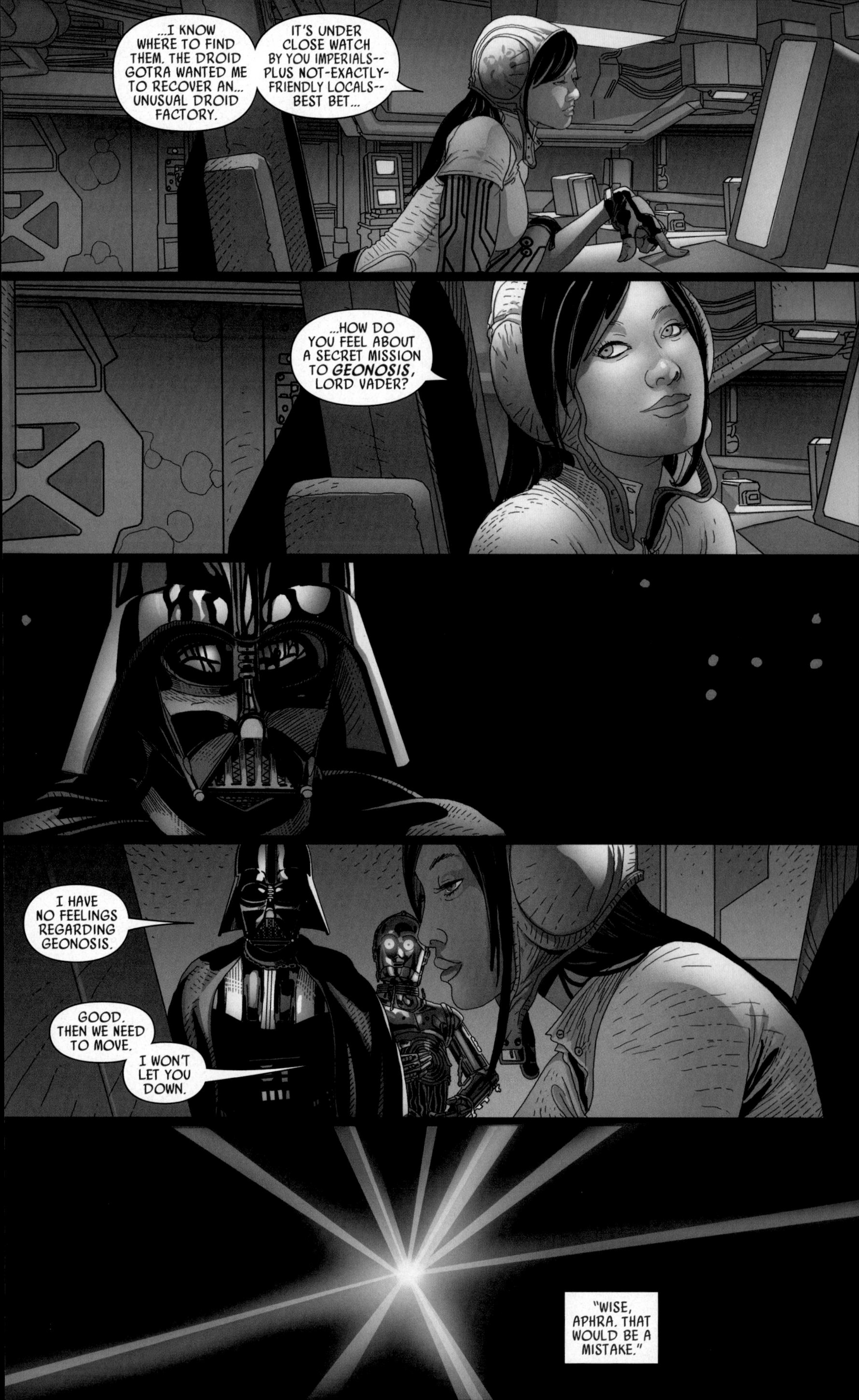
...I KNOW WHERE TO FIND THEM. THE DROID GOTRA WANTED ME TO RECOVER AN... UNUSUAL DROID FACTORY.
IT'S UNDER CLOSE WATCH BY YOU IMPERIALS-- PLUS NOT-EXACTLY-FRIENDLY LOCALS-- BEST BET...
...HOW DO YOU FEEL ABOUT A SECRET MISSION TO GEONOSIS, LORD VADER?
I HAVE NO FEELINGS REGARDING GEONOSIS.
GOOD. THEN WE NEED TO MOVE.
I WON'T LET YOU DOWN.
"WISE, APHRA. THAT WOULD BE A MISTAKE."

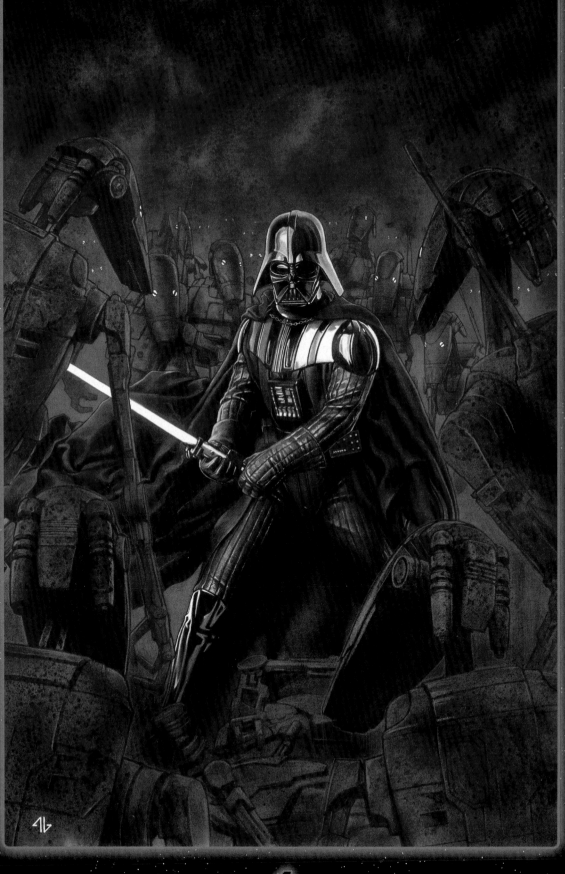

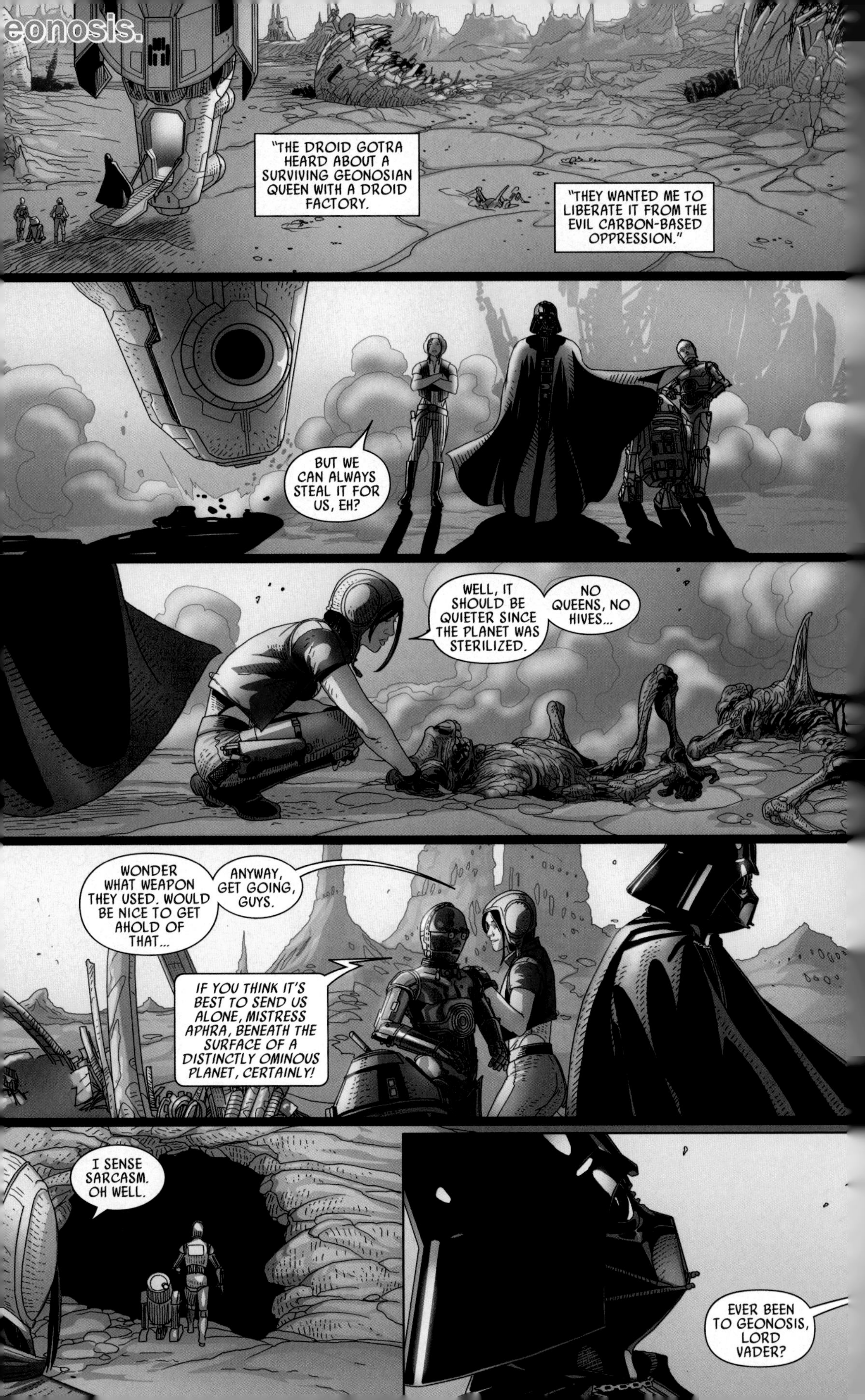
eonosis.
"THE DROID GOTRA HEARD ABOUT A SURVIVING GEONOSIAN QUEEN WITH A DROID FACTORY.
"THEY WANTED ME TO LIBERATE IT FROM THE EVIL CARBON-BASED OPPRESSION."
BUT WE CAN ALWAYS STEAL IT FOR US, EH?
WELL, IT SHOULD BE QUIETER SINCE THE PLANET WAS STERILIZED.
NO QUEENS, NO HIVES...
WONDER WHAT WEAPON THEY USED. WOULD BE NICE TO GET AHOLD OF THAT...
ANYWAY, GET GOING, GUYS.
IF YOU THINK IT'S BEST TO SEND US ALONE, MISTRESS APHRA, BENEATH THE SURFACE OF A DISTINCTLY OMINOUS PLANET, CERTAINLY!
I SENSE SARCASM. OH WELL.
EVER BEEN TO GEONOSIS, LORD VADER?

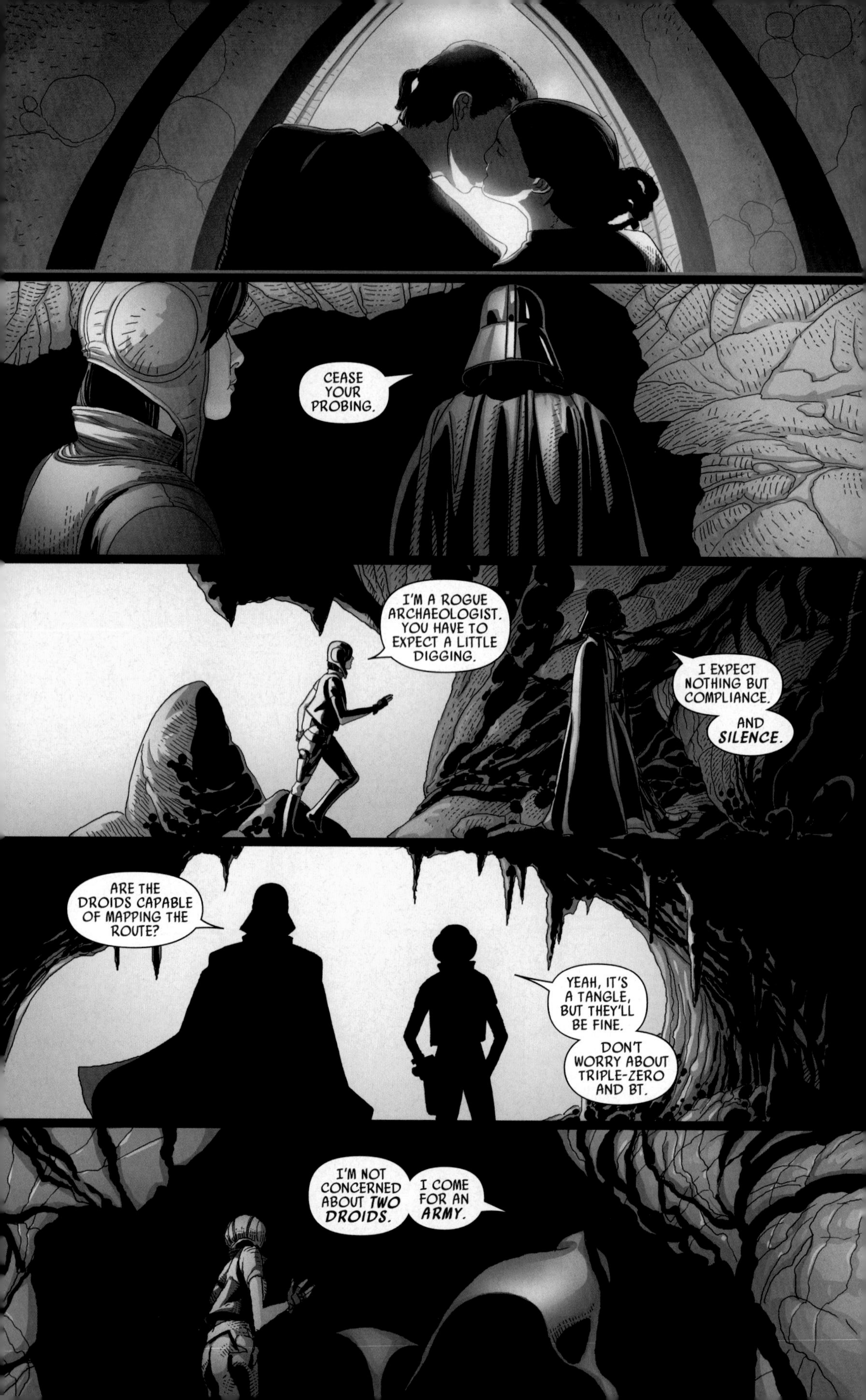
CEASE YOUR PROBING.
I'M A ROGUE ARCHAEOLOGIST. YOU HAVE TO EXPECT A LITTLE DIGGING.
I EXPECT NOTHING BUT COMPLIANCE.
AND SILENCE.
ARE THE DROIDS CAPABLE OF MAPPING THE ROUTE?
YEAH, IT'S A TANGLE, BUT THEY'LL BE FINE.
DON'T WORRY ABOUT TRIPLE-ZERO AND BT.
I'M NOT CONCERNED ABOUT TWO DROIDS.
I COME FOR AN ARMY.

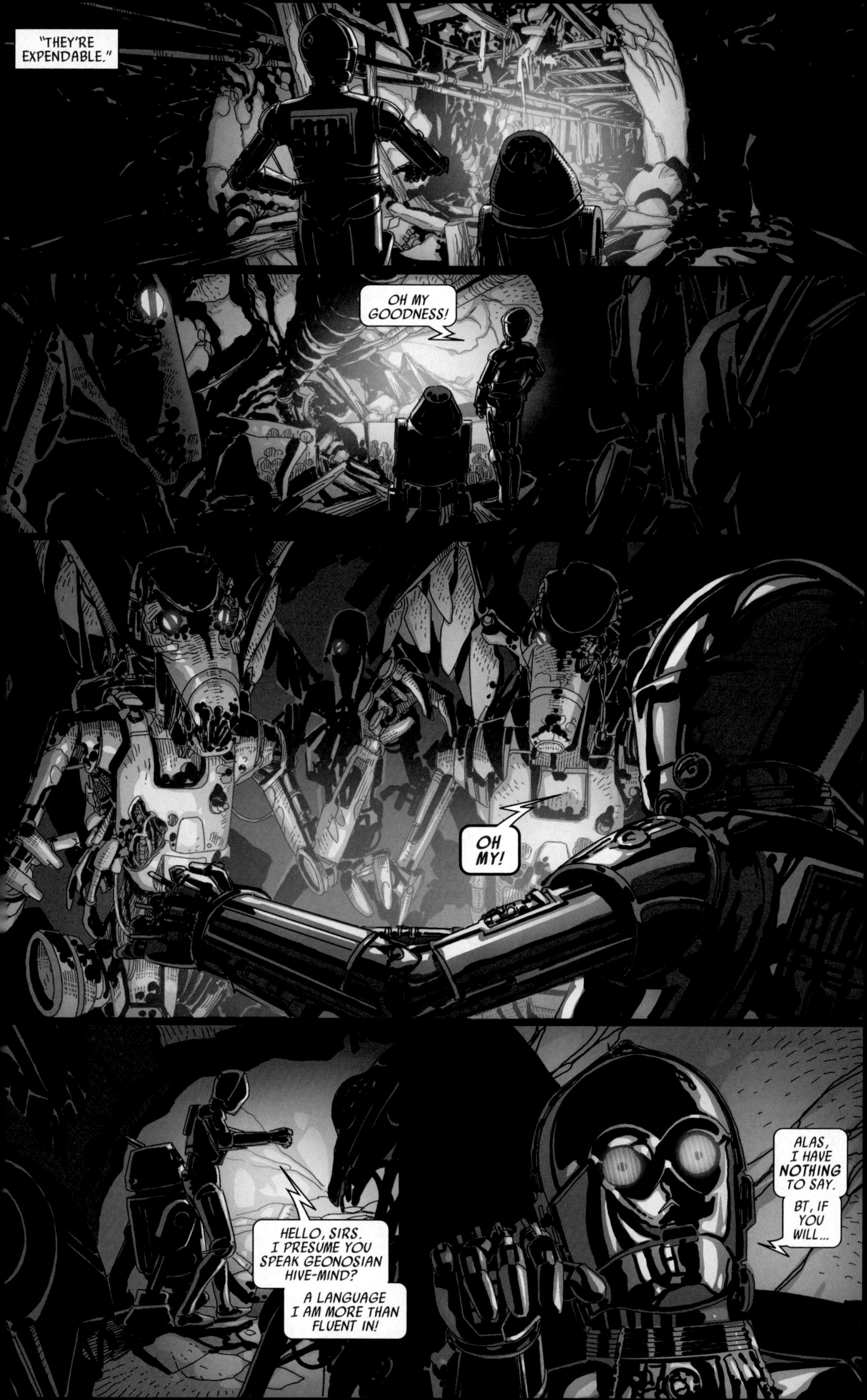
"THEY'RE EXPENDABLE."
OH MY GOODNESS!
OH MY!
HELLO, SIRS. I PRESUME YOU SPEAK GEONOSIAN HIVE-MIND?
A LANGUAGE I AM MORE THAN FLUENT IN!
ALAS, I HAVE NOTHING TO SAY.
BT, IF YOU WILL...

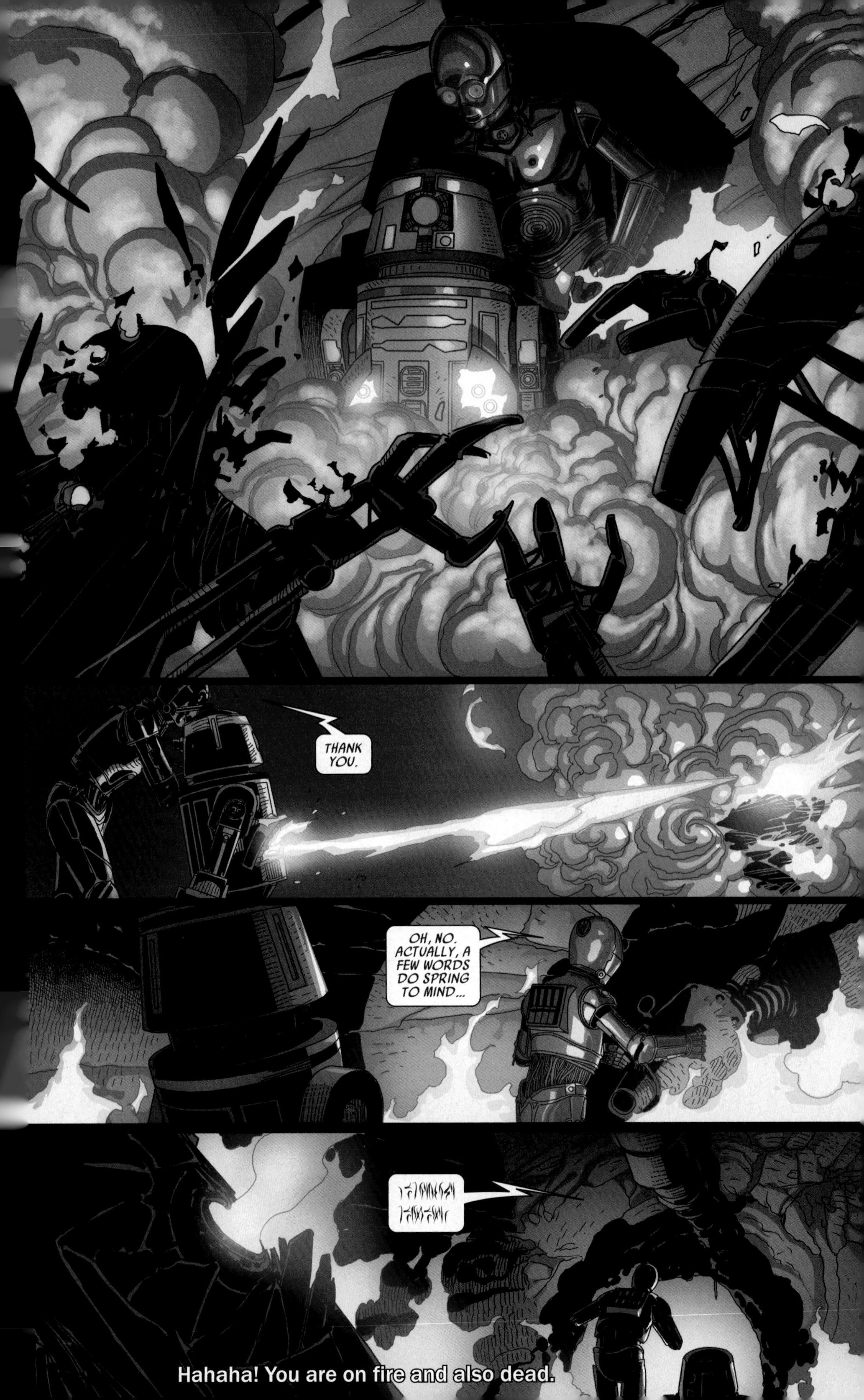
THANK YOU.
OH, NO. ACTUALLY, A FEW WORDS DO SPRING TO MIND...
Hahaha! You are on fire and also dead.

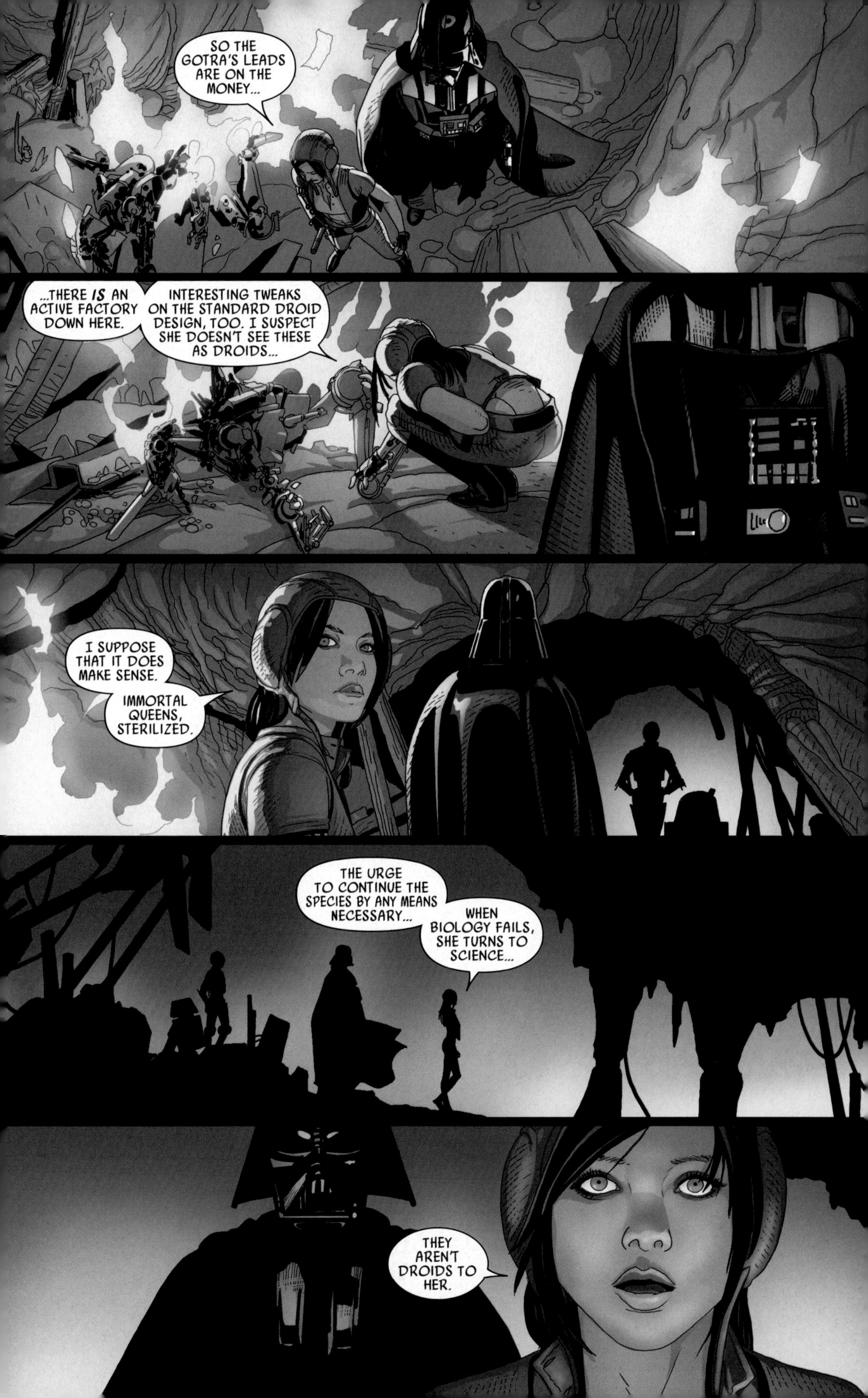
SO THE GOTRA'S LEADS ARE ON THE MONEY...
...THERE IS AN ACTIVE FACTORY DOWN HERE.
INTERESTING TWEAKS ON THE STANDARD DROID DESIGN, TOO. I SUSPECT SHE DOESN'T SEE THESE AS DROIDS...
I SUPPOSE THAT IT DOES MAKE SENSE.
IMMORTAL QUEENS, STERILIZED.
THE URGE TO CONTINUE THE SPECIES BY ANY MEANS NECESSARY...
WHEN BIOLOGY FAILS, SHE TURNS TO SCIENCE...
THEY AREN'T DROIDS TO HER.

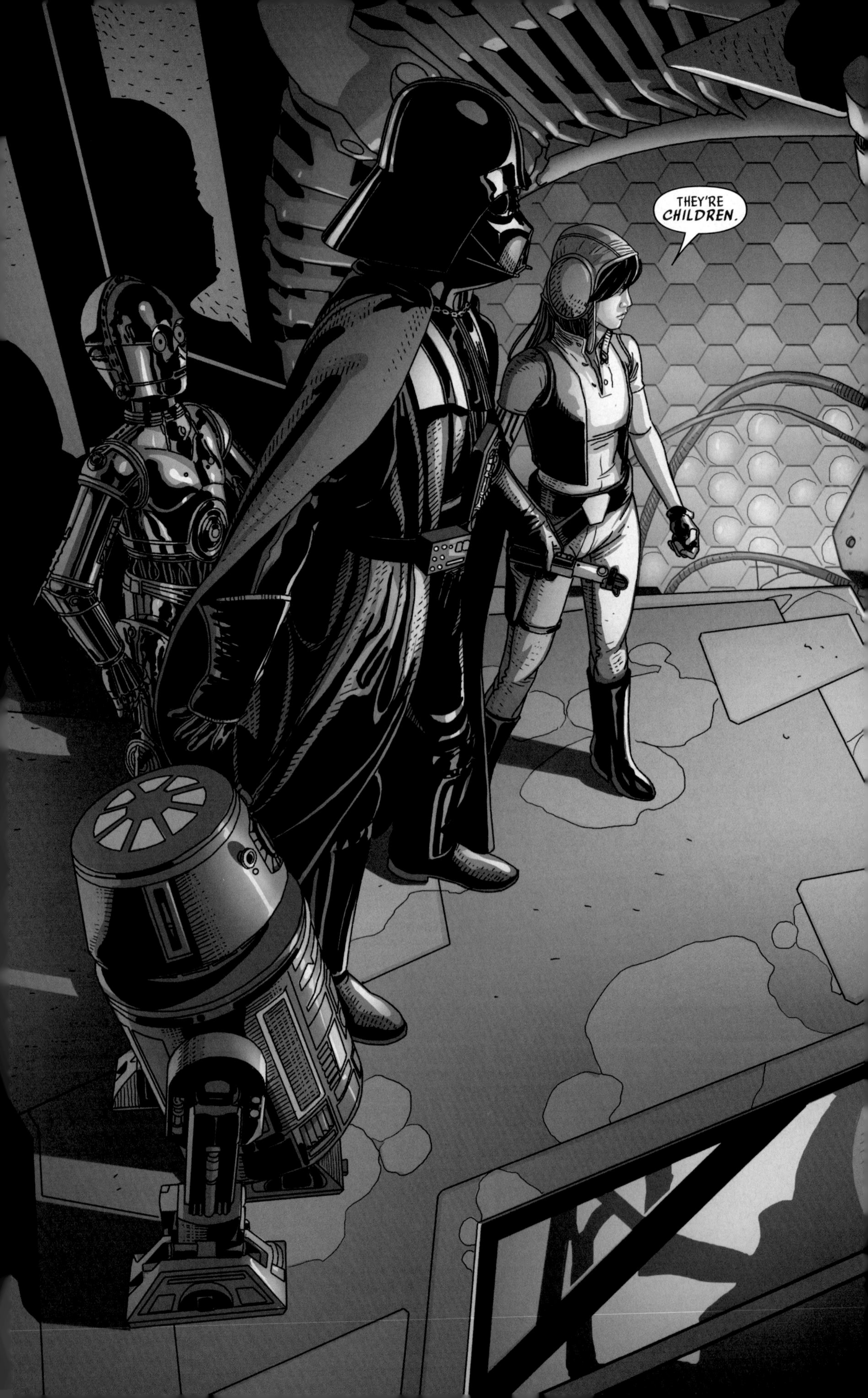
THEY'RE CHILDREN.

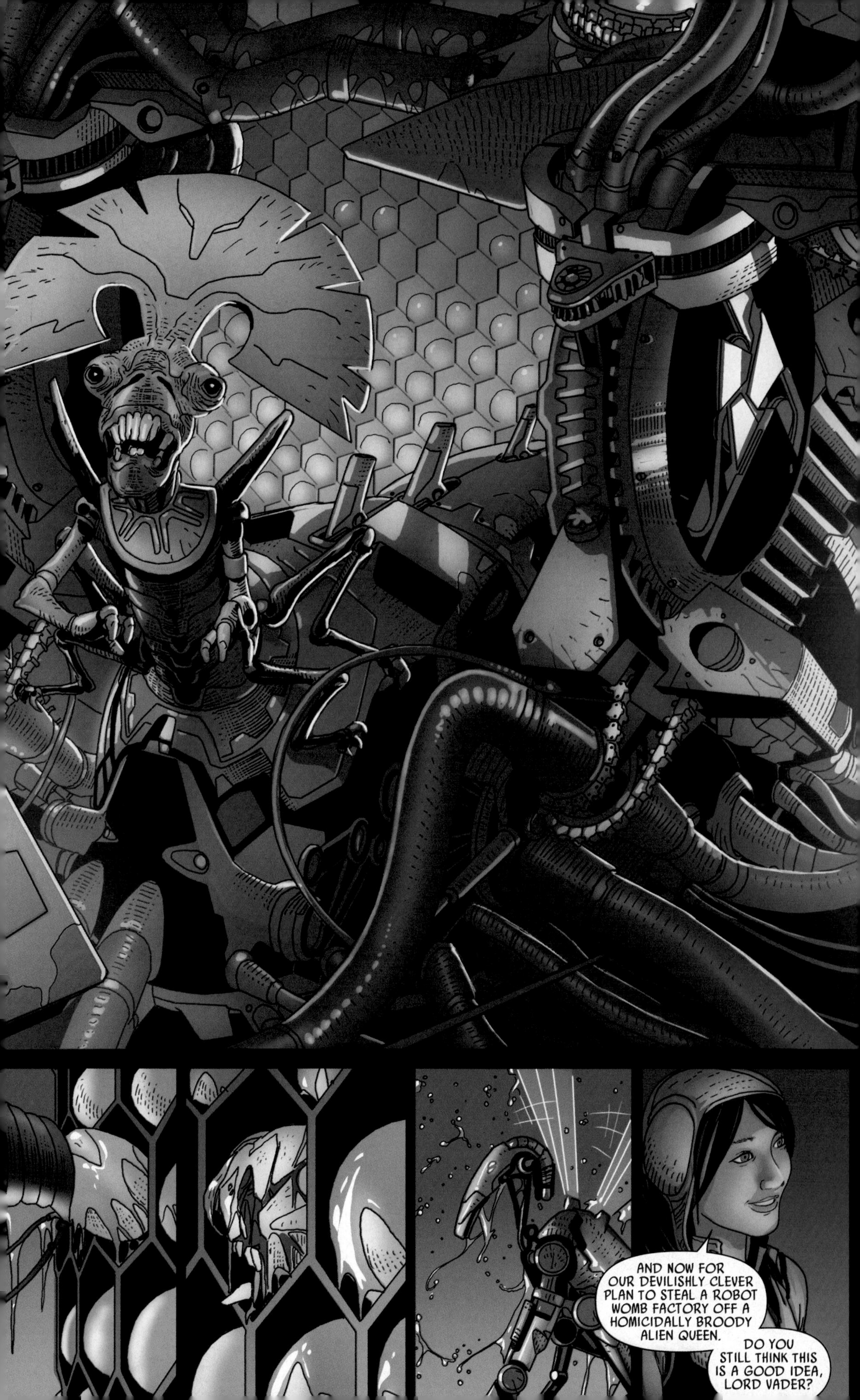
AND NOW FOR OUR DEVILISHLY CLEVER PLAN TO STEAL A ROBOT WOMB FACTORY OFF A HOMICIDALLY BROODY ALIEN QUEEN.
DO YOU STILL THINK THIS IS A GOOD IDEA, LORD VADER?

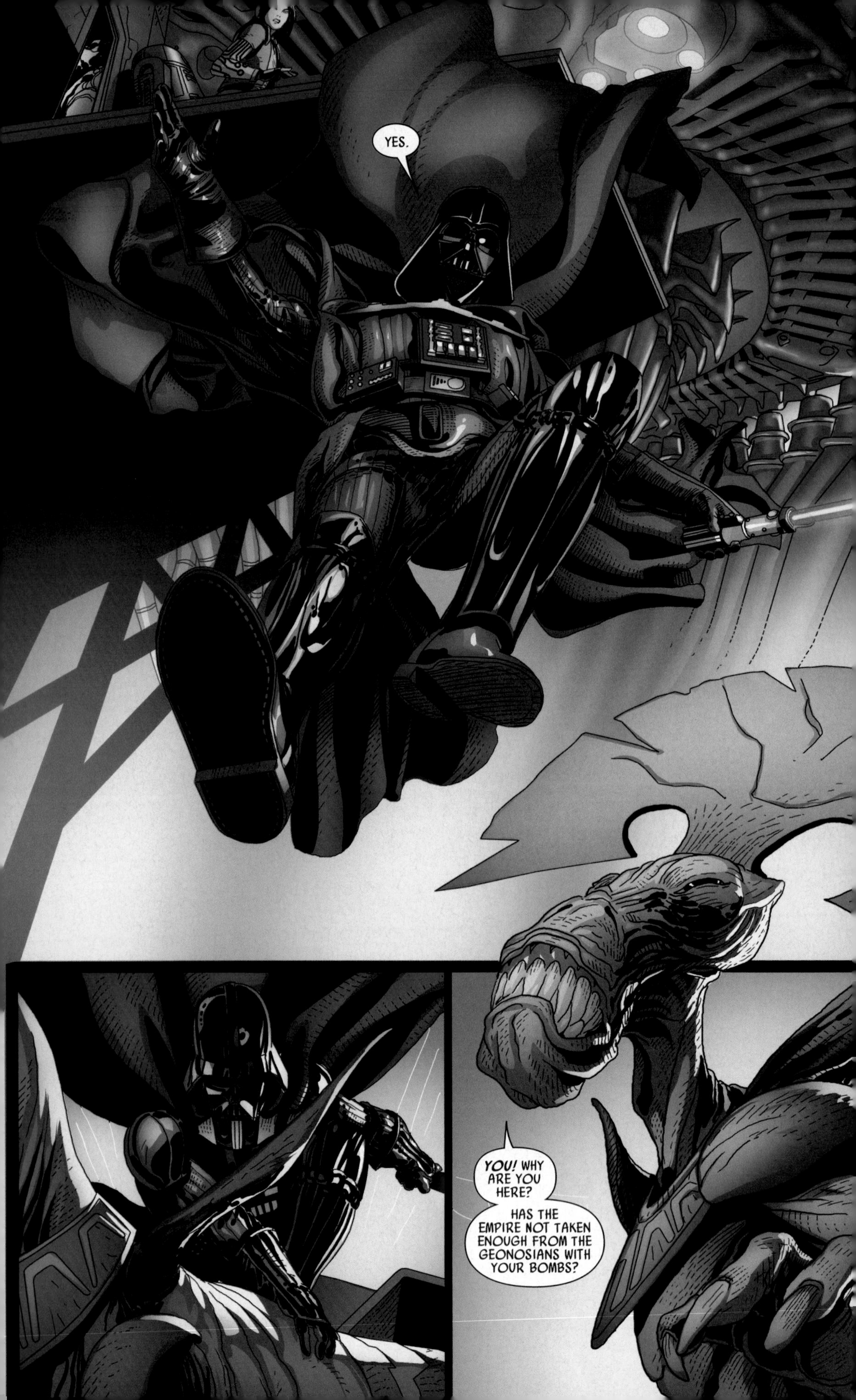
YES.
YOU! WHY ARE YOU HERE?
HAS THE EMPIRE NOT TAKEN ENOUGH FROM THE GEONOSIANS WITH YOUR BOMBS?

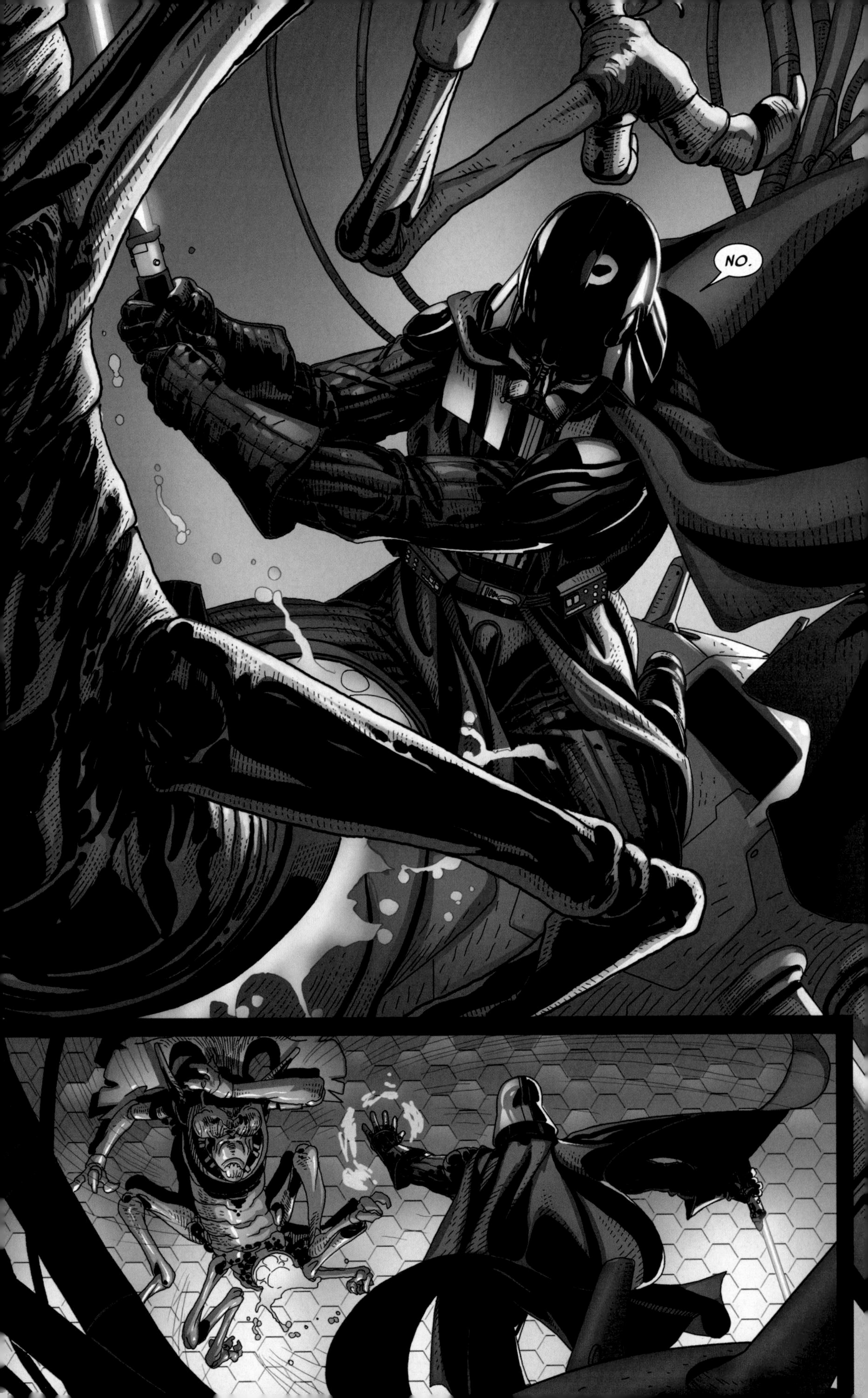
NO.

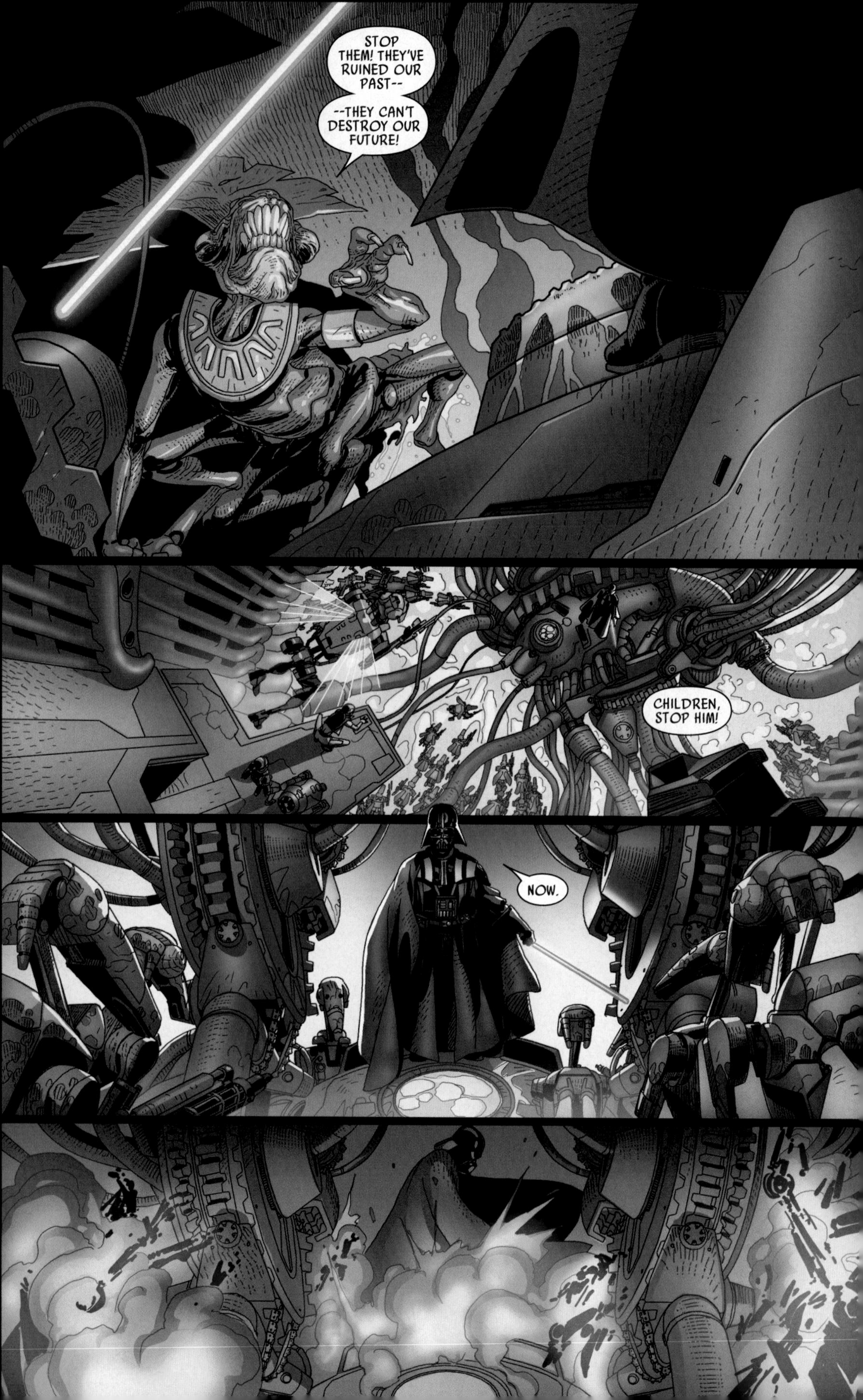
STOP THEM! THEY'VE RUINED OUR PAST--
--THEY CAN'T DESTROY OUR FUTURE!
CHILDREN, STOP HIM!
NOW.

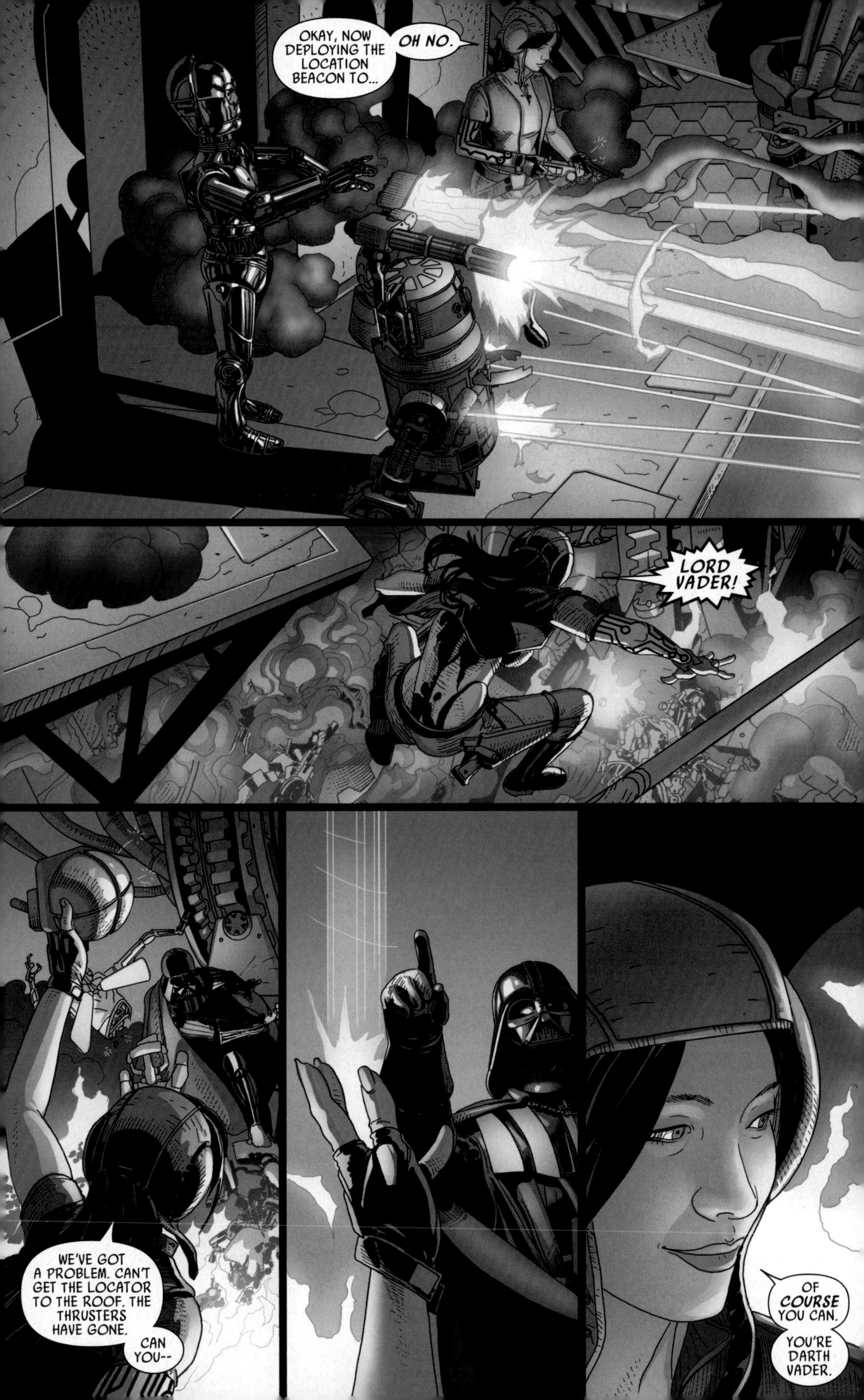
OKAY, NOW DEPLOYING THE LOCATION BEACON TO...
OH NO.
LORD VADER!
WE'VE GOT A PROBLEM. CAN'T GET THE LOCATOR TO THE ROOF. THE THRUSTERS HAVE GONE.
CAN YOU--
OF COURSE YOU CAN.
YOU'RE DARTH VADER.

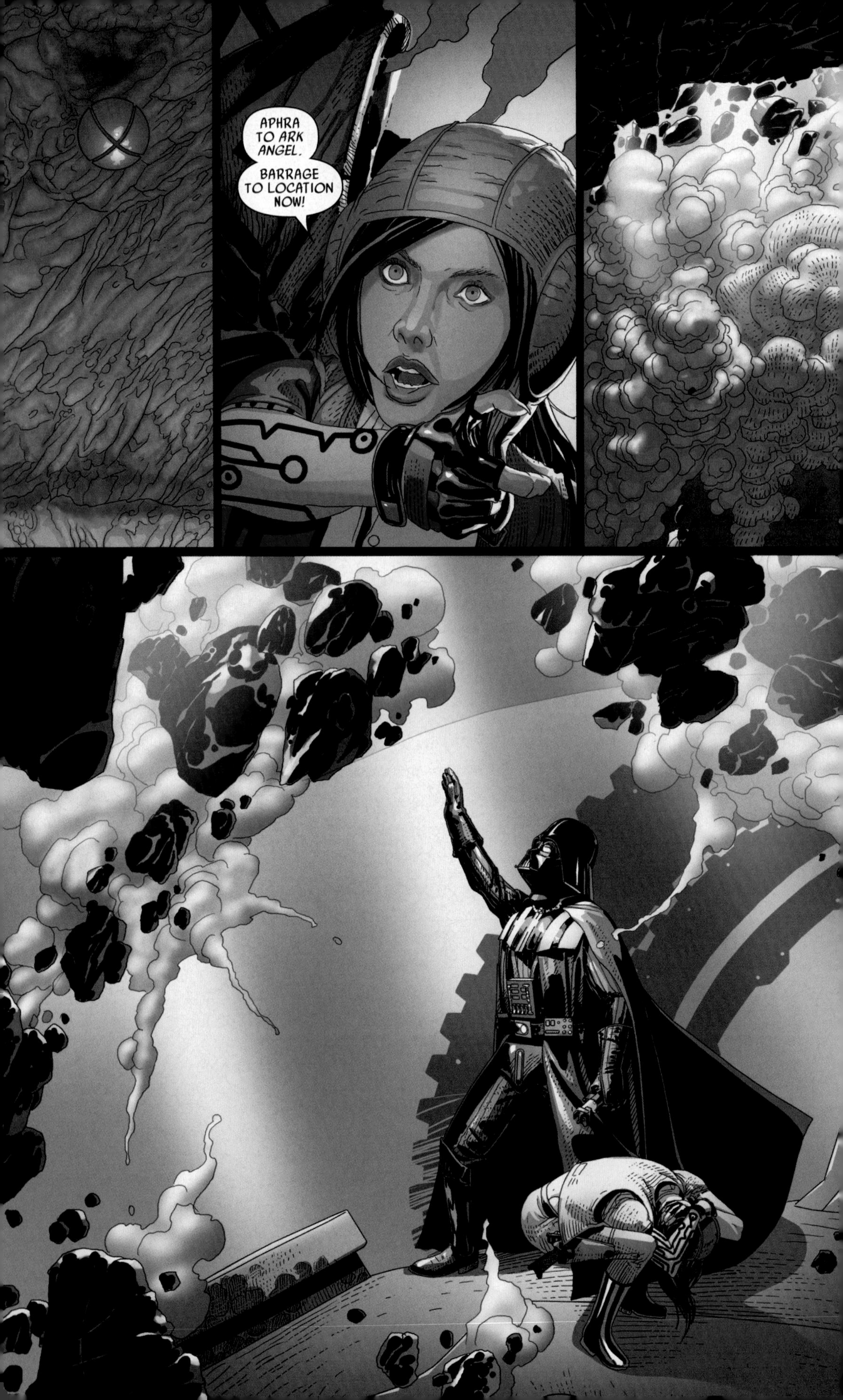
APHRA TO ARK ANGEL.
BARRAGE TO LOCATION NOW!

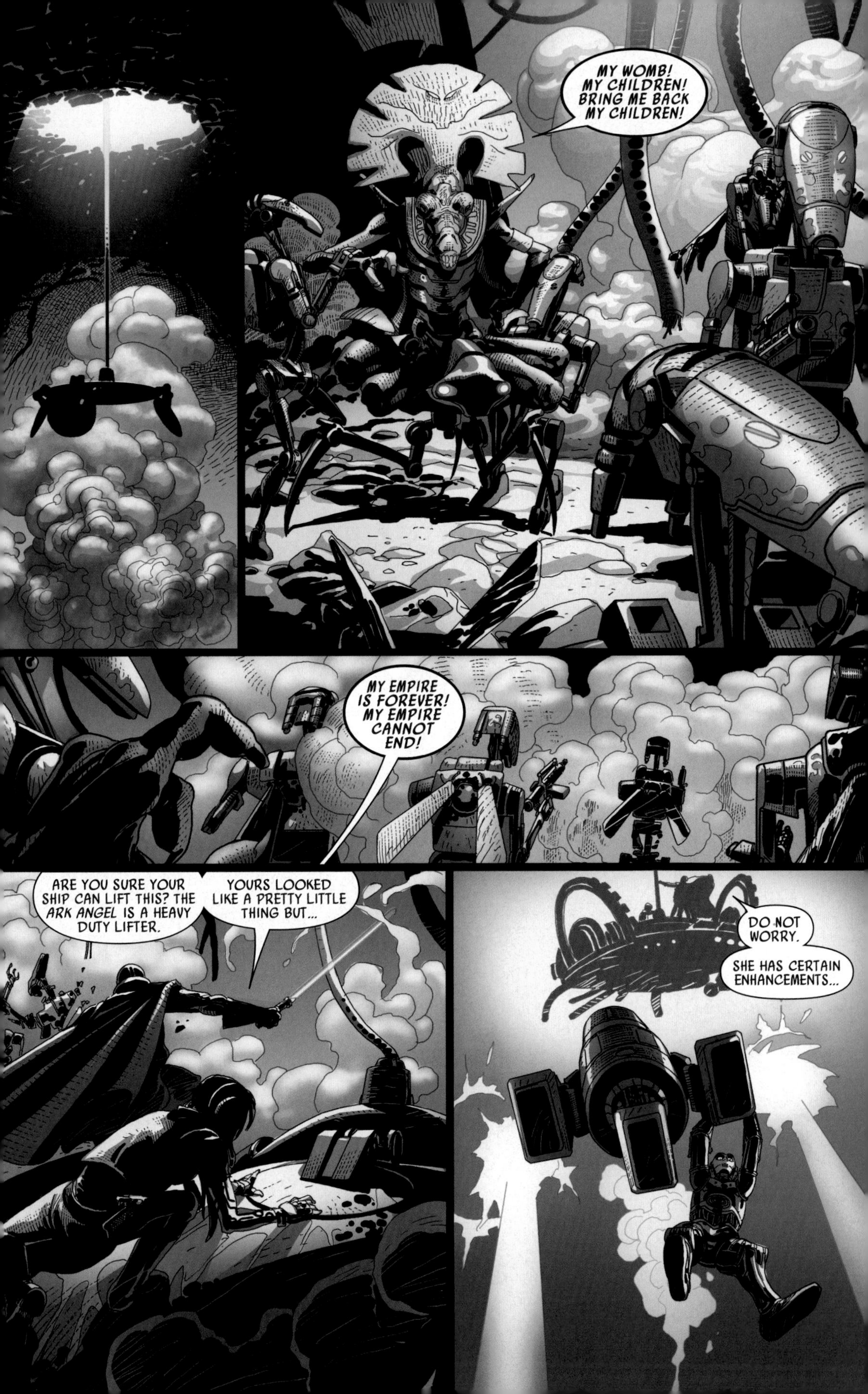
MY WOMB! MY CHILDREN! BRING ME BACK MY CHILDREN!
MY EMPIRE IS FOREVER! MY EMPIRE CANNOT END!
ARE YOU SURE YOUR SHIP CAN LIFT THIS? THE ARK ANGEL IS A HEAVY DUTY LIFTER.
YOURS LOOKED LIKE A PRETTY LITTLE THING BUT...
DO NOT WORRY.
SHE HAS CERTAIN ENHANCEMENTS...

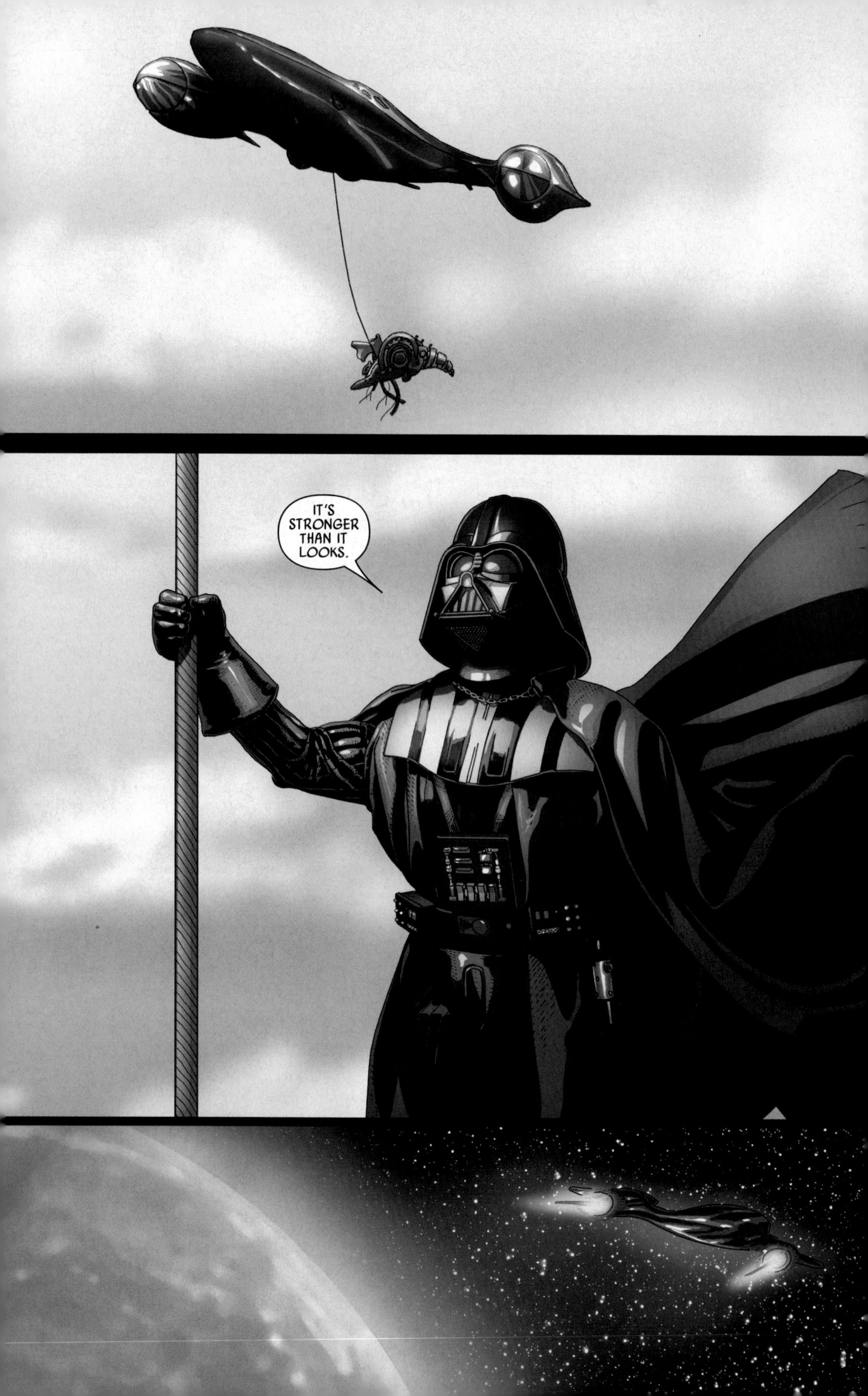
IT'S STRONGER THAN IT LOOKS.

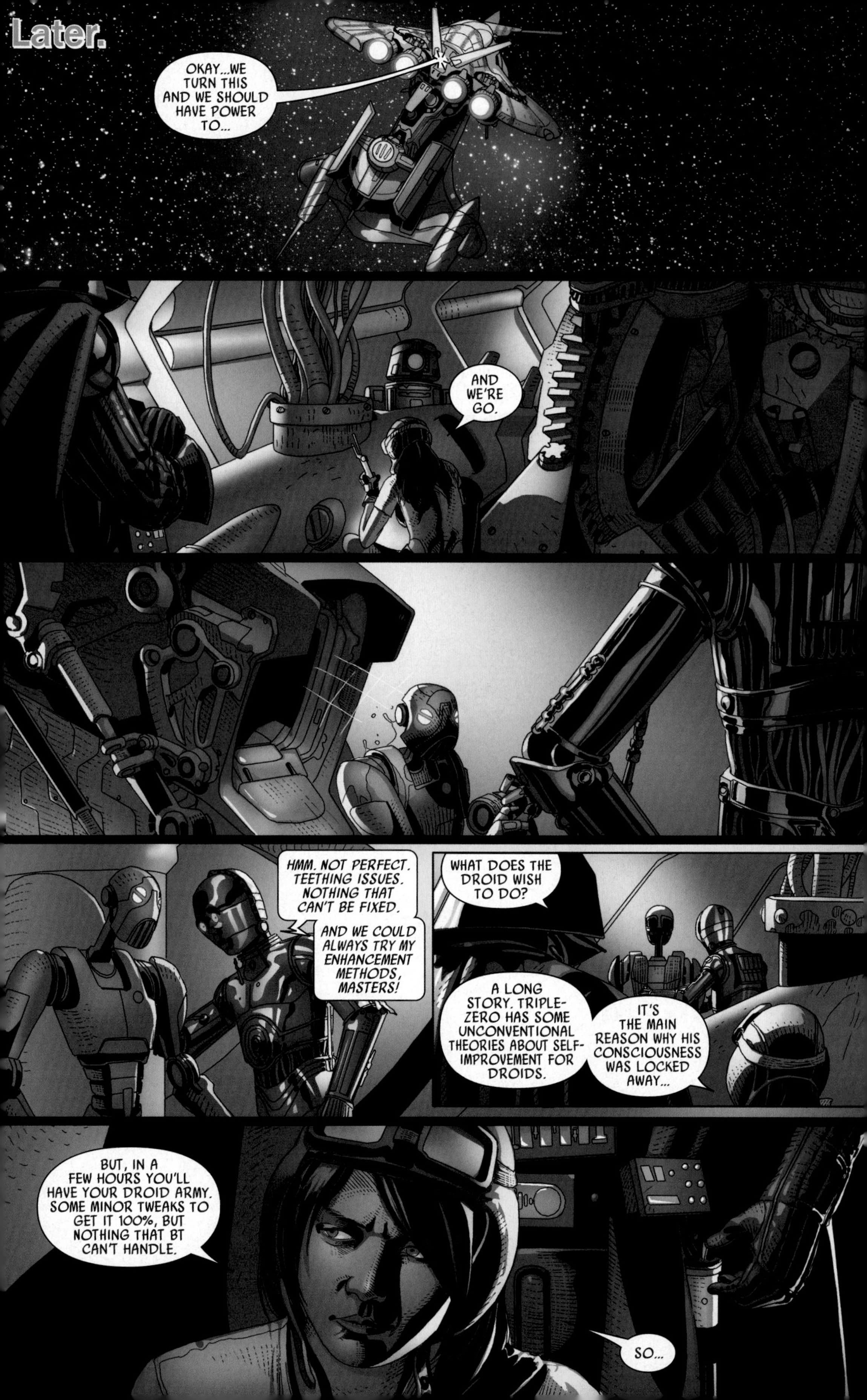
Later.
OKAY...WE TURN THIS AND WE SHOULD HAVE POWER TO...
AND WE'RE GO.
HMM. NOT PERFECT. TEETHING ISSUES. NOTHING THAT CAN'T BE FIXED.
AND WE COULD ALWAYS TRY MY ENHANCEMENT METHODS, MASTERS!
WHAT DOES THE DROID WISH TO DO?
A LONG STORY. TRIPLE-ZERO HAS SOME UNCONVENTIONAL THEORIES ABOUT SELF-IMPROVEMENT FOR DROIDS.
IT'S THE MAIN REASON WHY HIS CONSCIOUSNESS WAS LOCKED AWAY...
BUT, IN A FEW HOURS YOU'LL HAVE YOUR DROID ARMY. SOME MINOR TWEAKS TO GET IT 100%, BUT NOTHING THAT BT CAN'T HANDLE.
SO...

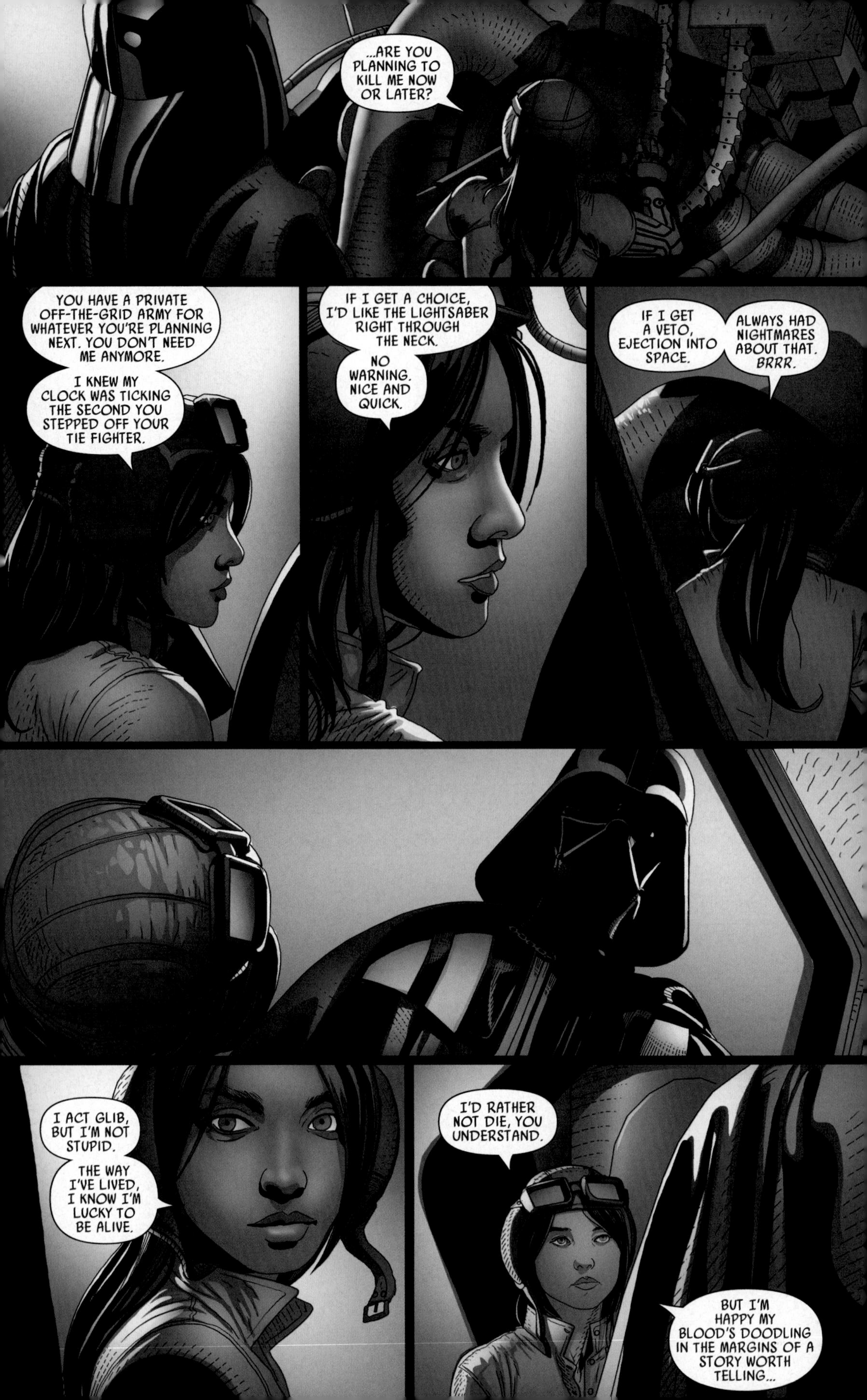
...ARE YOU PLANNING TO KILL ME NOW OR LATER?
YOU HAVE A PRIVATE OFF-THE-GRID ARMY FOR WHATEVER YOU'RE PLANNING NEXT. YOU DON'T NEED ME ANYMORE.
I KNEW MY CLOCK WAS TICKING THE SECOND YOU STEPPED OFF YOUR TIE FIGHTER.
IF I GET A CHOICE, I'D LIKE THE LIGHTSABER RIGHT THROUGH THE NECK.
NO WARNING. NICE AND QUICK.
IF I GET A VETO, EJECTION INTO SPACE.
ALWAYS HAD NIGHTMARES ABOUT THAT. BRRR.
I ACT GLIB, BUT I'M NOT STUPID.
THE WAY I'VE LIVED, I KNOW I'M LUCKY TO BE ALIVE.
I'D RATHER NOT DIE, YOU UNDERSTAND.
BUT I'M HAPPY MY BLOOD'S DOODLING IN THE MARGINS OF A STORY WORTH TELLING...

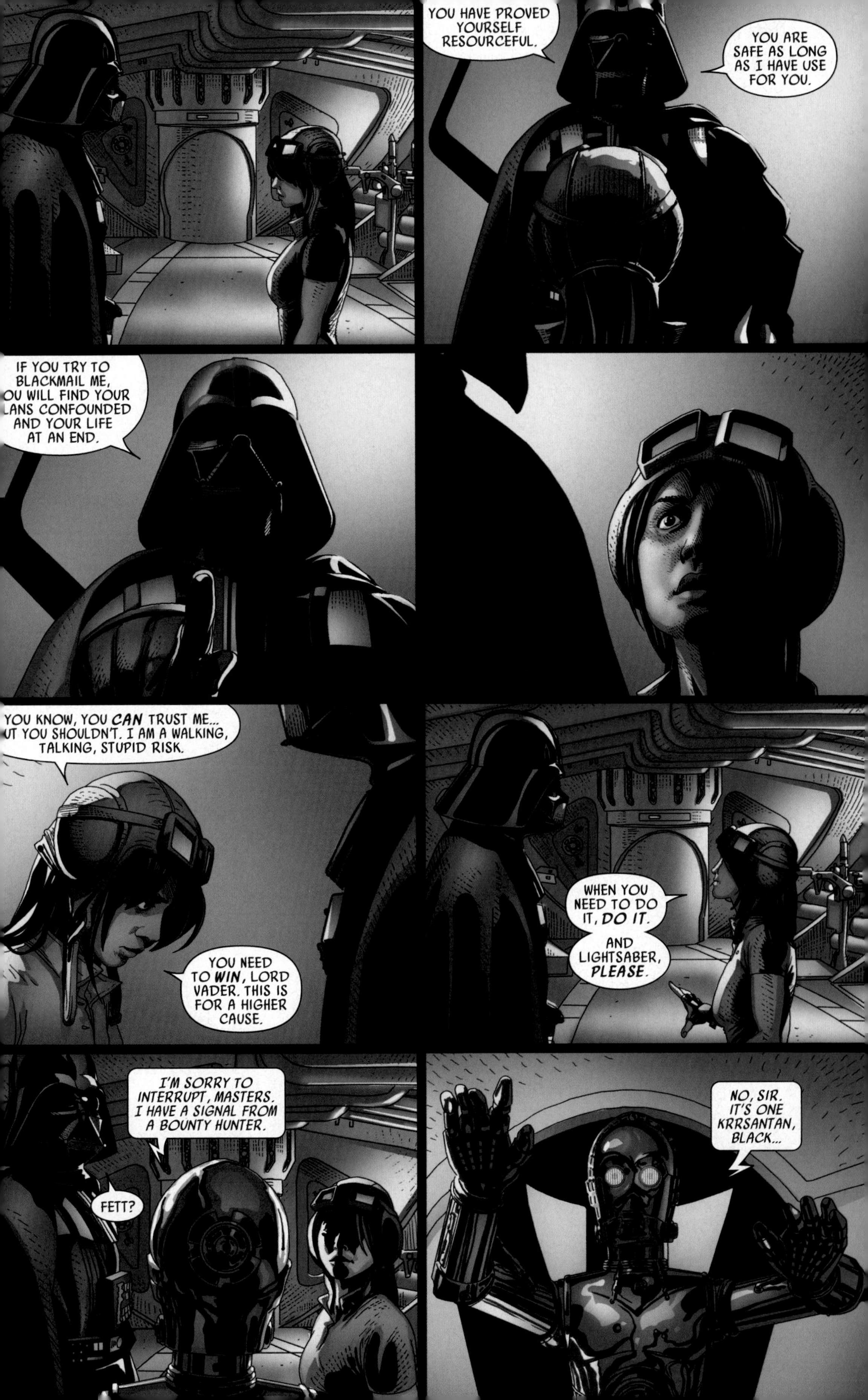
YOU HAVE PROVED YOURSELF RESOURCEFUL.
YOU ARE SAFE AS LONG AS I HAVE USE FOR YOU.
IF YOU TRY TO BLACKMAIL ME, OU WILL FIND YOUR LANS CONFOUNDED AND YOUR LIFE AT AN END.
YOU KNOW, YOU CAN TRUST ME... UT YOU SHOULDN'T. I AM A WALKING, TALKING, STUPID RISK.
YOU NEED TO WIN, LORD VADER. THIS IS FOR A HIGHER CAUSE.
WHEN YOU NEED TO DO IT, DO IT.
AND LIGHTSABER, PLEASE.
I'M SORRY TO INTERRUPT, MASTERS. I HAVE A SIGNAL FROM A BOUNTY HUNTER.
FETT?
NO, SIR. IT'S ONE KRRSANTAN, BLACK...

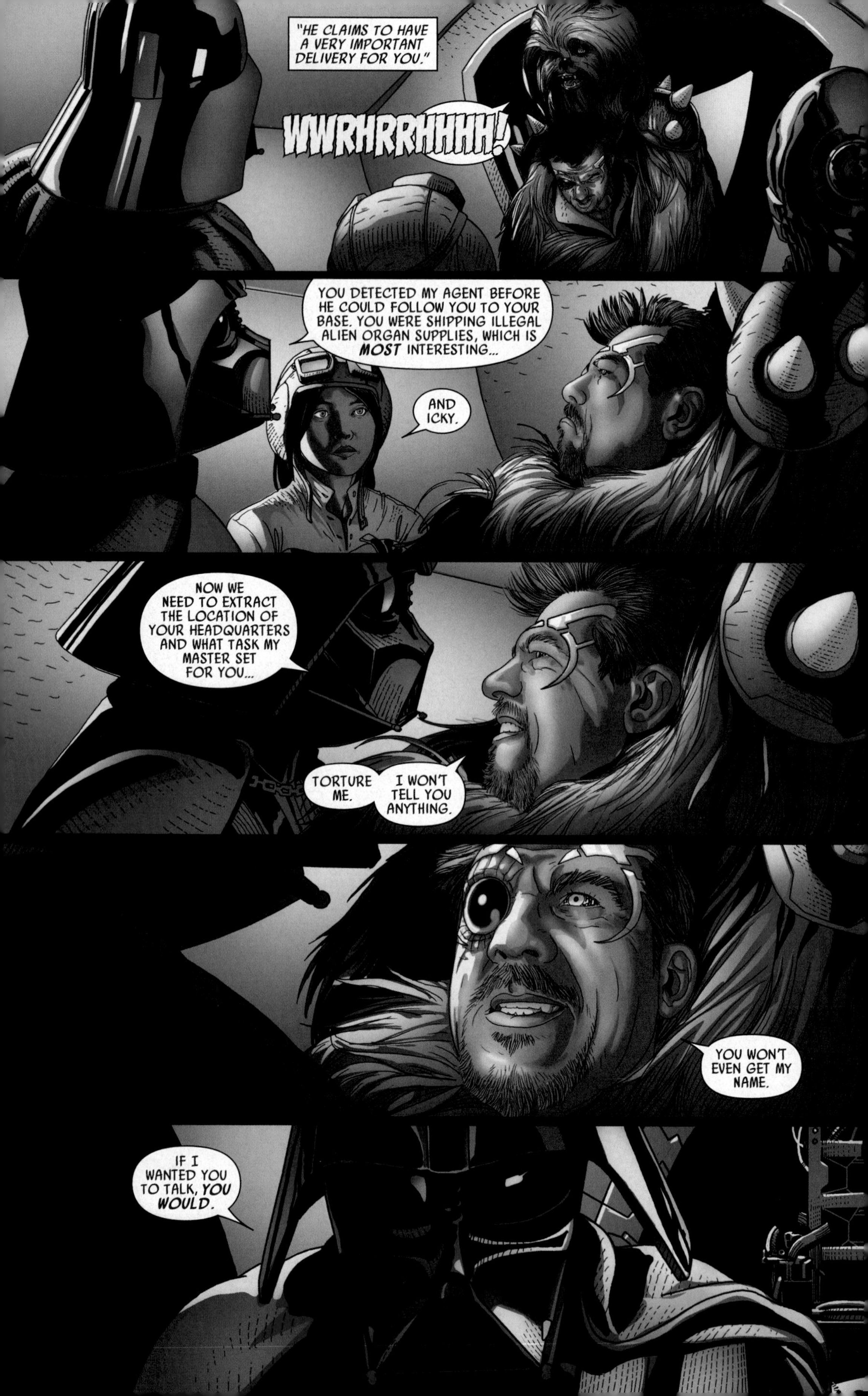
"HE CLAIMS TO HAVE A VERY IMPORTANT DELIVERY FOR YOU."
WWRHRRHHHH!
YOU DETECTED MY AGENT BEFORE HE COULD FOLLOW YOU TO YOUR BASE. YOU WERE SHIPPING ILLEGAL ALIEN ORGAN SUPPLIES, WHICH IS MOST INTERESTING...
AND ICKY.
NOW WE NEED TO EXTRACT THE LOCATION OF YOUR HEADQUARTERS AND WHAT TASK MY MASTER SET FOR YOU...
TORTURE ME.
I WON'T TELL YOU ANYTHING.
YOU WON'T EVEN GET MY NAME.
IF I WANTED YOU TO TALK, YOU WOULD.

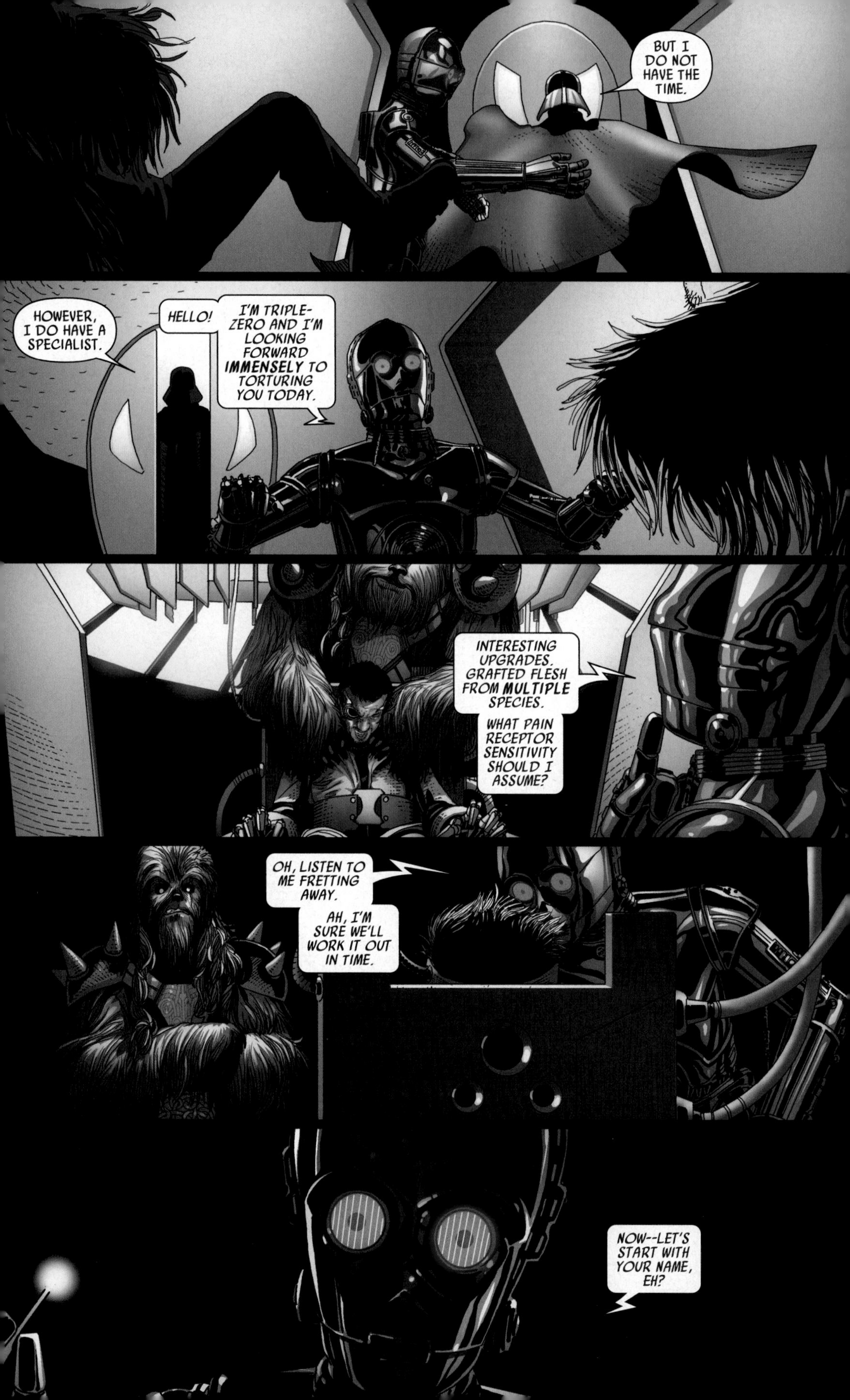
BUT I DO NOT HAVE THE TIME.
HOWEVER, I DO HAVE A SPECIALIST.
HELLO!
I'M TRIPLE-ZERO AND I'M LOOKING FORWARD IMMENSELY TO TORTURING YOU TODAY.
INTERESTING UPGRADES. GRAFTED FLESH FROM MULTIPLE SPECIES.
WHAT PAIN RECEPTOR SENSITIVITY SHOULD I ASSUME?
OH, LISTEN TO ME FRETTING AWAY.
AH, I'M SURE WE'LL WORK IT OUT IN TIME.
NOW--LET'S START WITH YOUR NAME, EH?

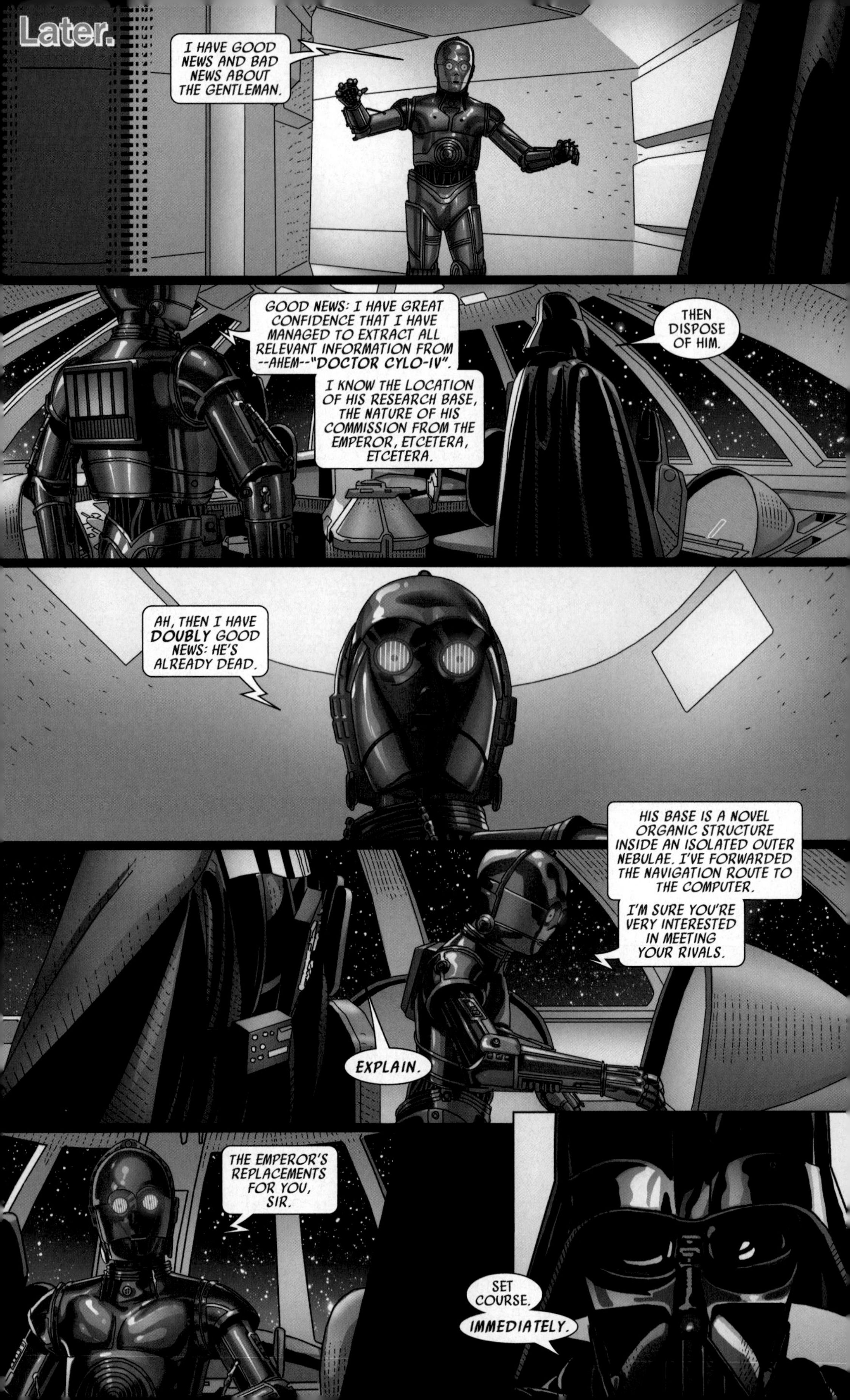
Later.
I HAVE GOOD NEWS AND BAD NEWS ABOUT THE GENTLEMAN.
GOOD NEWS: I HAVE GREAT CONFIDENCE THAT I HAVE MANAGED TO EXTRACT ALL RELEVANT INFORMATION FROM --AHEM--"DOCTOR CYLO-IV".
I KNOW THE LOCATION OF HIS RESEARCH BASE, THE NATURE OF HIS COMMISSION FROM THE EMPEROR, ETCETERA, ETCETERA.
THEN DISPOSE OF HIM.
AH, THEN I HAVE DOUBLY GOOD NEWS: HE'S ALREADY DEAD.
EXPLAIN.
HIS BASE IS A NOVEL ORGANIC STRUCTURE INSIDE AN ISOLATED OUTER NEBULAE. I'VE FORWARDED THE NAVIGATION ROUTE TO THE COMPUTER.
I'M SURE YOU'RE VERY INTERESTED IN MEETING YOUR RIVALS.
THE EMPEROR'S REPLACEMENTS FOR YOU, SIR.
SET COURSE.
IMMEDIATELY.

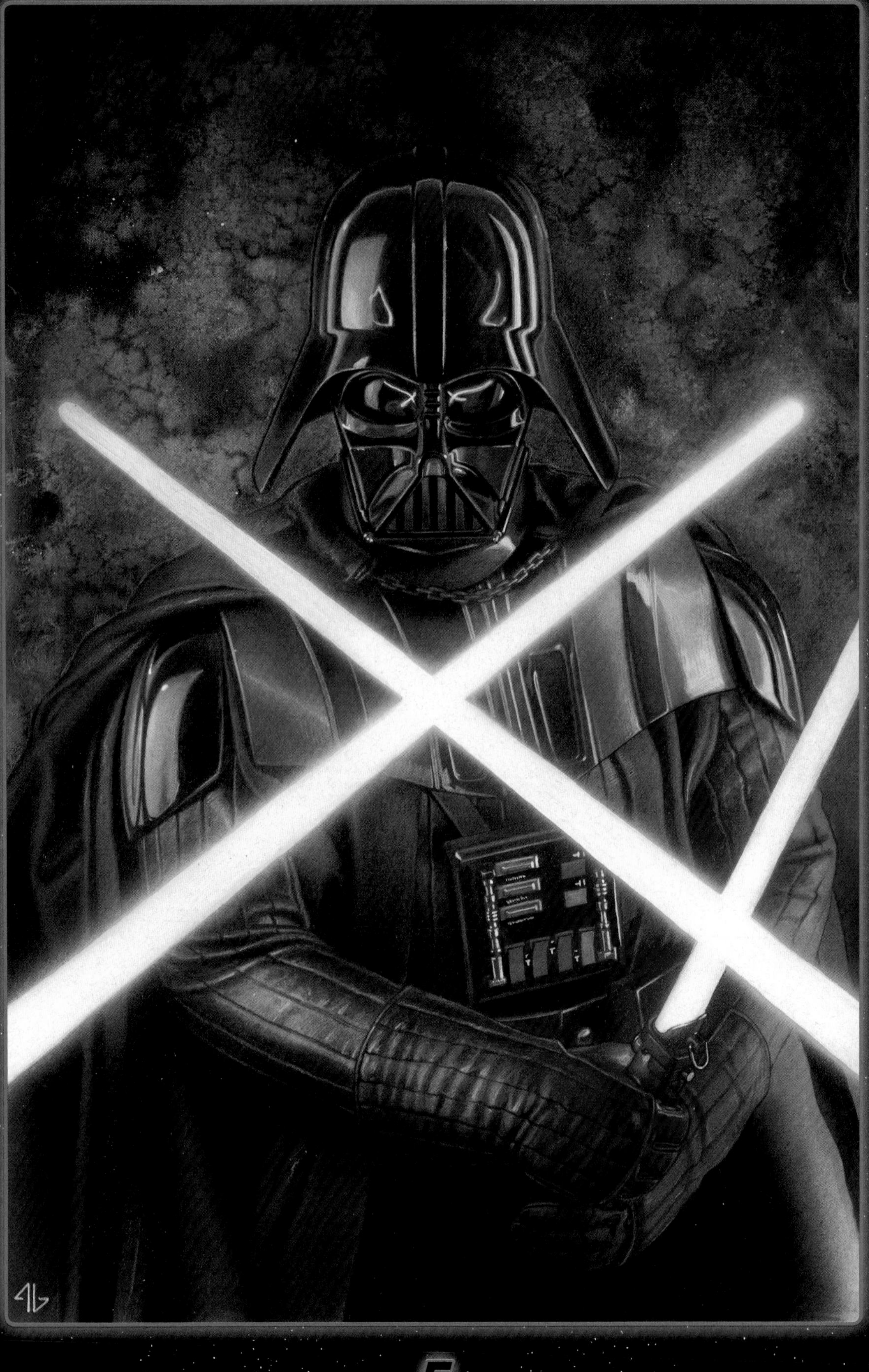

5

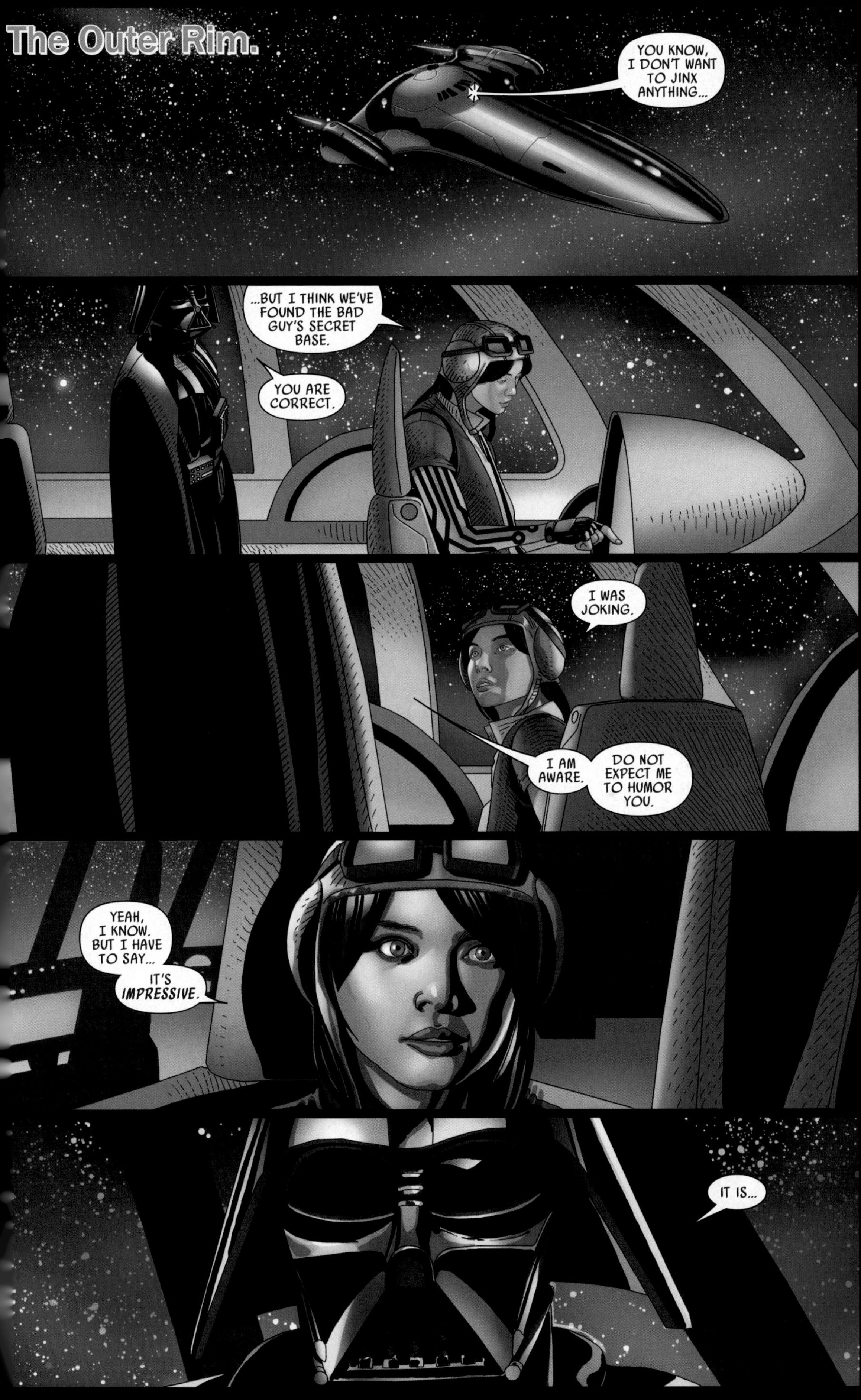
The Outer Rim.
YOU KNOW, I DON'T WANT TO JINX ANYTHING...
...BUT I THINK WE'VE FOUND THE BAD GUY'S SECRET BASE.
YOU ARE CORRECT.
I WAS JOKING.
I AM AWARE.
DO NOT EXPECT ME TO HUMOR YOU.
YEAH, I KNOW. BUT I HAVE TO SAY...
IT'S IMPRESSIVE.
IT IS...

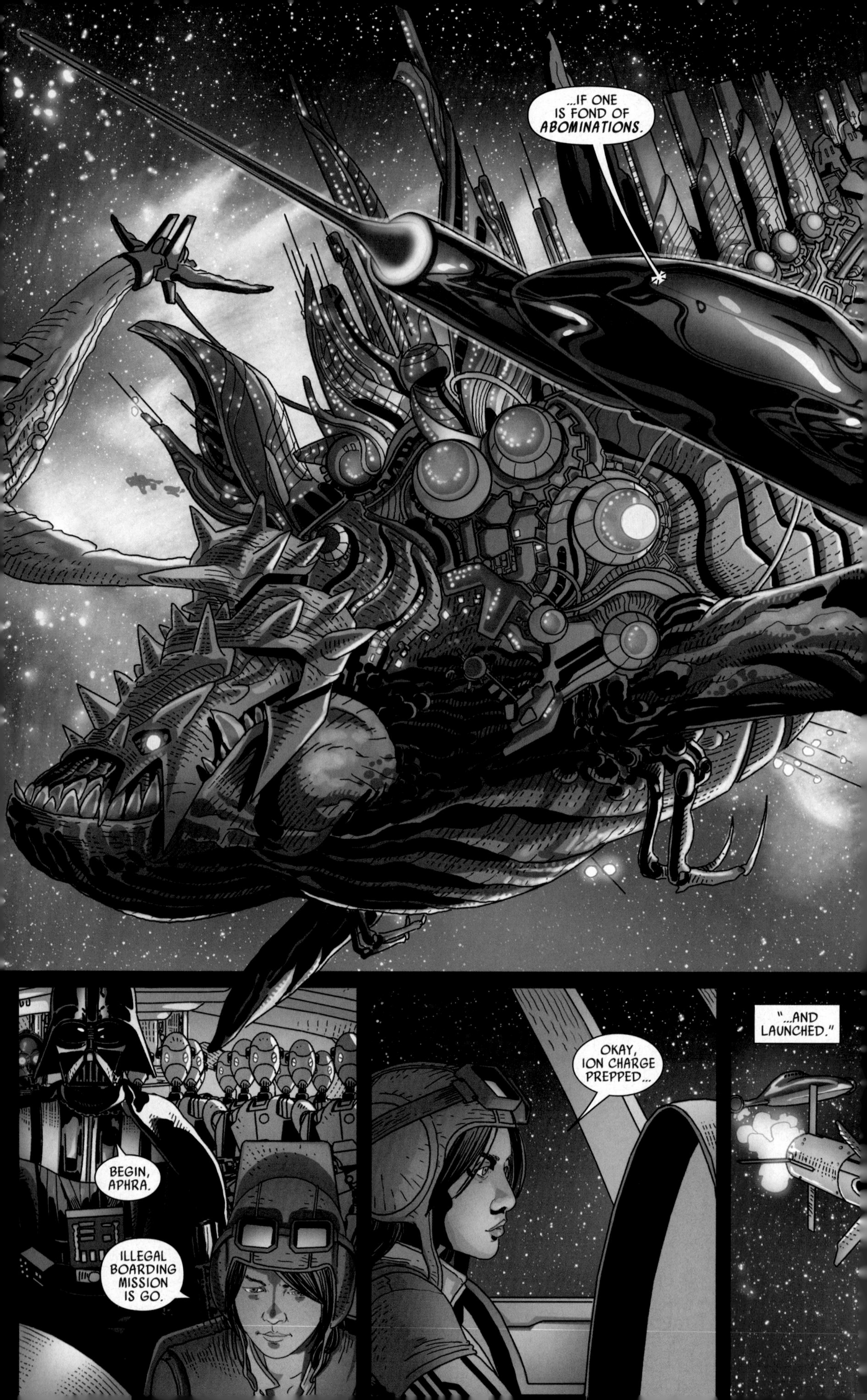
...IF ONE IS FOND OF ABOMINATIONS.
BEGIN, APHRA.
ILLEGAL BOARDING MISSION IS GO.
OKAY, ION CHARGE PREPPED...
"...AND LAUNCHED."

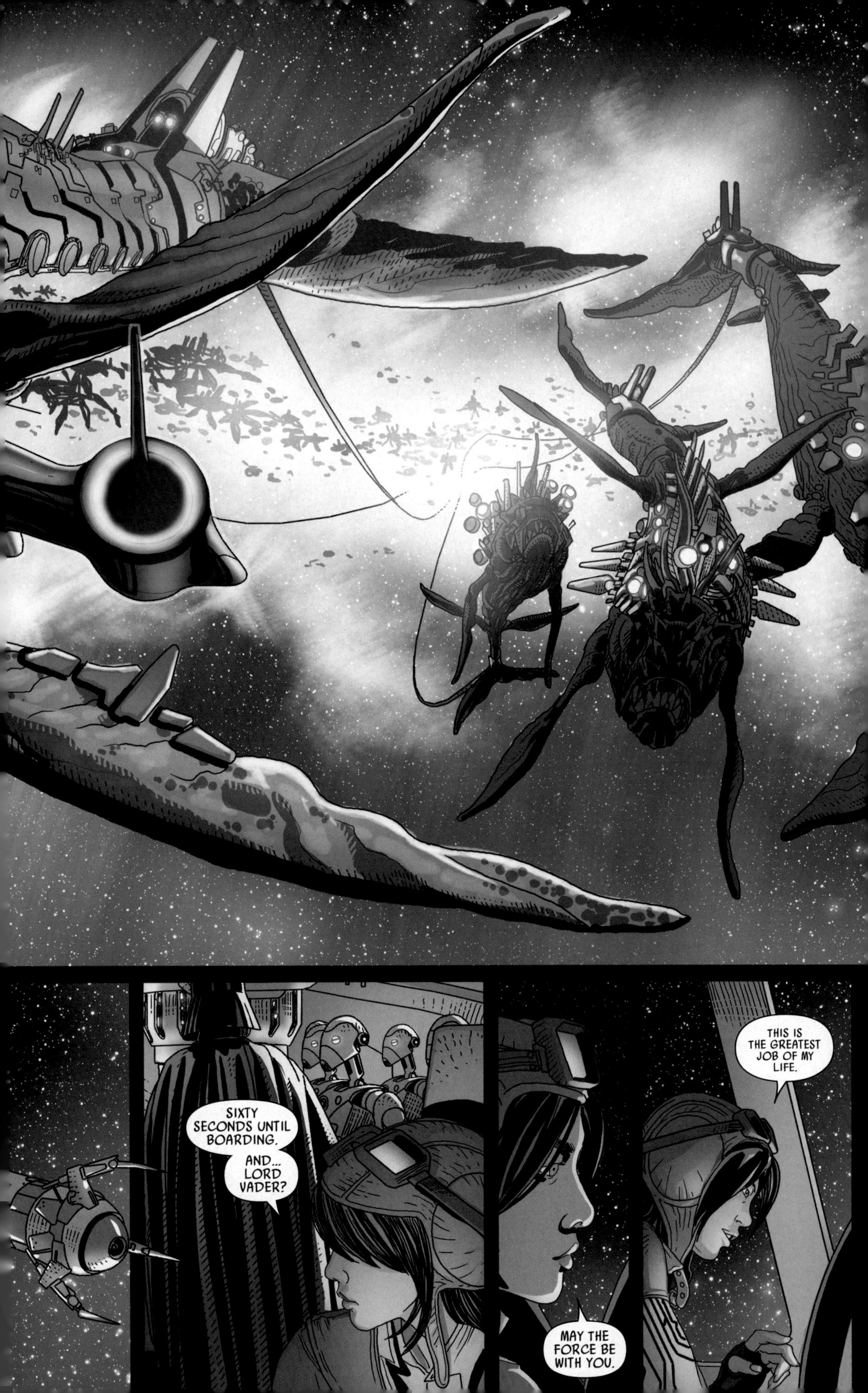
SIXTY SECONDS UNTIL BOARDING.
AND... LORD VADER?
MAY THE FORCE BE WITH YOU.
THIS IS THE GREATEST JOB OF MY LIFE.

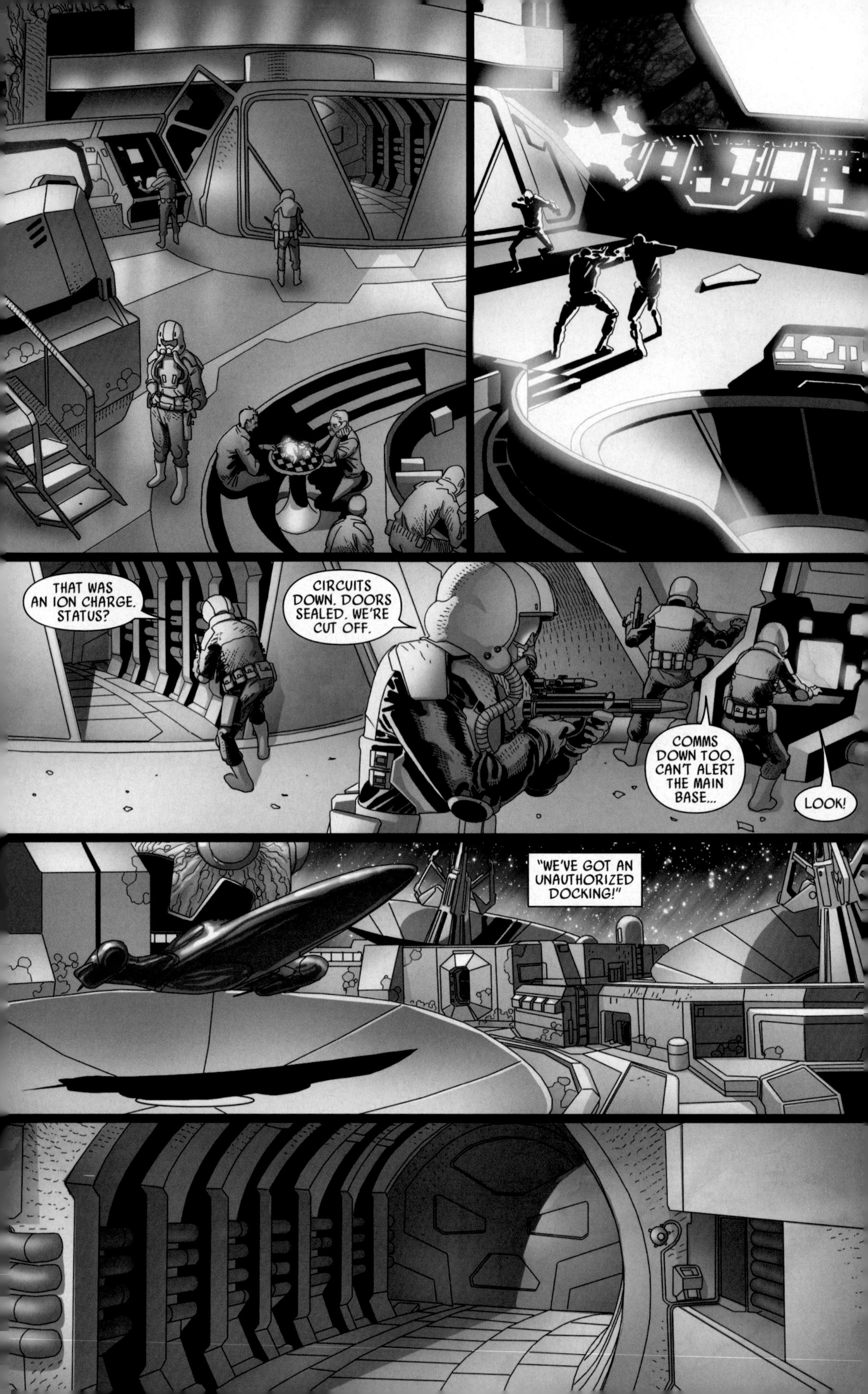
THAT WAS AN ION CHARGE. STATUS?
CIRCUITS DOWN. DOORS SEALED. WE'RE CUT OFF.
COMMS DOWN TOO. CAN'T ALERT THE MAIN BASE...
LOOK!
"WE'VE GOT AN UNAUTHORIZED DOCKING!"

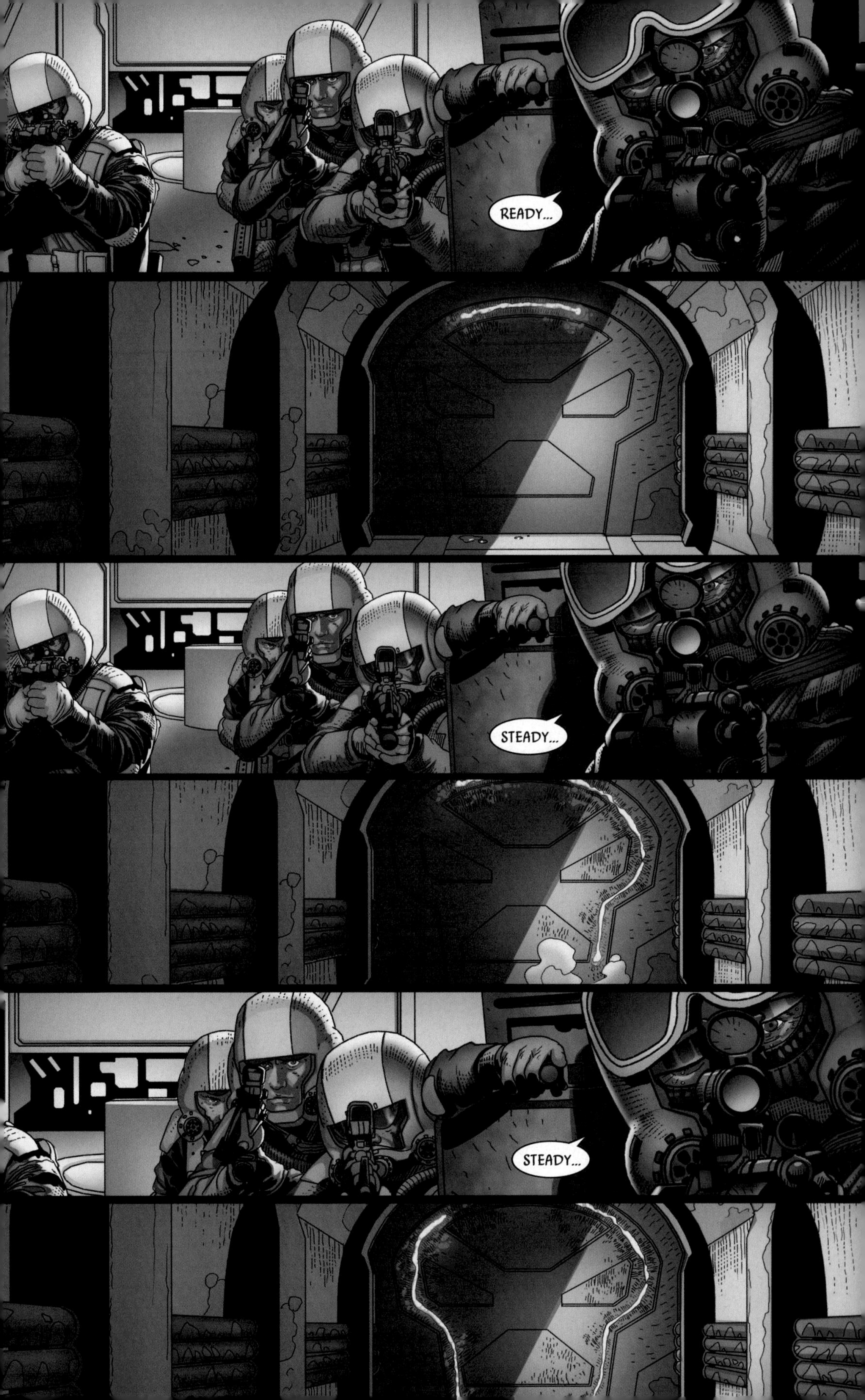
READY...
STEADY...
STEADY...

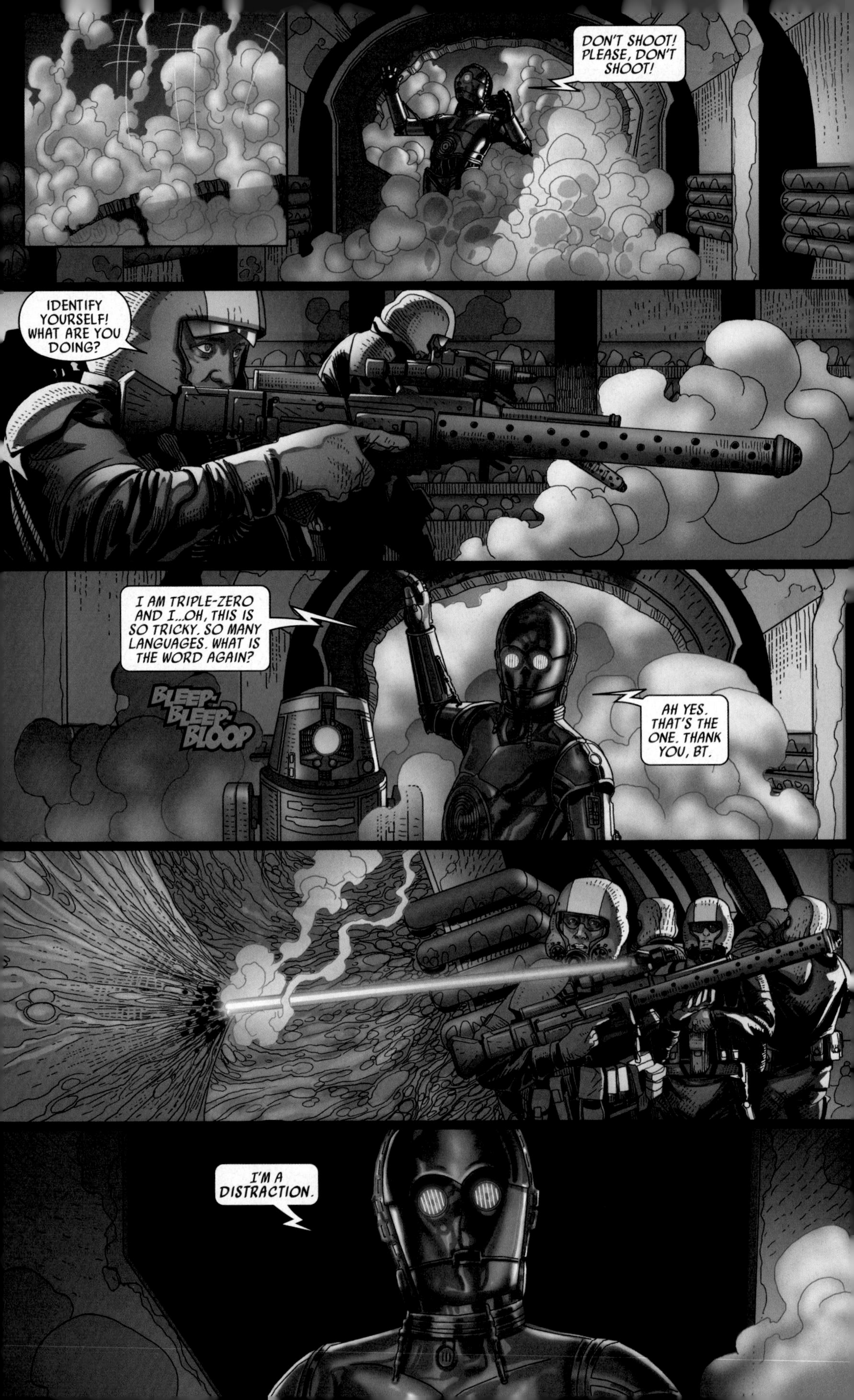
DON'T SHOOT! PLEASE, DON'T SHOOT!
IDENTIFY YOURSELF! WHAT ARE YOU DOING?
I AM TRIPLE-ZERO AND I...OH, THIS IS SO TRICKY. SO MANY LANGUAGES. WHAT IS THE WORD AGAIN?
BLEEP-BLEEP-BLOOP
AH YES. THAT'S THE ONE. THANK YOU, BT.
I'M A DISTRACTION.

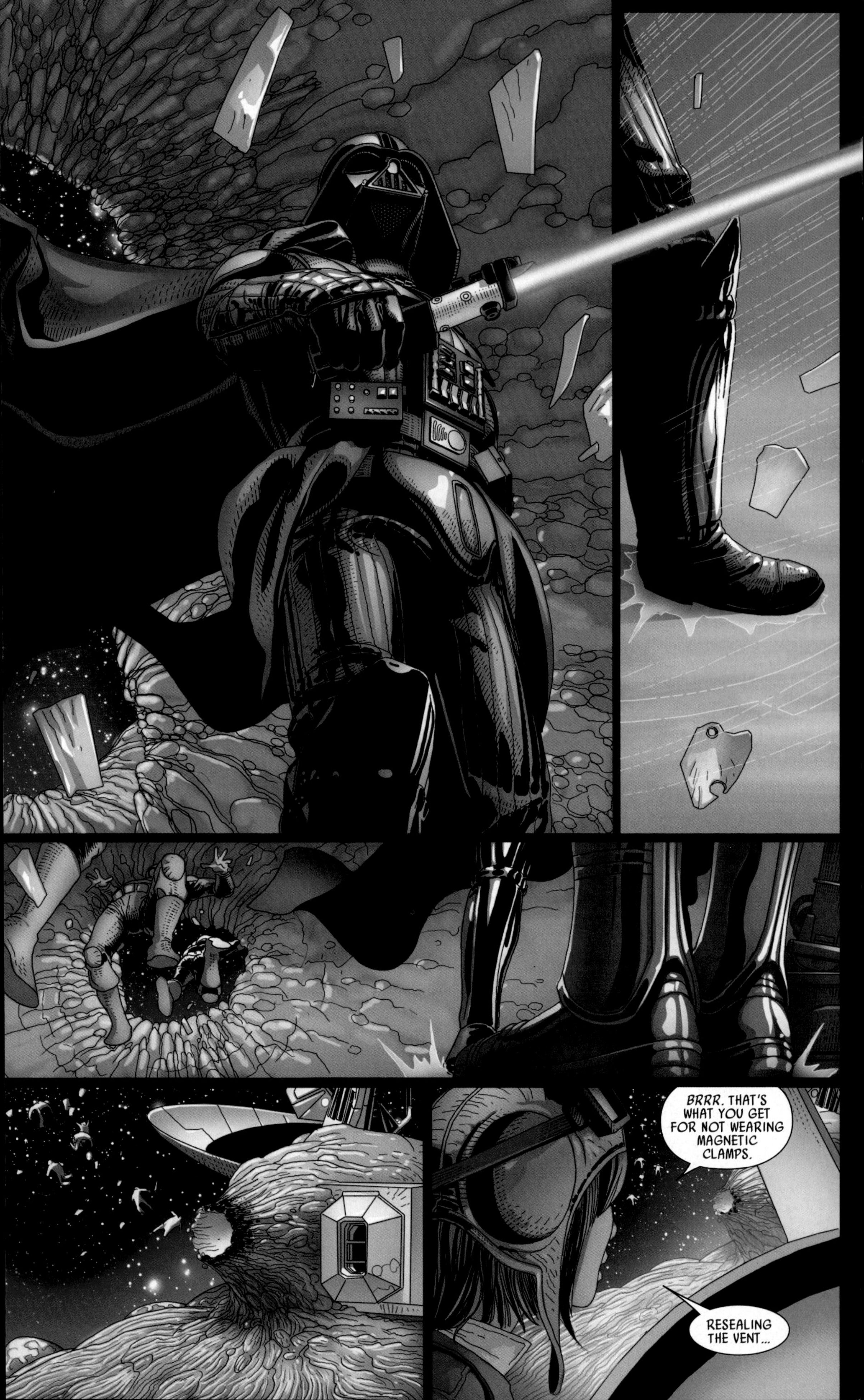
BRRR. THAT'S WHAT YOU GET FOR NOT WEARING MAGNETIC CLAMPS.
RESEALING THE VENT...

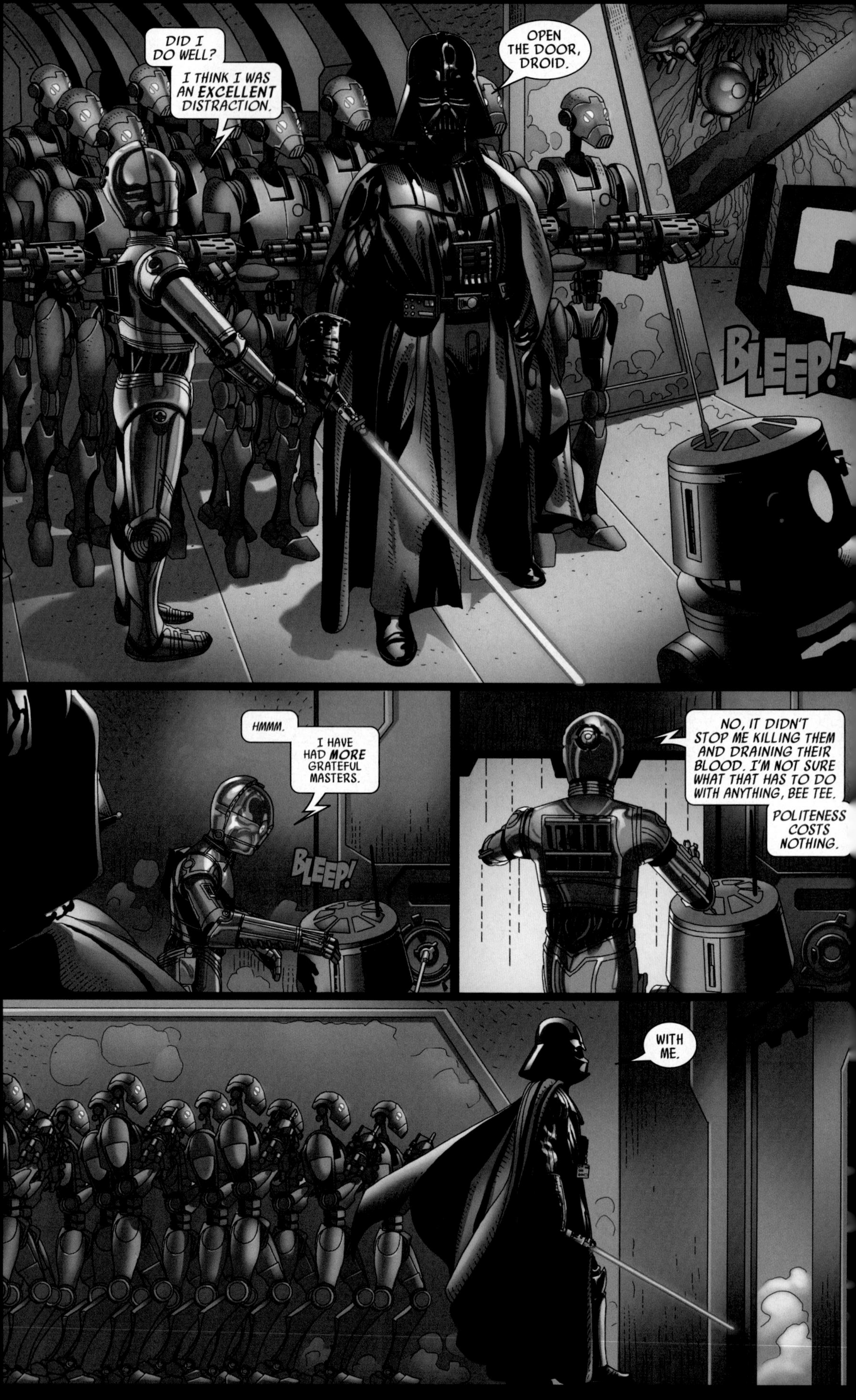
DID I DO WELL?
I THINK I WAS AN EXCELLENT DISTRACTION.
OPEN THE DOOR, DROID.
BLEEP!
HMMM.
I HAVE HAD MORE GRATEFUL MASTERS.
BLEEP!
NO, IT DIDN'T STOP ME KILLING THEM AND DRAINING THEIR BLOOD. I'M NOT SURE WHAT THAT HAS TO DO WITH ANYTHING, BEE TEE.
POLITENESS COSTS NOTHING.
WITH ME.

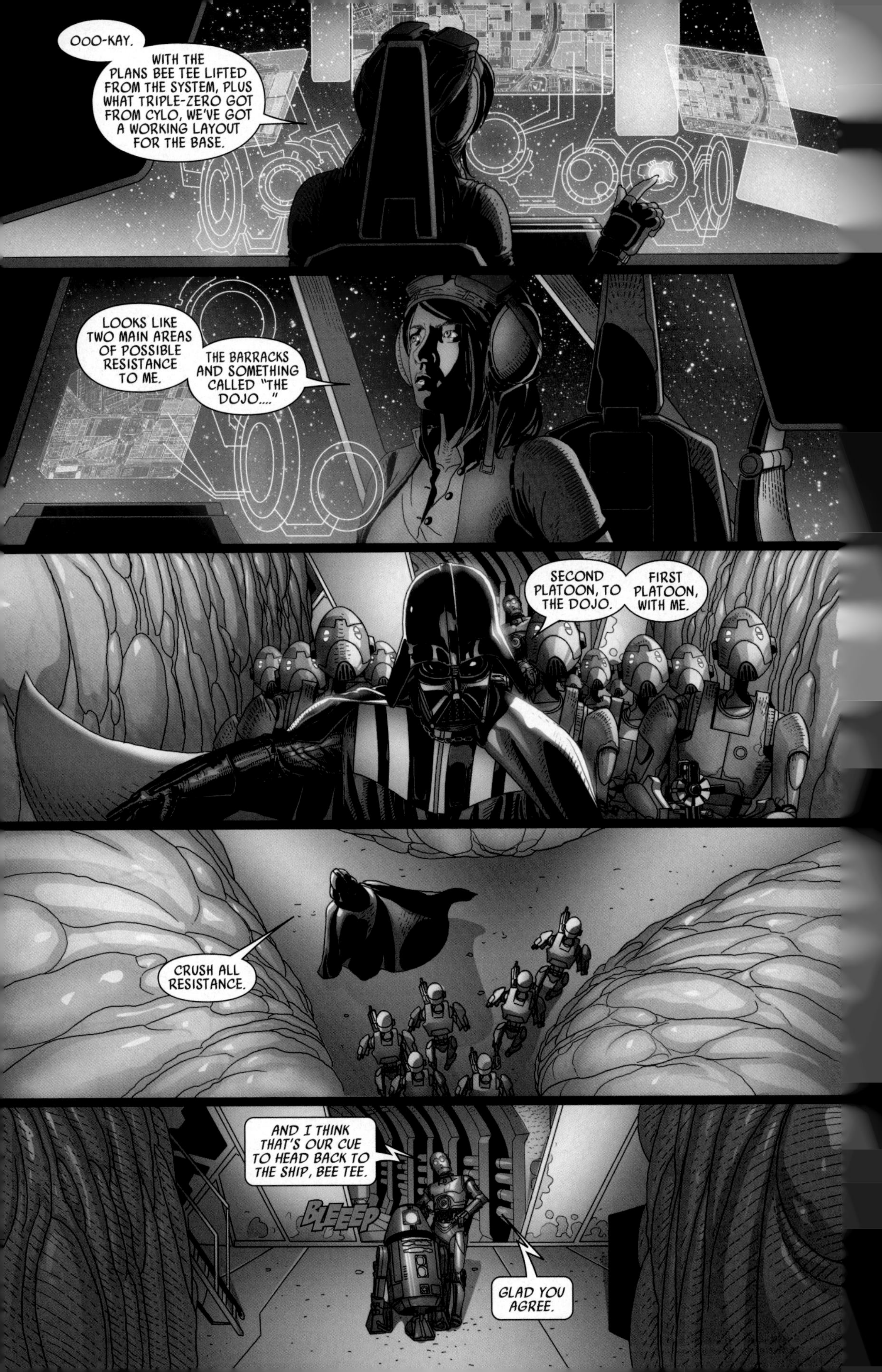
OOO-KAY.
WITH THE PLANS BEE TEE LIFTED FROM THE SYSTEM, PLUS WHAT TRIPLE-ZERO GOT FROM CYLO, WE'VE GOT A WORKING LAYOUT FOR THE BASE.
LOOKS LIKE TWO MAIN AREAS OF POSSIBLE RESISTANCE TO ME.
THE BARRACKS AND SOMETHING CALLED "THE DOJO...."
SECOND PLATOON, TO THE DOJO.
FIRST PLATOON, WITH ME.
CRUSH ALL RESISTANCE.
AND I THINK THAT'S OUR CUE TO HEAD BACK TO THE SHIP, BEE TEE.
BLEEEP
GLAD YOU AGREE.

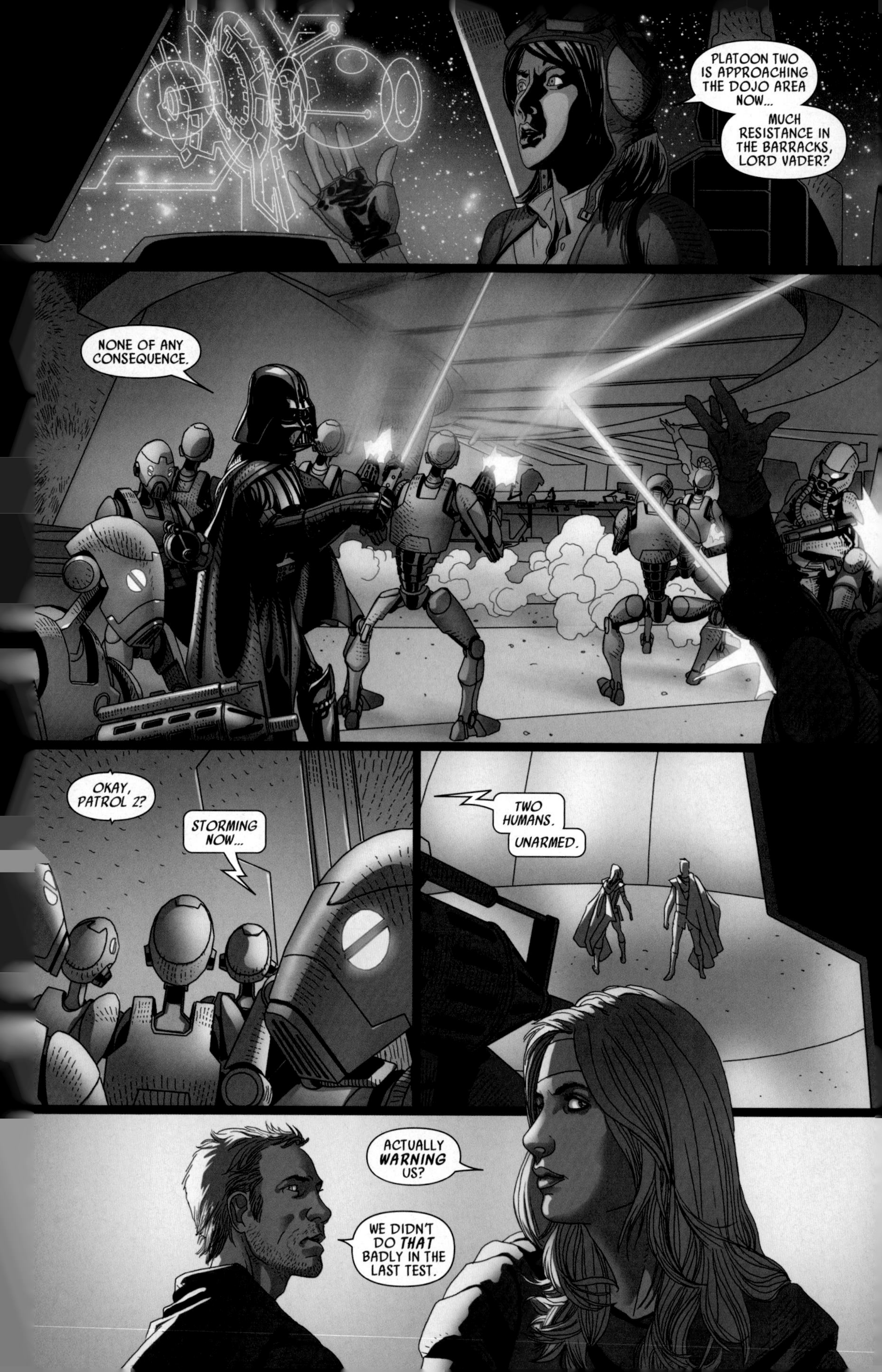
PLATOON TWO IS APPROACHING THE DOJO AREA NOW...
MUCH RESISTANCE IN THE BARRACKS, LORD VADER?
NONE OF ANY CONSEQUENCE.
OKAY, PATROL 2?
STORMING NOW...
TWO HUMANS.
UNARMED.
ACTUALLY WARNING US?
WE DIDN'T DO THAT BADLY IN THE LAST TEST.

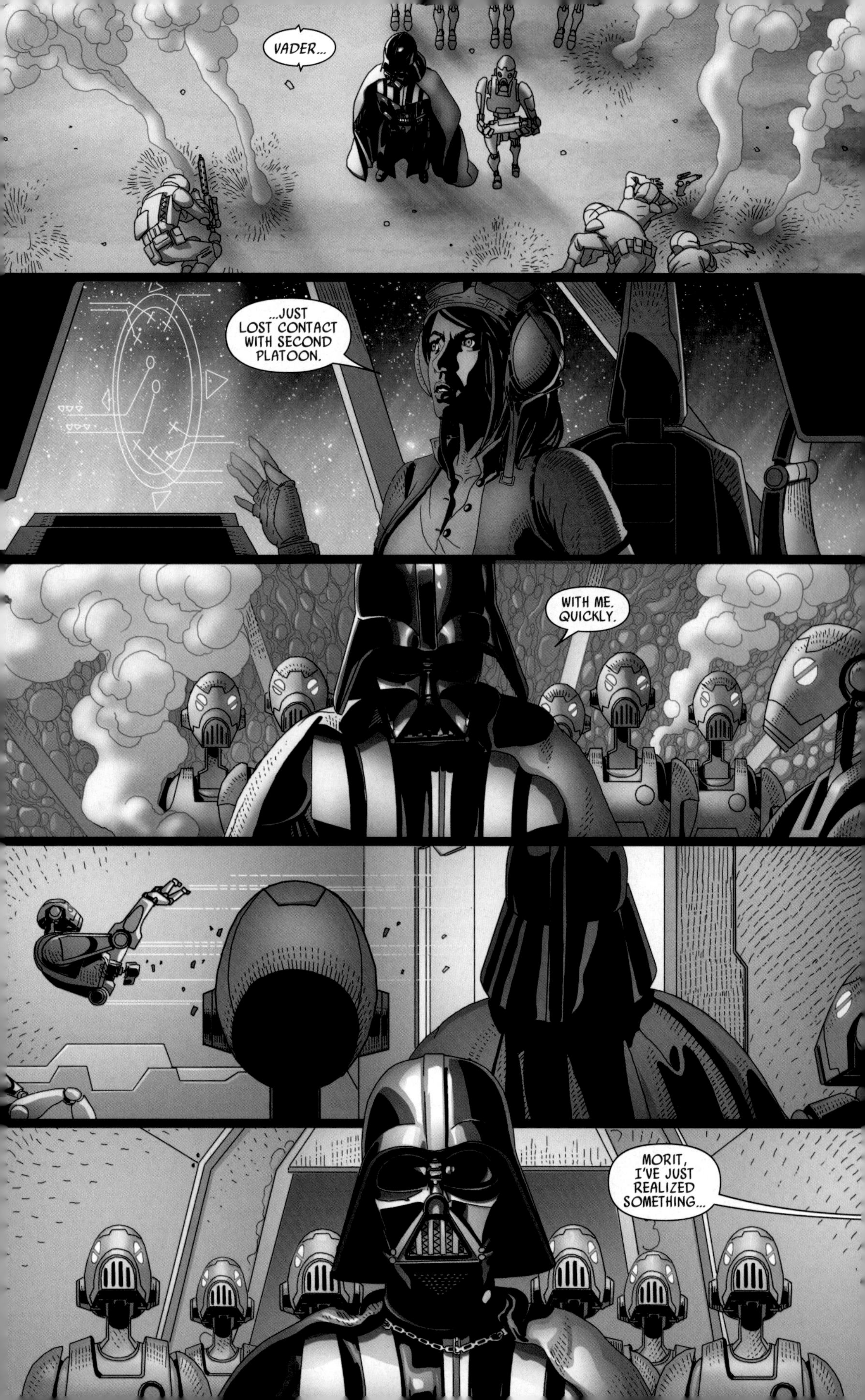
VADER...
...JUST LOST CONTACT WITH SECOND PLATOON.
WITH ME. QUICKLY.
MORIT, I'VE JUST REALIZED SOMETHING...

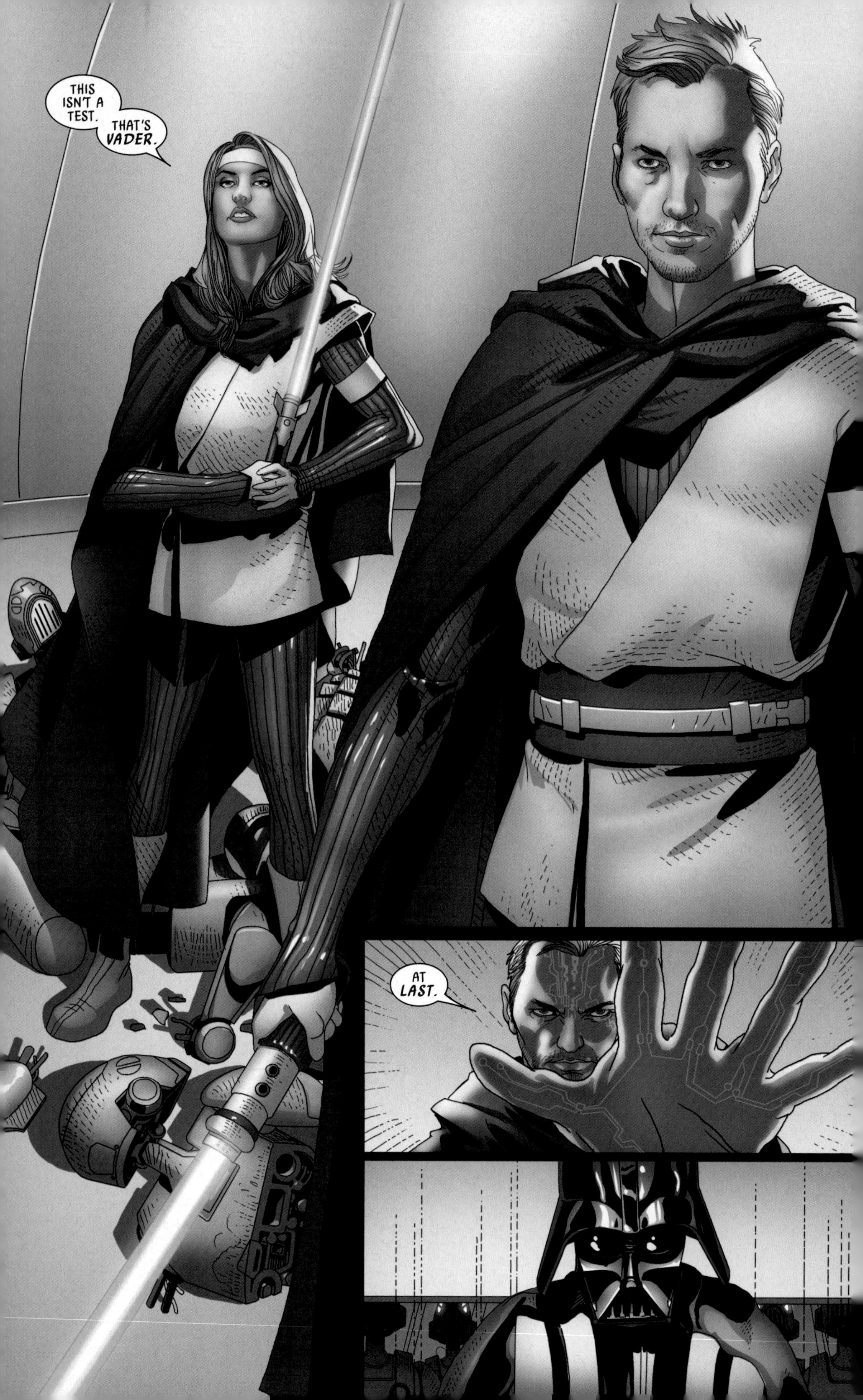
THIS ISN'T A TEST.
THAT'S VADER.
AT LAST.

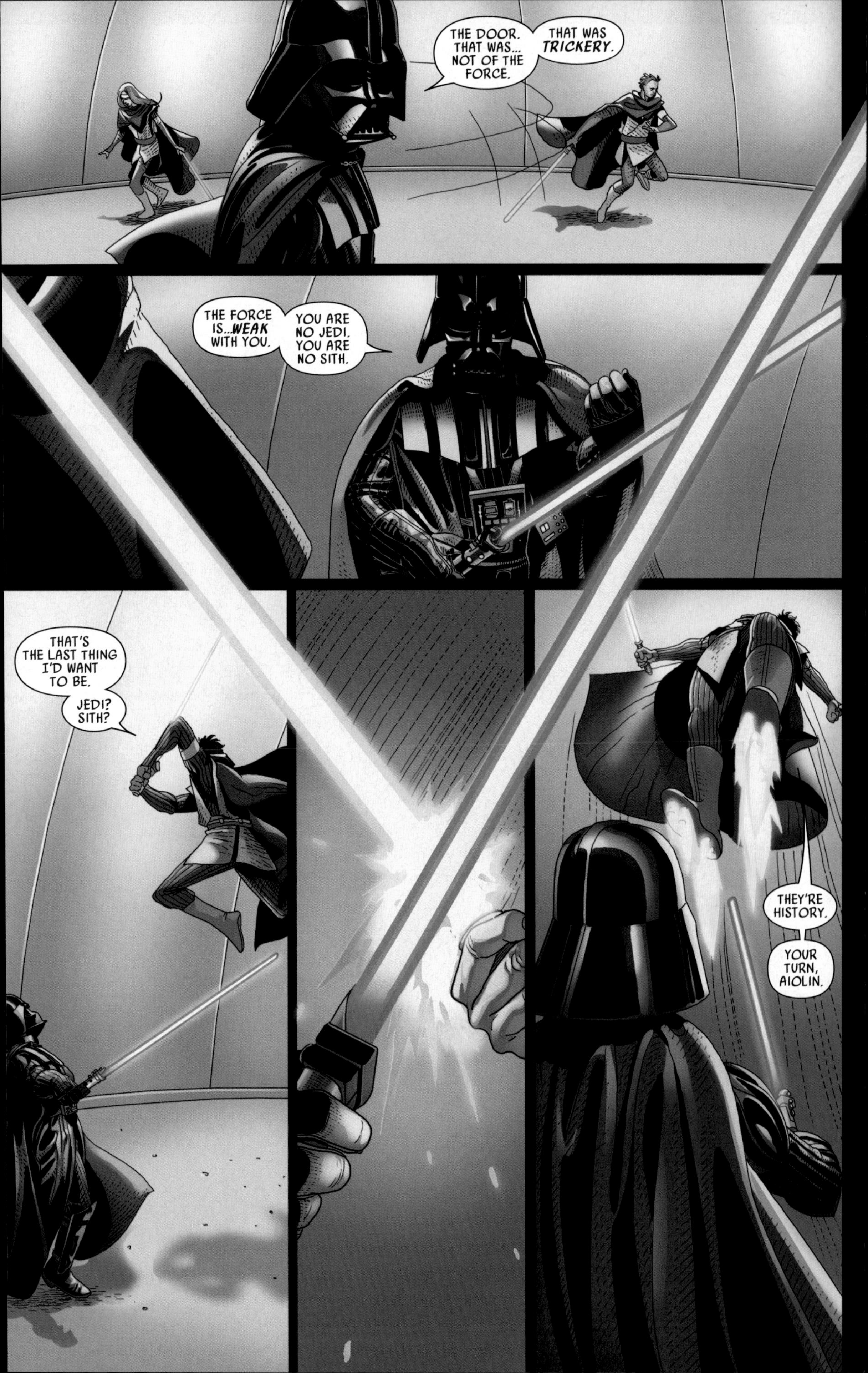
THE DOOR. THAT WAS... NOT OF THE FORCE.
THAT WAS TRICKERY.
THE FORCE IS...WEAK WITH YOU.
YOU ARE NO JEDI. YOU ARE NO SITH.
THAT'S THE LAST THING I'D WANT TO BE.
JEDI? SITH?
THEY'RE HISTORY.
YOUR TURN, AIOLIN.

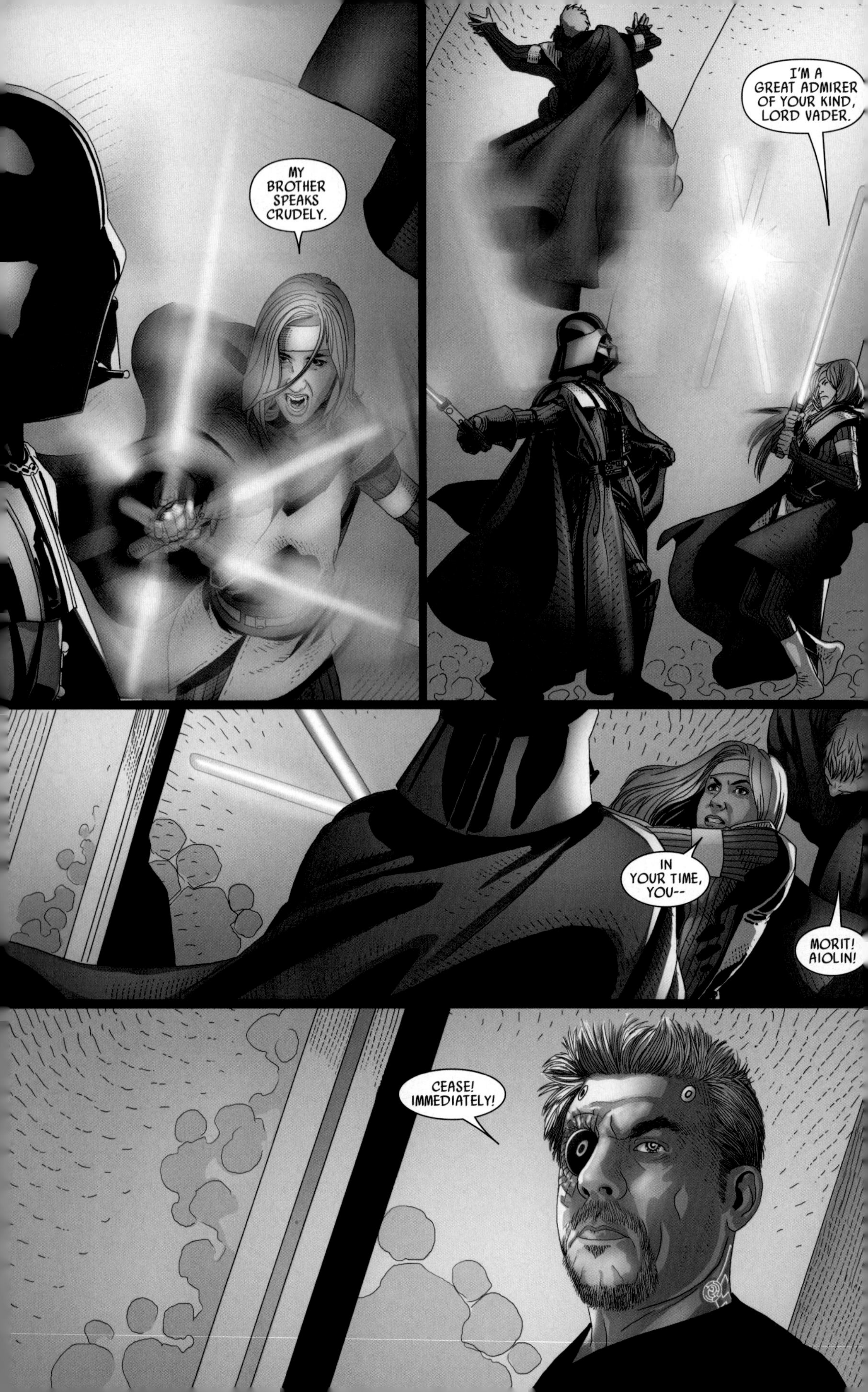
MY BROTHER SPEAKS CRUDELY.
I'M A GREAT ADMIRER OF YOUR KIND, LORD VADER.
IN YOUR TIME, YOU--
MORIT! AIOLIN!
CEASE! IMMEDIATELY!

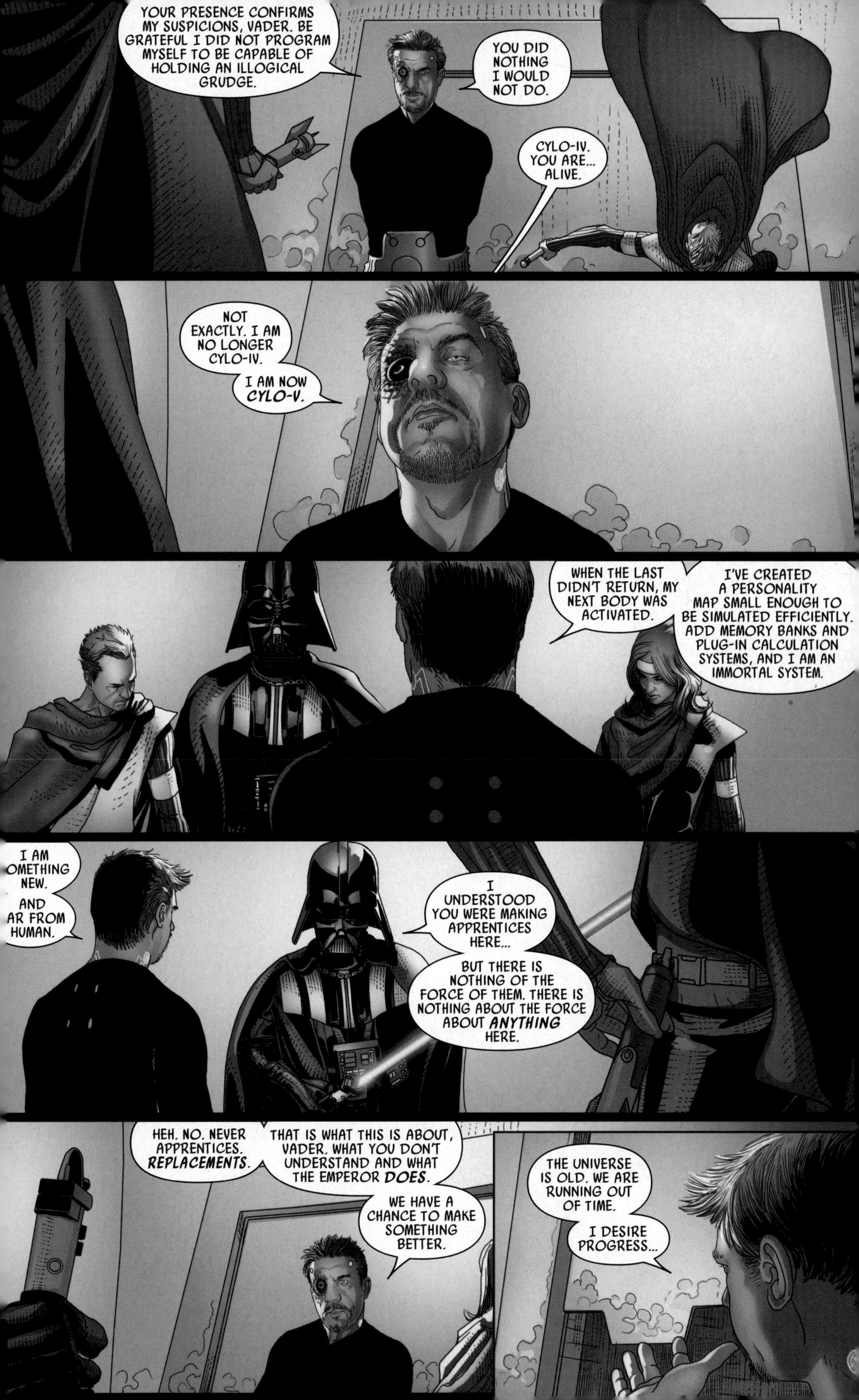
YOUR PRESENCE CONFIRMS MY SUSPICIONS, VADER. BE GRATEFUL I DID NOT PROGRAM MYSELF TO BE CAPABLE OF HOLDING AN ILLOGICAL GRUDGE.
YOU DID NOTHING I WOULD NOT DO.
CYLO-IV. YOU ARE... ALIVE.
NOT EXACTLY. I AM NO LONGER CYLO-IV.
I AM NOW *CYLO-V.*
WHEN THE LAST DIDN'T RETURN, MY NEXT BODY WAS ACTIVATED.
I'VE CREATED A PERSONALITY MAP SMALL ENOUGH TO BE SIMULATED EFFICIENTLY. ADD MEMORY BANKS AND PLUG-IN CALCULATION SYSTEMS, AND I AM AN IMMORTAL SYSTEM.
I AM OMETHING NEW.
AND AR FROM HUMAN.
I UNDERSTOOD YOU WERE MAKING APPRENTICES HERE...
BUT THERE IS NOTHING OF THE FORCE OF THEM. THERE IS NOTHING ABOUT THE FORCE ABOUT *ANYTHING* HERE.
HEH. NO. NEVER APPRENTICES. *REPLACEMENTS.*
THAT IS WHAT THIS IS ABOUT, VADER. WHAT YOU DON'T UNDERSTAND AND WHAT THE EMPEROR *DOES.*
WE HAVE A CHANCE TO MAKE SOMETHING BETTER.
THE UNIVERSE IS OLD. WE ARE RUNNING OUT OF TIME.
I DESIRE PROGRESS...

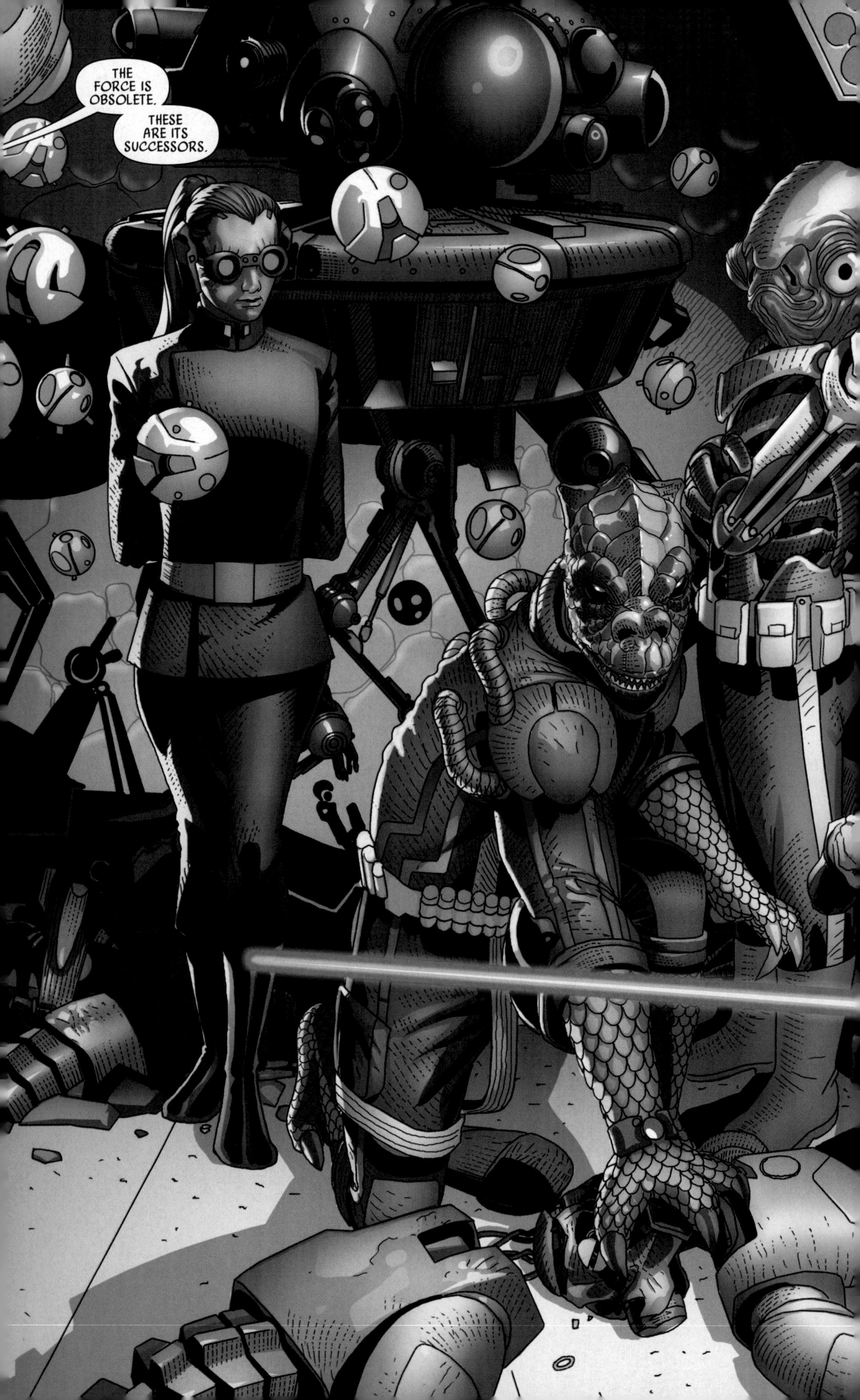

THE FORCE IS OBSOLETE.
THESE ARE ITS SUCCESSORS.

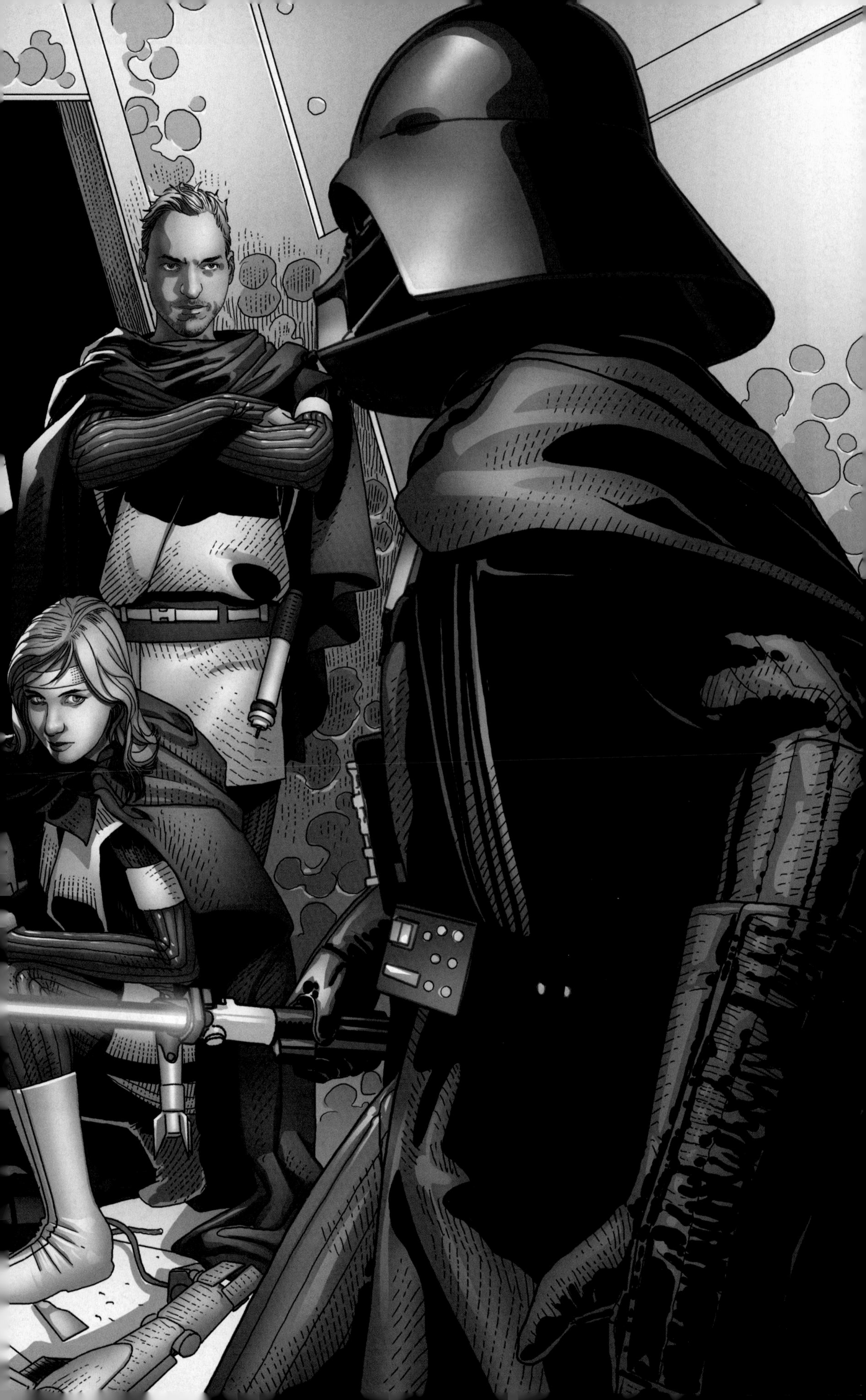

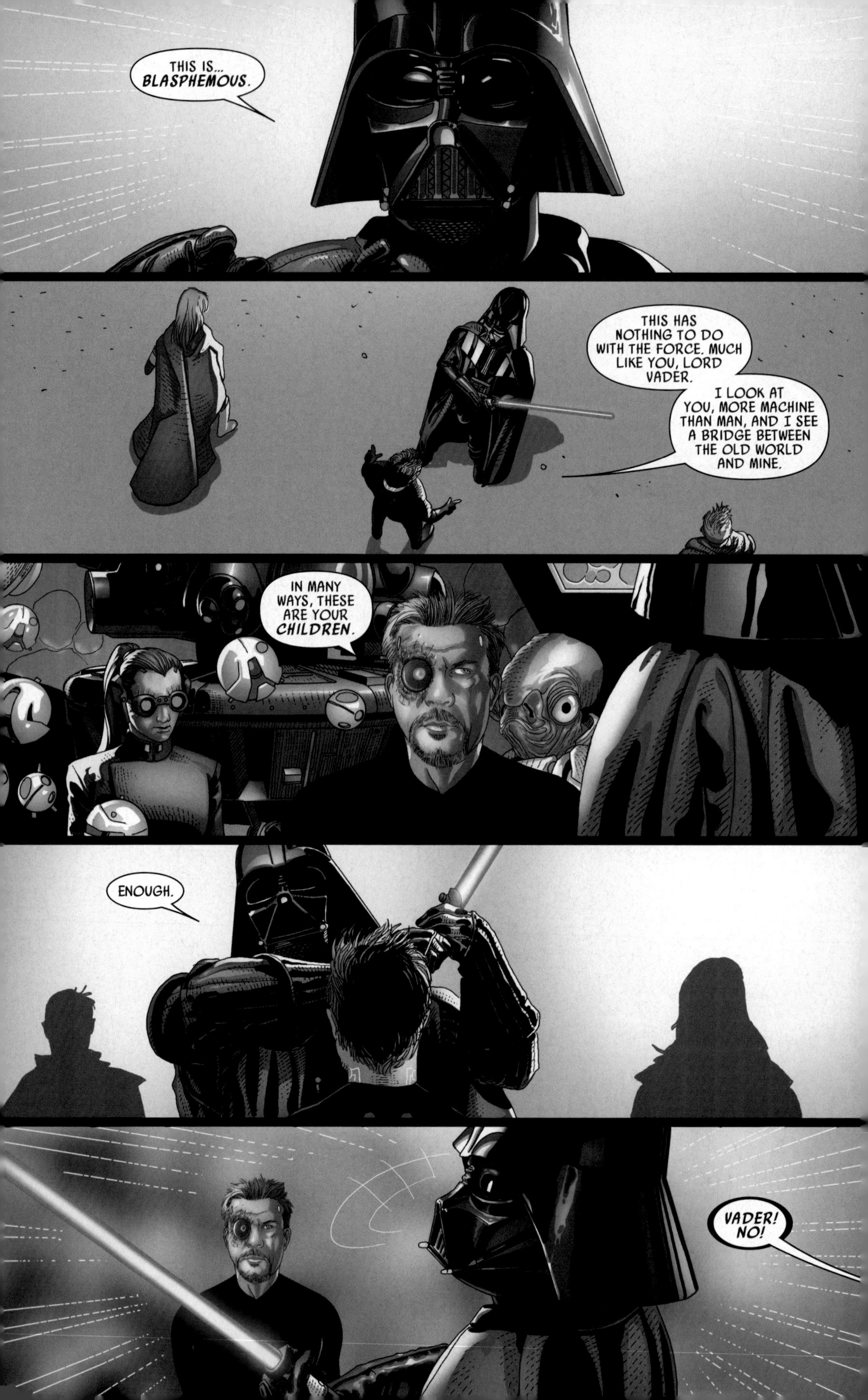
THIS IS... BLASPHEMOUS.
THIS HAS NOTHING TO DO WITH THE FORCE. MUCH LIKE YOU, LORD VADER.
I LOOK AT YOU, MORE MACHINE THAN MAN, AND I SEE A BRIDGE BETWEEN THE OLD WORLD AND MINE.
IN MANY WAYS, THESE ARE YOUR CHILDREN.
ENOUGH.
VADER! NO!

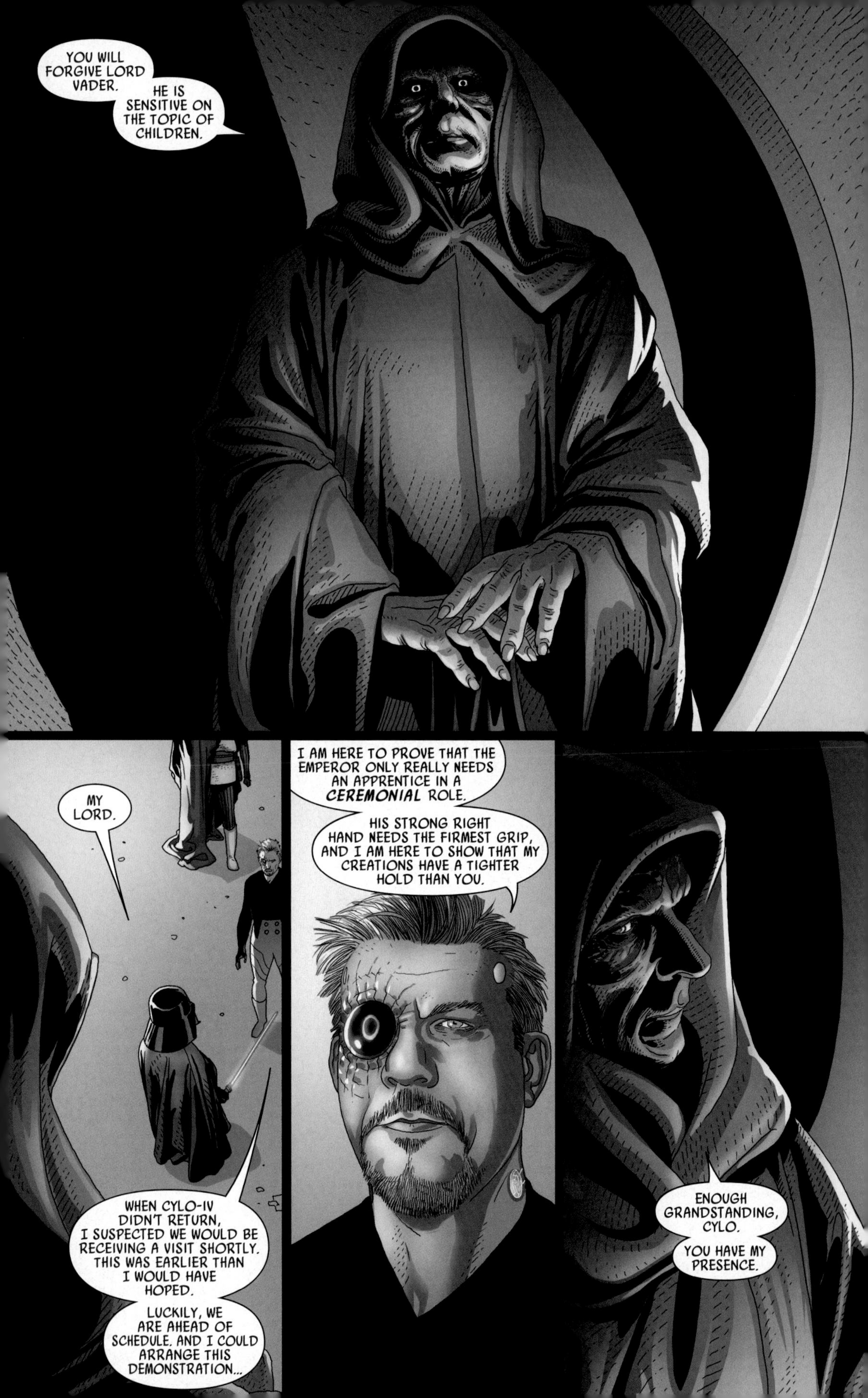
YOU WILL FORGIVE LORD VADER.
HE IS SENSITIVE ON THE TOPIC OF CHILDREN.
MY LORD.
WHEN CYLO-IV DIDN'T RETURN, I SUSPECTED WE WOULD BE RECEIVING A VISIT SHORTLY. THIS WAS EARLIER THAN I WOULD HAVE HOPED.
LUCKILY, WE ARE AHEAD OF SCHEDULE. AND I COULD ARRANGE THIS DEMONSTRATION...
I AM HERE TO PROVE THAT THE EMPEROR ONLY REALLY NEEDS AN APPRENTICE IN A *CEREMONIAL* ROLE.
HIS STRONG RIGHT HAND NEEDS THE FIRMEST GRIP, AND I AM HERE TO SHOW THAT MY CREATIONS HAVE A TIGHTER HOLD THAN YOU.
ENOUGH GRANDSTANDING, CYLO.
YOU HAVE MY PRESENCE.

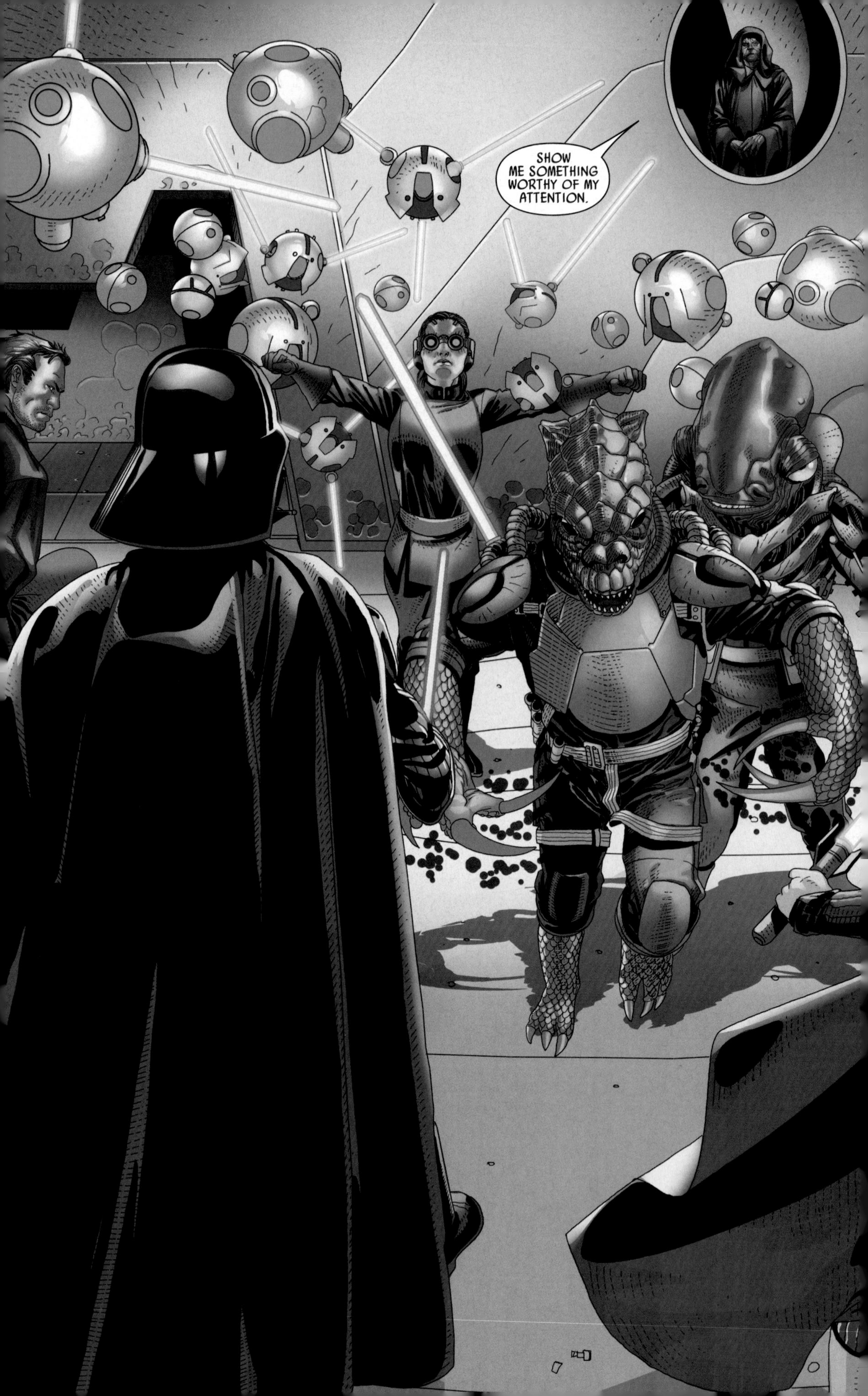
SHOW ME SOMETHING WORTHY OF MY ATTENTION.

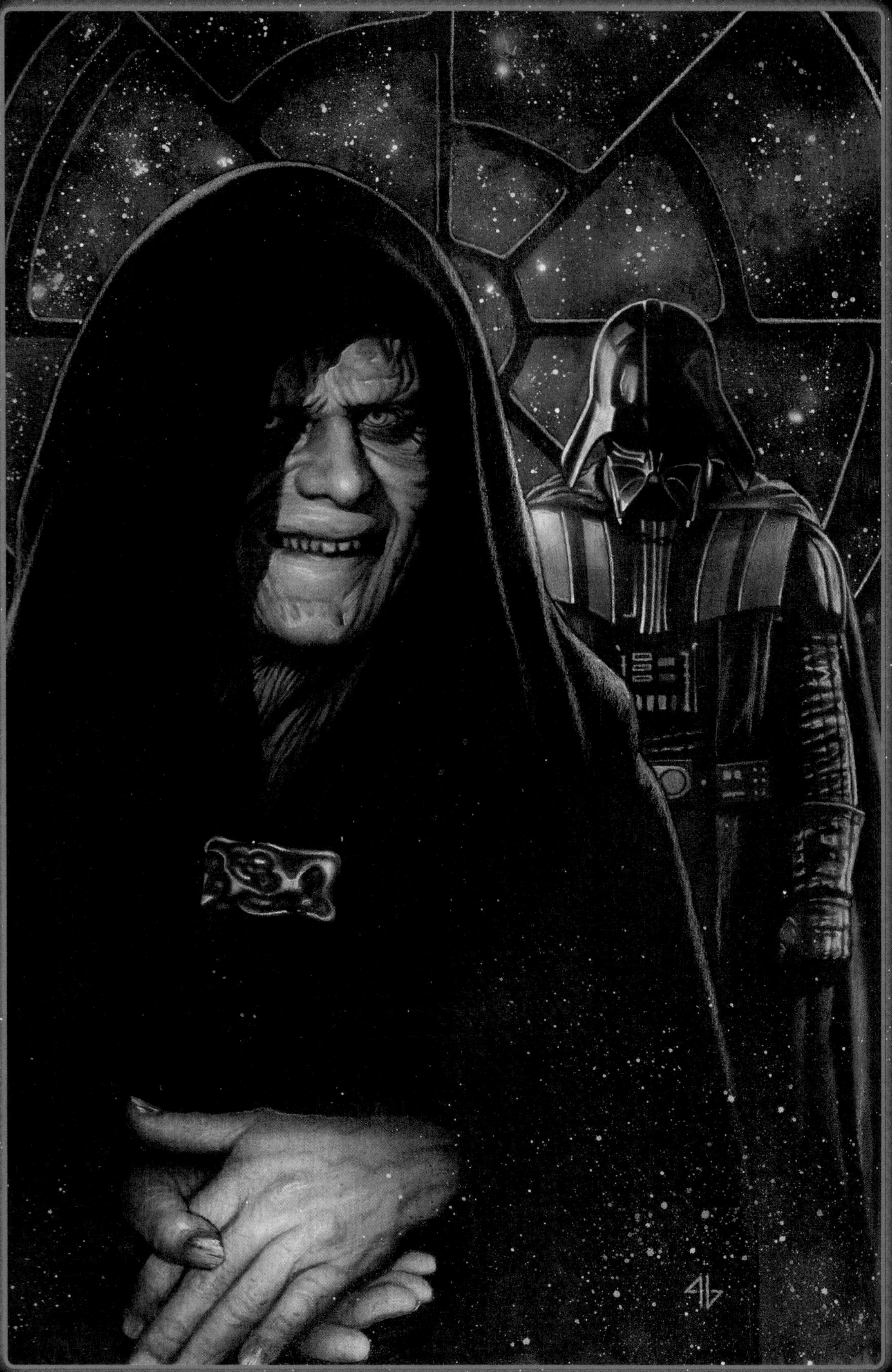

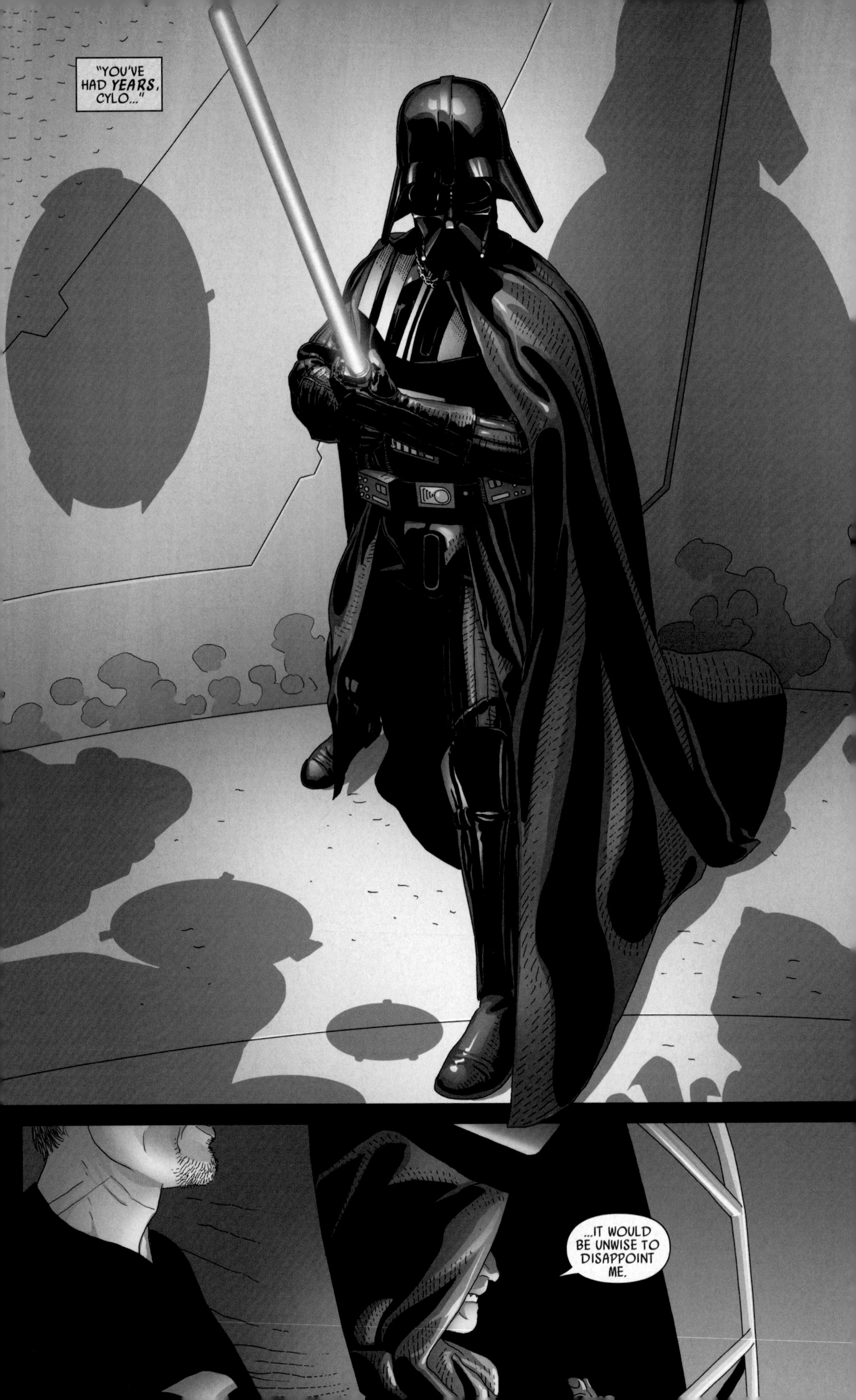
"YOU'VE HAD YEARS, CYLO..."
...IT WOULD BE UNWISE TO DISAPPOINT ME.

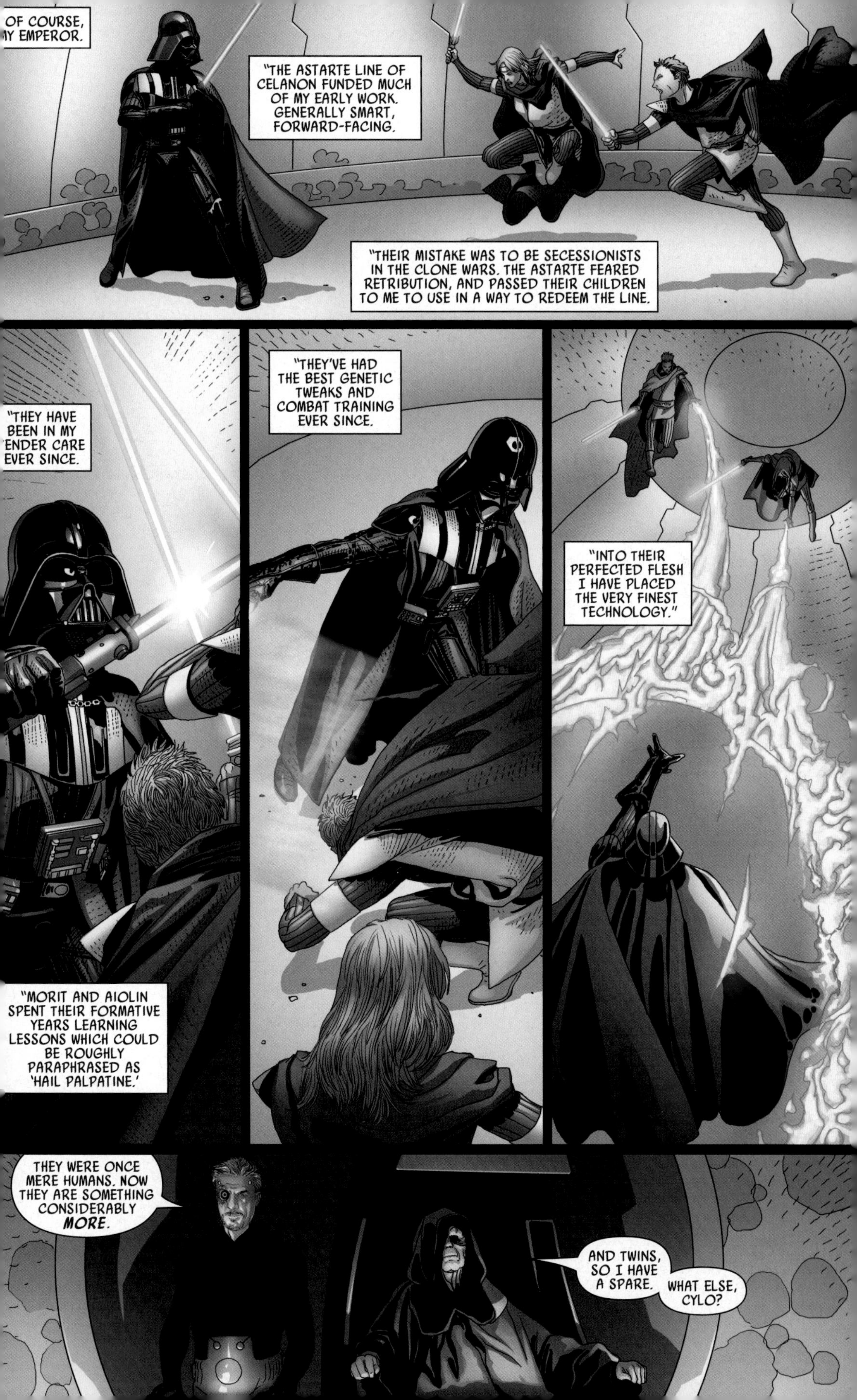
OF COURSE, MY EMPEROR.
"THE ASTARTE LINE OF CELANON FUNDED MUCH OF MY EARLY WORK. GENERALLY SMART, FORWARD-FACING.
"THEIR MISTAKE WAS TO BE SECESSIONISTS IN THE CLONE WARS. THE ASTARTE FEARED RETRIBUTION, AND PASSED THEIR CHILDREN TO ME TO USE IN A WAY TO REDEEM THE LINE.
"THEY HAVE BEEN IN MY ENDER CARE EVER SINCE.
"MORIT AND AIOLIN SPENT THEIR FORMATIVE YEARS LEARNING LESSONS WHICH COULD BE ROUGHLY PARAPHRASED AS 'HAIL PALPATINE.'
"THEY'VE HAD THE BEST GENETIC TWEAKS AND COMBAT TRAINING EVER SINCE.
"INTO THEIR PERFECTED FLESH I HAVE PLACED THE VERY FINEST TECHNOLOGY."
THEY WERE ONCE MERE HUMANS. NOW THEY ARE SOMETHING CONSIDERABLY MORE.
AND TWINS, SO I HAVE A SPARE.
WHAT ELSE, CYLO?

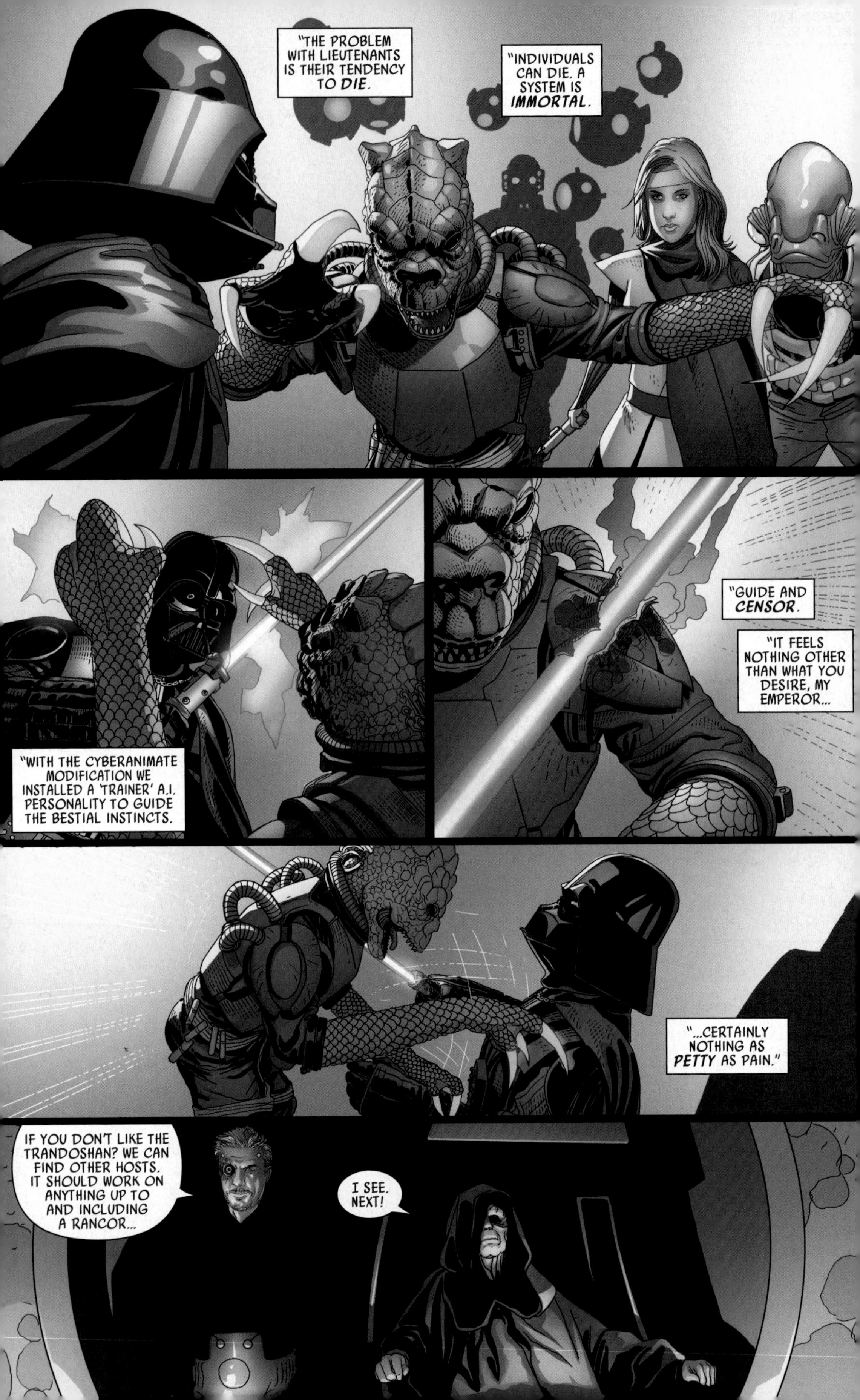
"THE PROBLEM WITH LIEUTENANTS IS THEIR TENDENCY TO DIE.
"INDIVIDUALS CAN DIE. A SYSTEM IS IMMORTAL.
"WITH THE CYBERANIMATE MODIFICATION WE INSTALLED A 'TRAINER' A.I. PERSONALITY TO GUIDE THE BESTIAL INSTINCTS.
"GUIDE AND CENSOR.
"IT FEELS NOTHING OTHER THAN WHAT YOU DESIRE, MY EMPEROR...
"...CERTAINLY NOTHING AS PETTY AS PAIN."
IF YOU DON'T LIKE THE TRANDOSHAN? WE CAN FIND OTHER HOSTS. IT SHOULD WORK ON ANYTHING UP TO AND INCLUDING A RANCOR...
I SEE. NEXT!

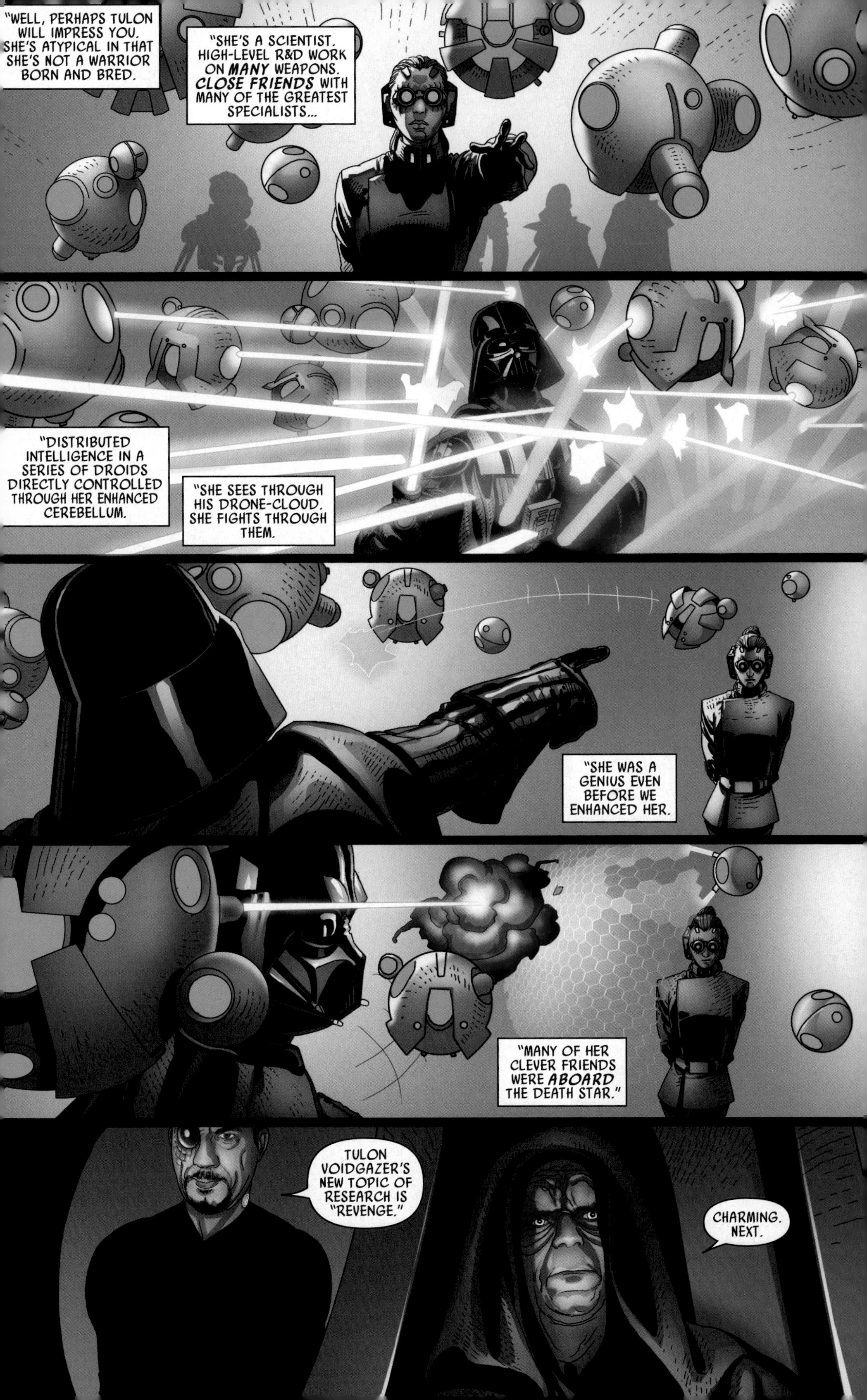
"WELL, PERHAPS TULON WILL IMPRESS YOU. SHE'S ATYPICAL IN THAT SHE'S NOT A WARRIOR BORN AND BRED.
"SHE'S A SCIENTIST. HIGH-LEVEL R&D WORK ON MANY WEAPONS. CLOSE FRIENDS WITH MANY OF THE GREATEST SPECIALISTS...
"DISTRIBUTED INTELLIGENCE IN A SERIES OF DROIDS DIRECTLY CONTROLLED THROUGH HER ENHANCED CEREBELLUM.
"SHE SEES THROUGH HIS DRONE-CLOUD. SHE FIGHTS THROUGH THEM.
"SHE WAS A GENIUS EVEN BEFORE WE ENHANCED HER.
"MANY OF HER CLEVER FRIENDS WERE ABOARD THE DEATH STAR."
TULON VOIDGAZER'S NEW TOPIC OF RESEARCH IS "REVENGE."
CHARMING. NEXT.

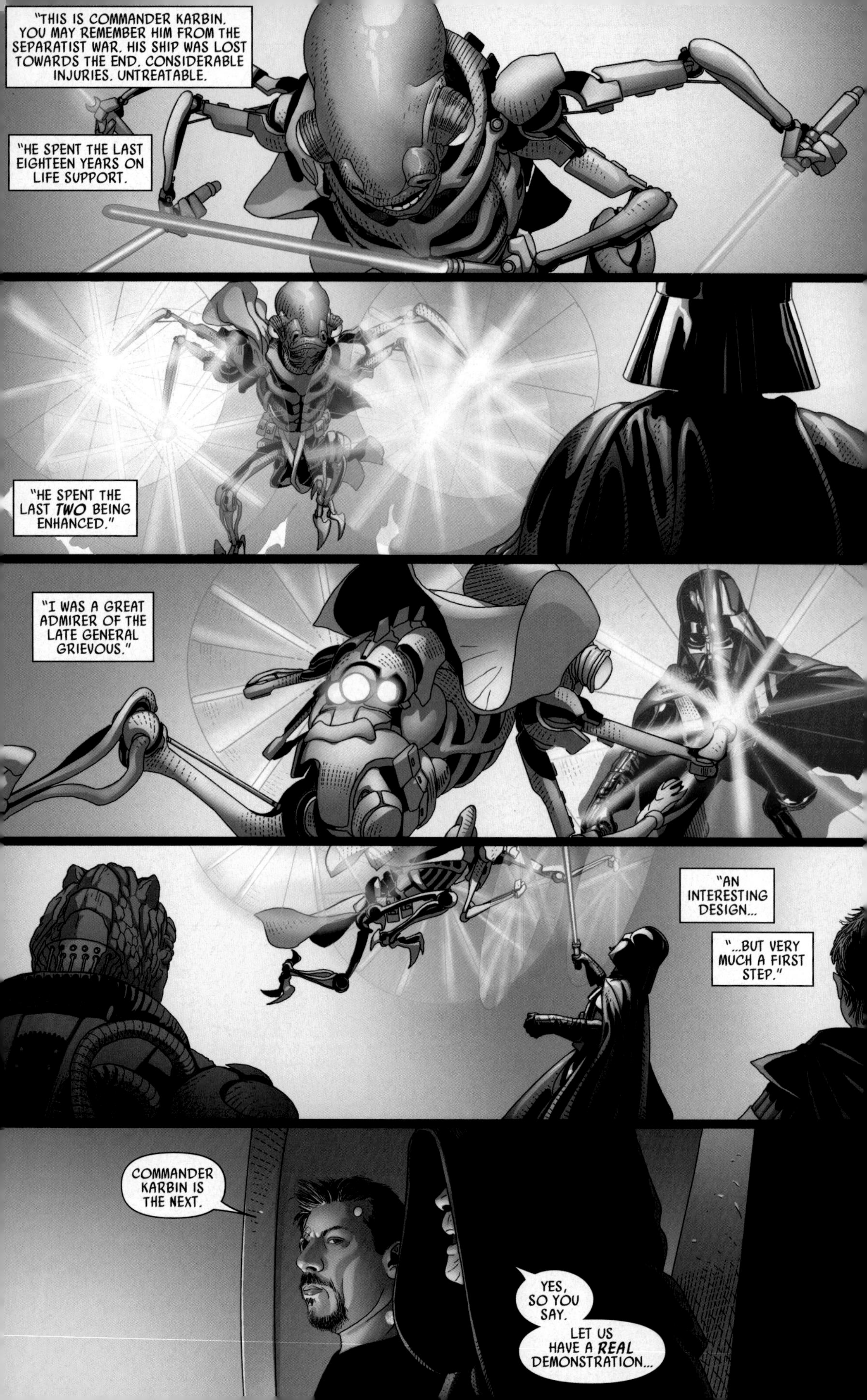
"THIS IS COMMANDER KARBIN. YOU MAY REMEMBER HIM FROM THE SEPARATIST WAR. HIS SHIP WAS LOST TOWARDS THE END. CONSIDERABLE INJURIES. UNTREATABLE.
"HE SPENT THE LAST EIGHTEEN YEARS ON LIFE SUPPORT.
"HE SPENT THE LAST TWO BEING ENHANCED."
"I WAS A GREAT ADMIRER OF THE LATE GENERAL GRIEVOUS."
"AN INTERESTING DESIGN...
"...BUT VERY MUCH A FIRST STEP."
COMMANDER KARBIN IS THE NEXT.
YES, SO YOU SAY.
LET US HAVE A REAL DEMONSTRATION...

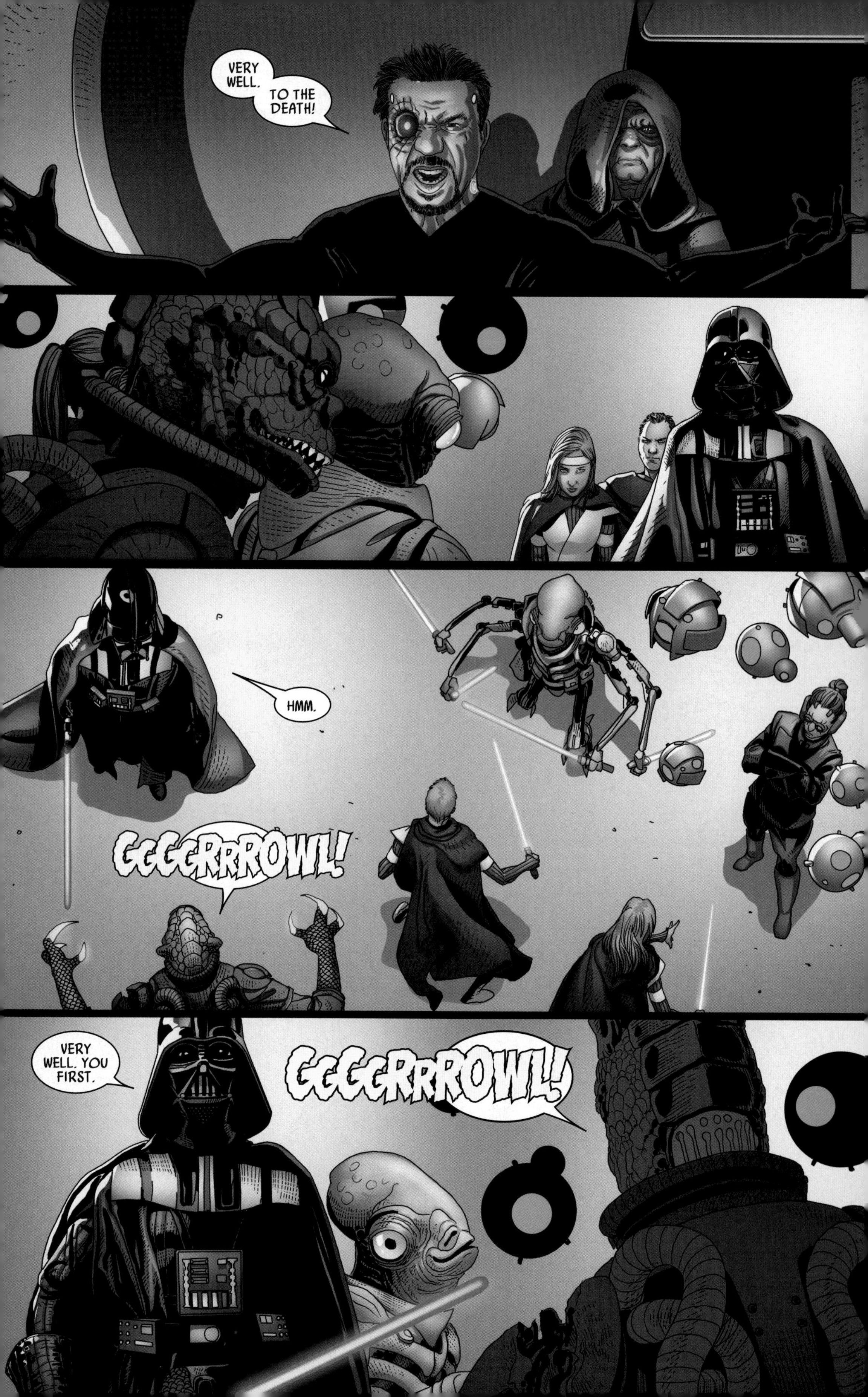
VERY WELL. TO THE DEATH!
HMM.
GGGGRRROWL!
VERY WELL. YOU FIRST.
GGGGRRROWL!

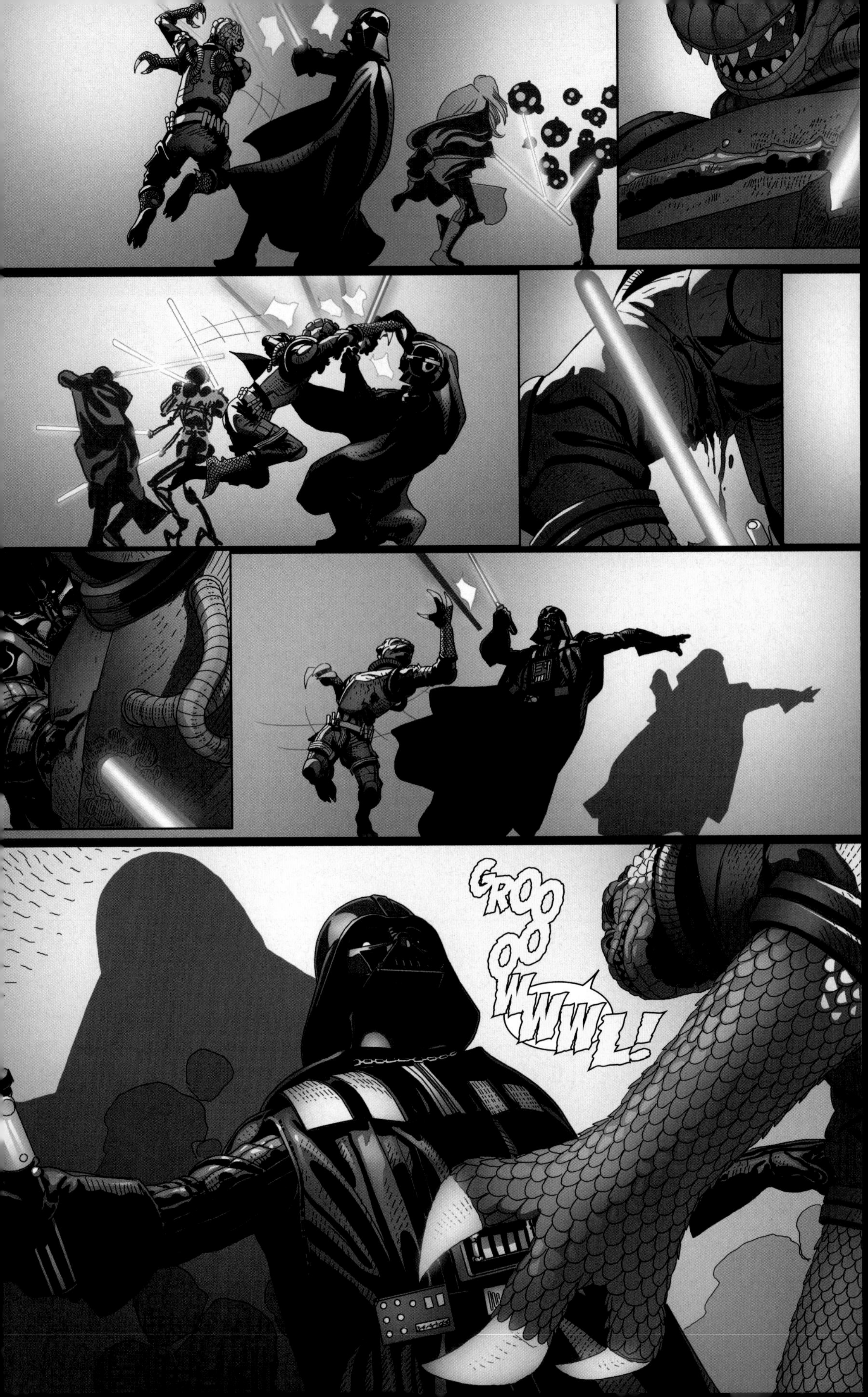
GROOOOWWWL!

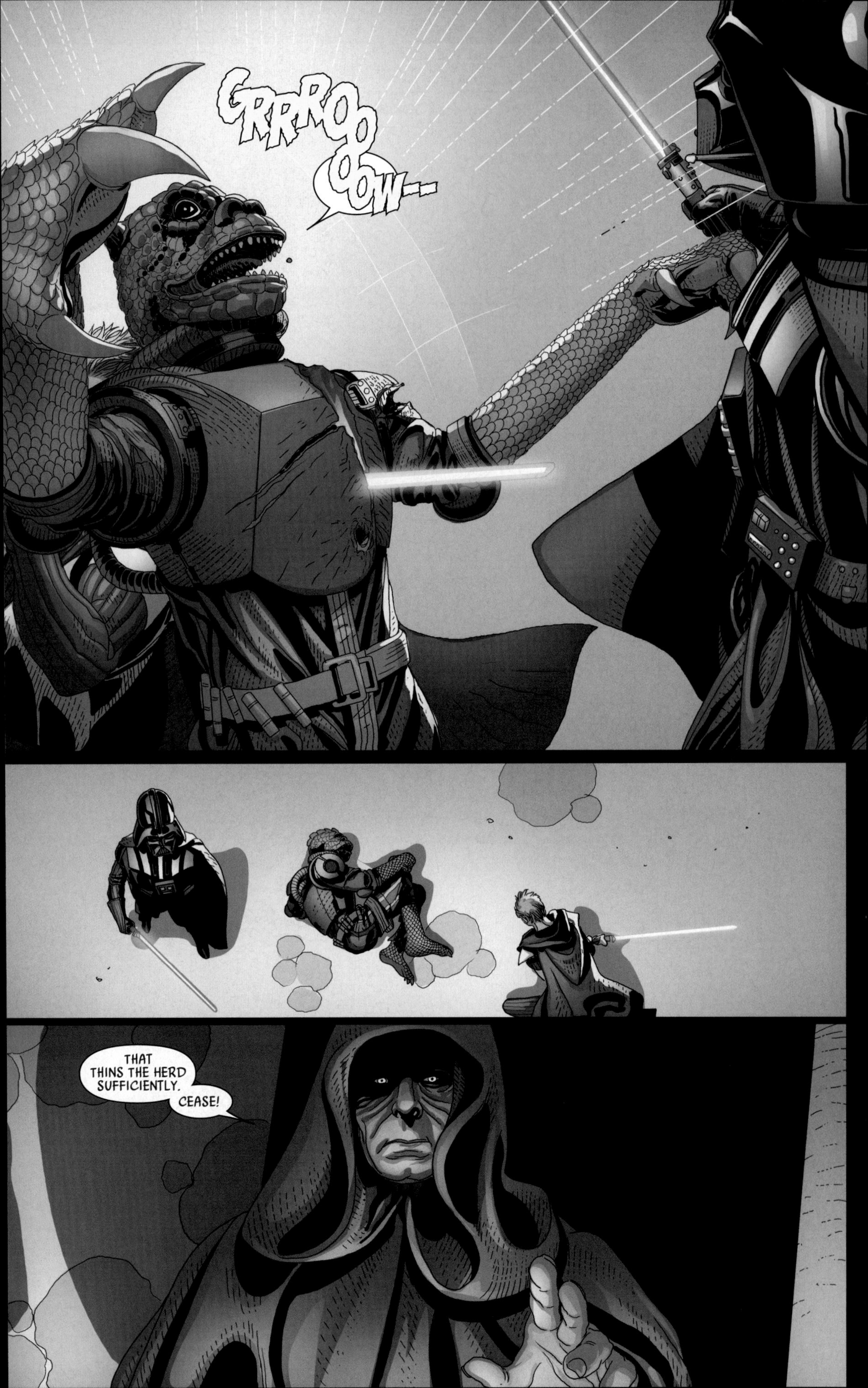
GRRROOOOW--
THAT THINS THE HERD SUFFICIENTLY.
CEASE!

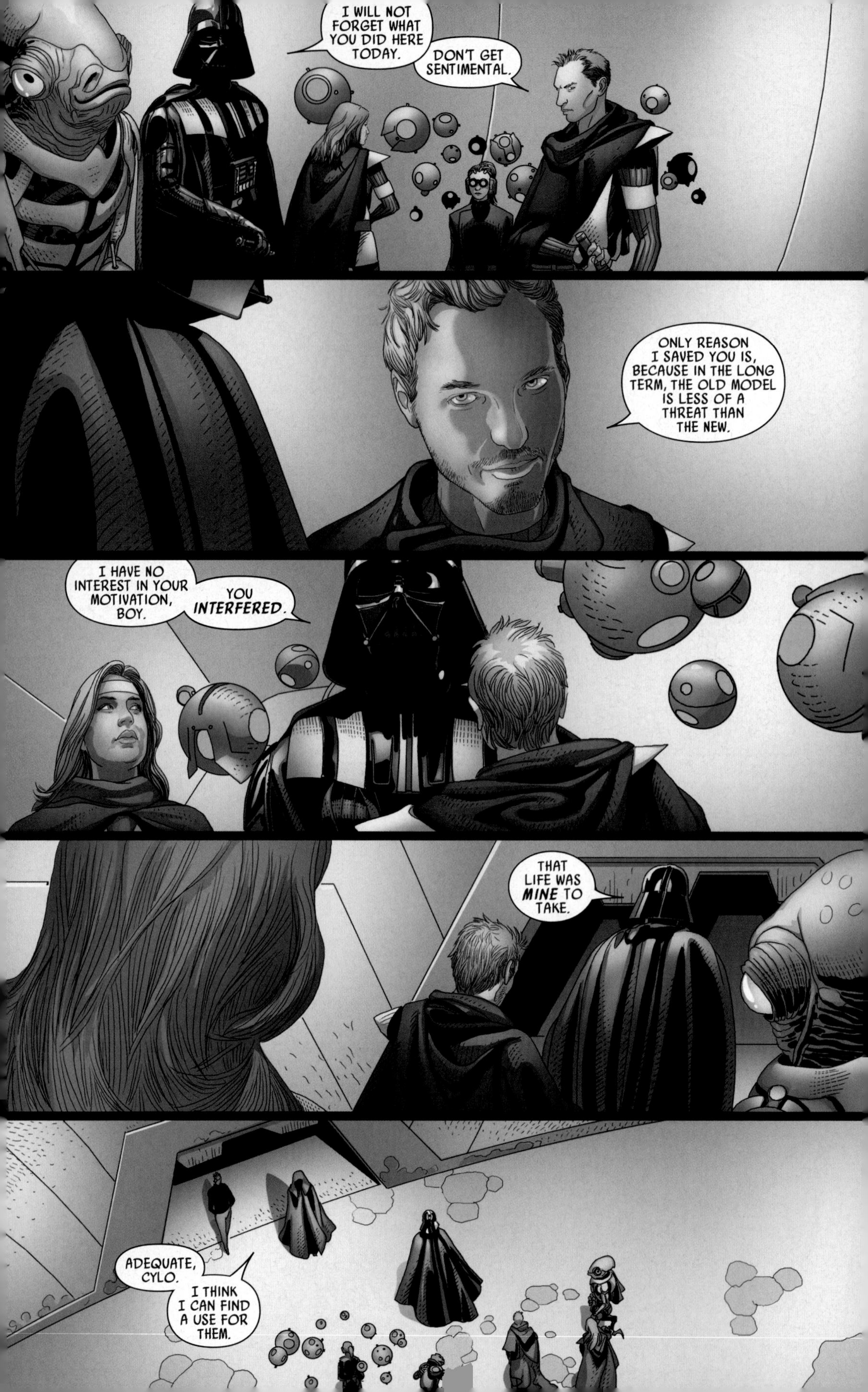
I WILL NOT FORGET WHAT YOU DID HERE TODAY.
DON'T GET SENTIMENTAL.
ONLY REASON I SAVED YOU IS, BECAUSE IN THE LONG TERM, THE OLD MODEL IS LESS OF A THREAT THAN THE NEW.
I HAVE NO INTEREST IN YOUR MOTIVATION, BOY.
YOU *INTERFERED*.
THAT LIFE WAS *MINE* TO TAKE.
ADEQUATE, CYLO.
I THINK I CAN FIND A USE FOR THEM.

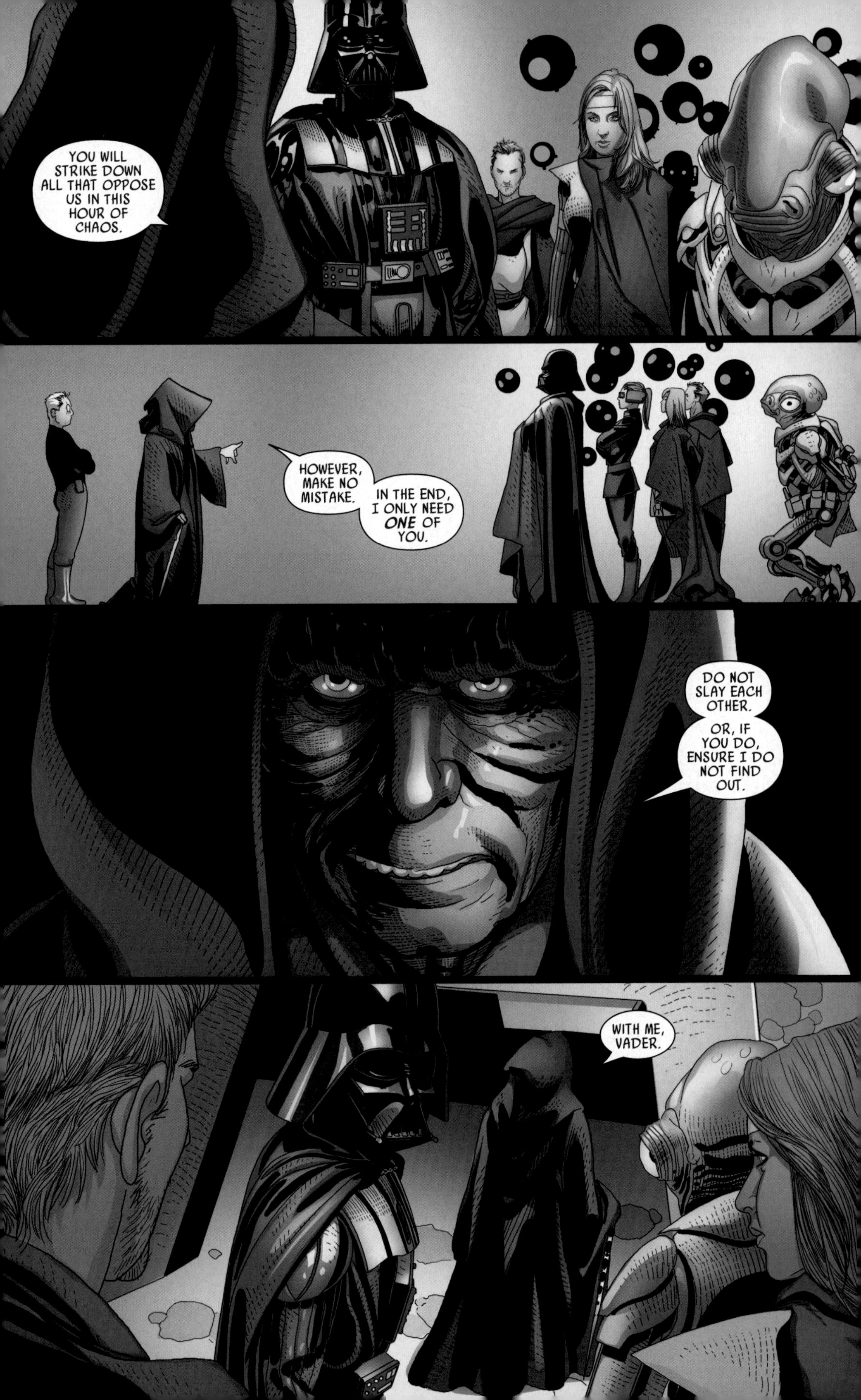
YOU WILL STRIKE DOWN ALL THAT OPPOSE US IN THIS HOUR OF CHAOS.
HOWEVER, MAKE NO MISTAKE.
IN THE END, I ONLY NEED ONE OF YOU.
DO NOT SLAY EACH OTHER.
OR, IF YOU DO, ENSURE I DO NOT FIND OUT.
WITH ME, VADER.

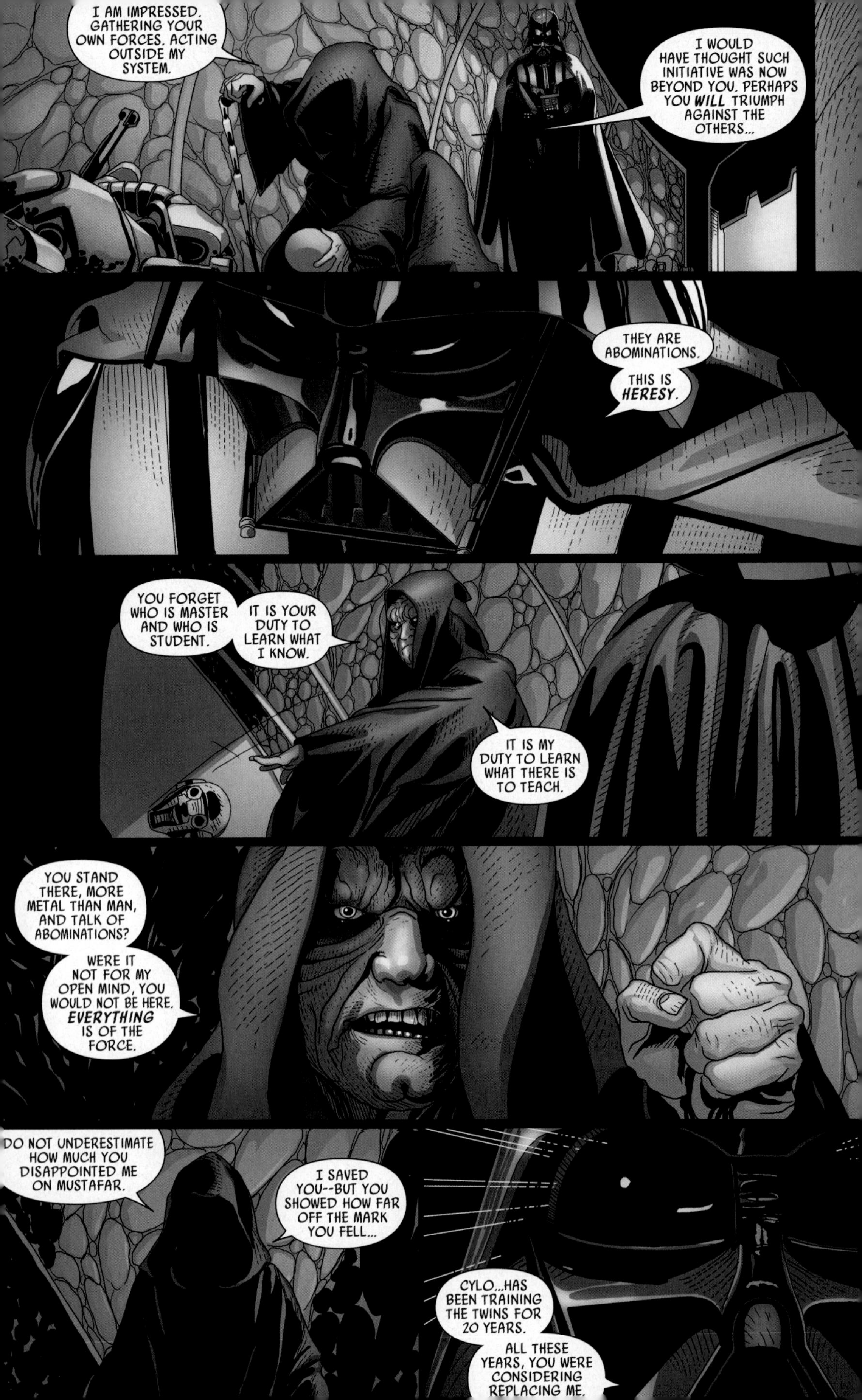
I AM IMPRESSED. GATHERING YOUR OWN FORCES. ACTING OUTSIDE MY SYSTEM.
I WOULD HAVE THOUGHT SUCH INITIATIVE WAS NOW BEYOND YOU. PERHAPS YOU *WILL* TRIUMPH AGAINST THE OTHERS...
THEY ARE ABOMINATIONS.
THIS IS *HERESY*.
YOU FORGET WHO IS MASTER AND WHO IS STUDENT.
IT IS YOUR DUTY TO LEARN WHAT I KNOW.
IT IS MY DUTY TO LEARN WHAT THERE IS TO TEACH.
YOU STAND THERE, MORE METAL THAN MAN, AND TALK OF ABOMINATIONS?
WERE IT NOT FOR MY OPEN MIND, YOU WOULD NOT BE HERE. *EVERYTHING* IS OF THE FORCE.
DO NOT UNDERESTIMATE HOW MUCH YOU DISAPPOINTED ME ON MUSTAFAR.
I SAVED YOU--BUT YOU SHOWED HOW FAR OFF THE MARK YOU FELL...
CYLO...HAS BEEN TRAINING THE TWINS FOR 20 YEARS.
ALL THESE YEARS, YOU WERE CONSIDERING REPLACING ME.

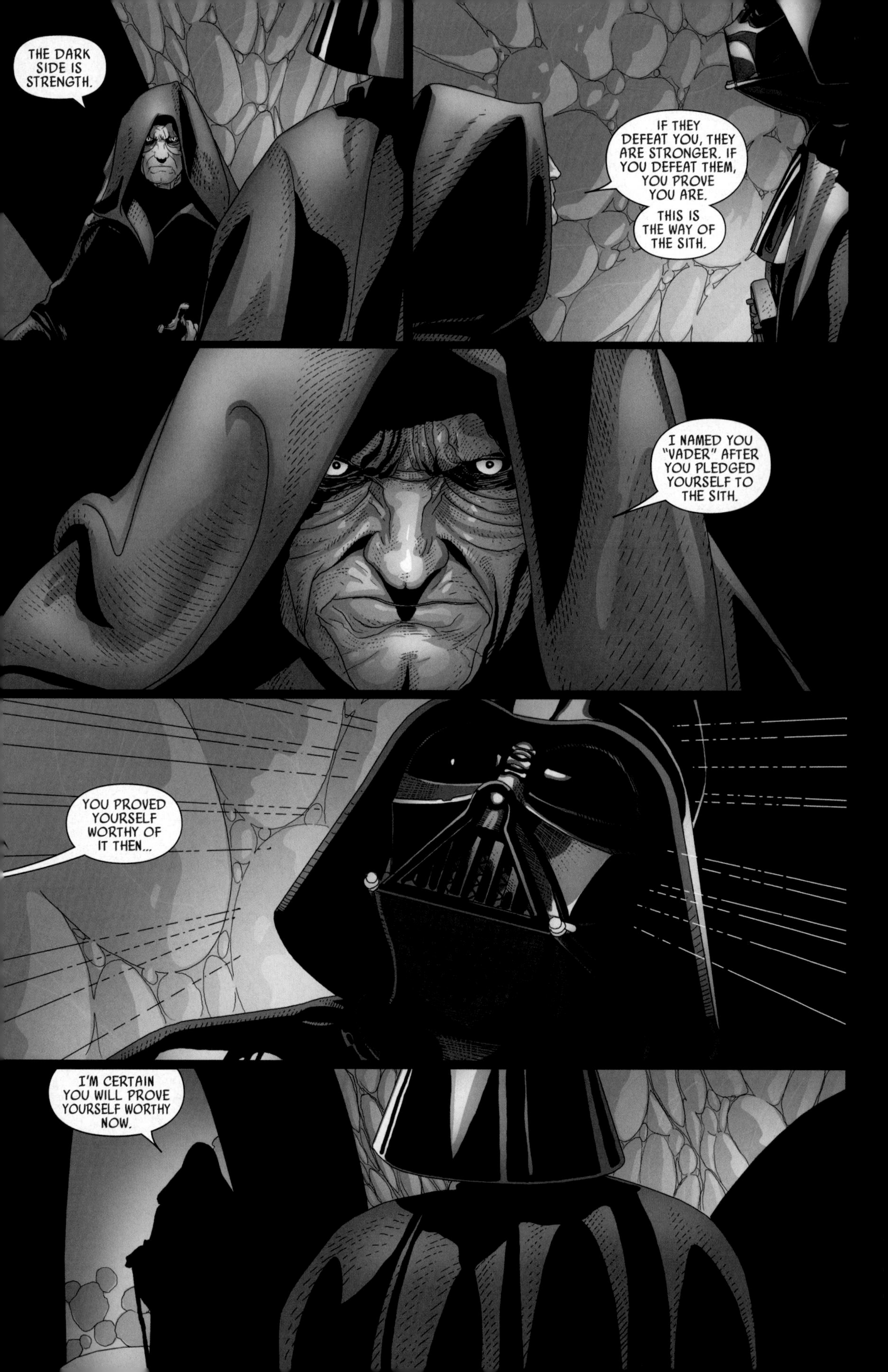
THE DARK SIDE IS STRENGTH.
IF THEY DEFEAT YOU, THEY ARE STRONGER. IF YOU DEFEAT THEM, YOU PROVE YOU ARE.
THIS IS THE WAY OF THE SITH.
I NAMED YOU "VADER" AFTER YOU PLEDGED YOURSELF TO THE SITH.
YOU PROVED YOURSELF WORTHY OF IT THEN...
I'M CERTAIN YOU WILL PROVE YOURSELF WORTHY NOW.

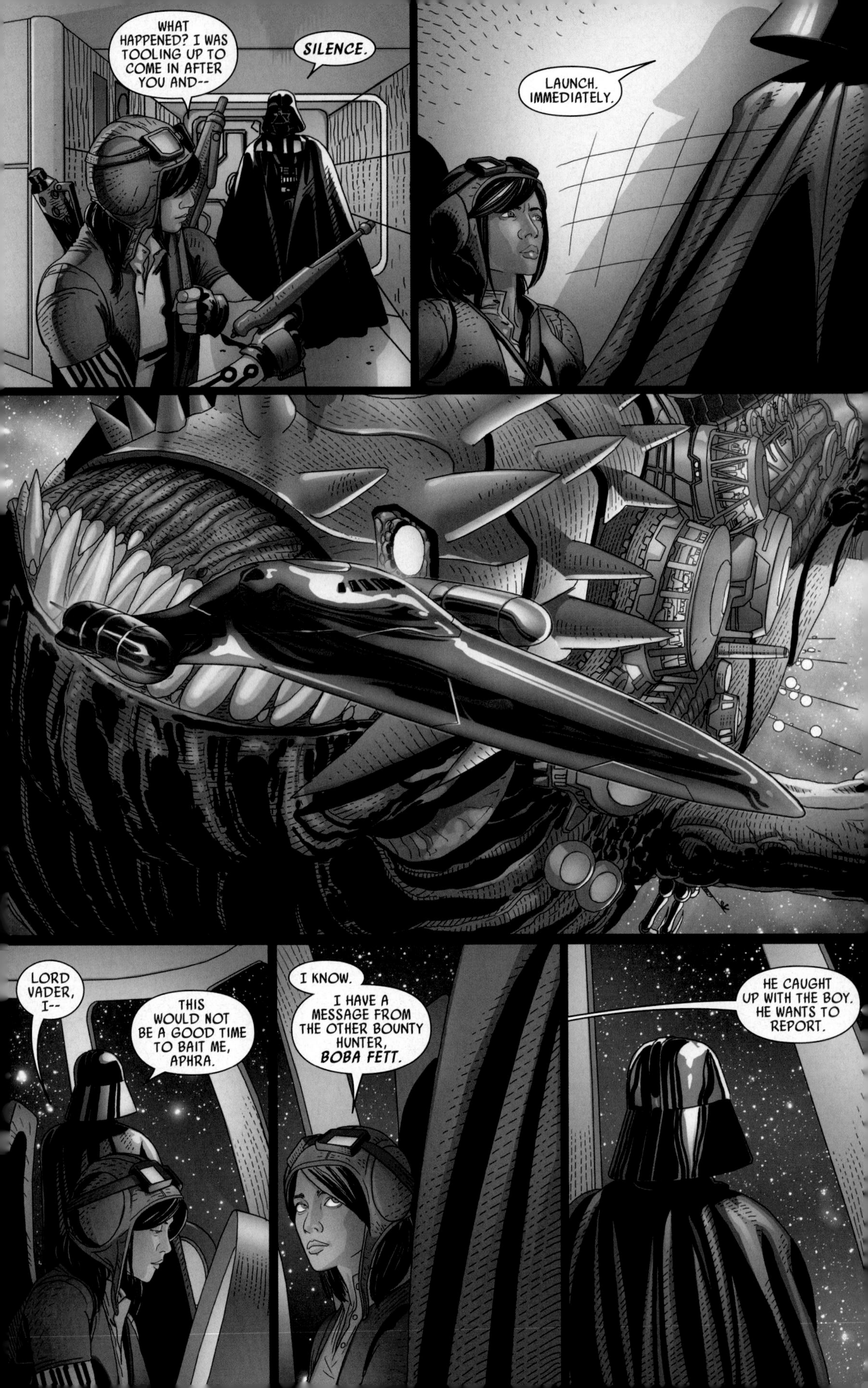
WHAT HAPPENED? I WAS TOOLING UP TO COME IN AFTER YOU AND--
SILENCE.
LAUNCH. IMMEDIATELY.
LORD VADER, I--
THIS WOULD NOT BE A GOOD TIME TO BAIT ME, APHRA.
I KNOW.
I HAVE A MESSAGE FROM THE OTHER BOUNTY HUNTER, BOBA FETT.
HE CAUGHT UP WITH THE BOY. HE WANTS TO REPORT.

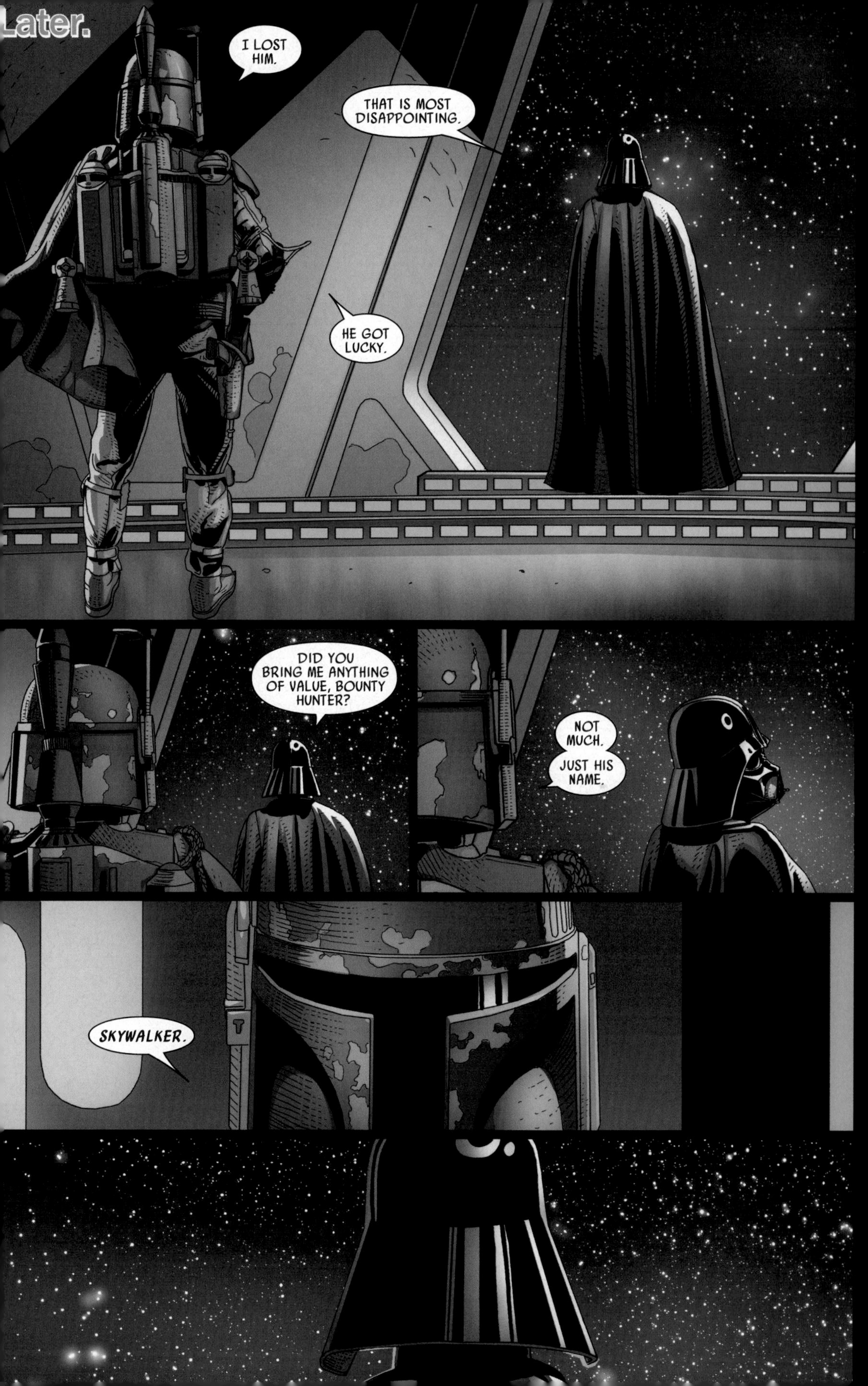
Later.
I LOST HIM.
THAT IS MOST DISAPPOINTING.
HE GOT LUCKY.
DID YOU BRING ME ANYTHING OF VALUE, BOUNTY HUNTER?
NOT MUCH.
JUST HIS NAME.
SKYWALKER.

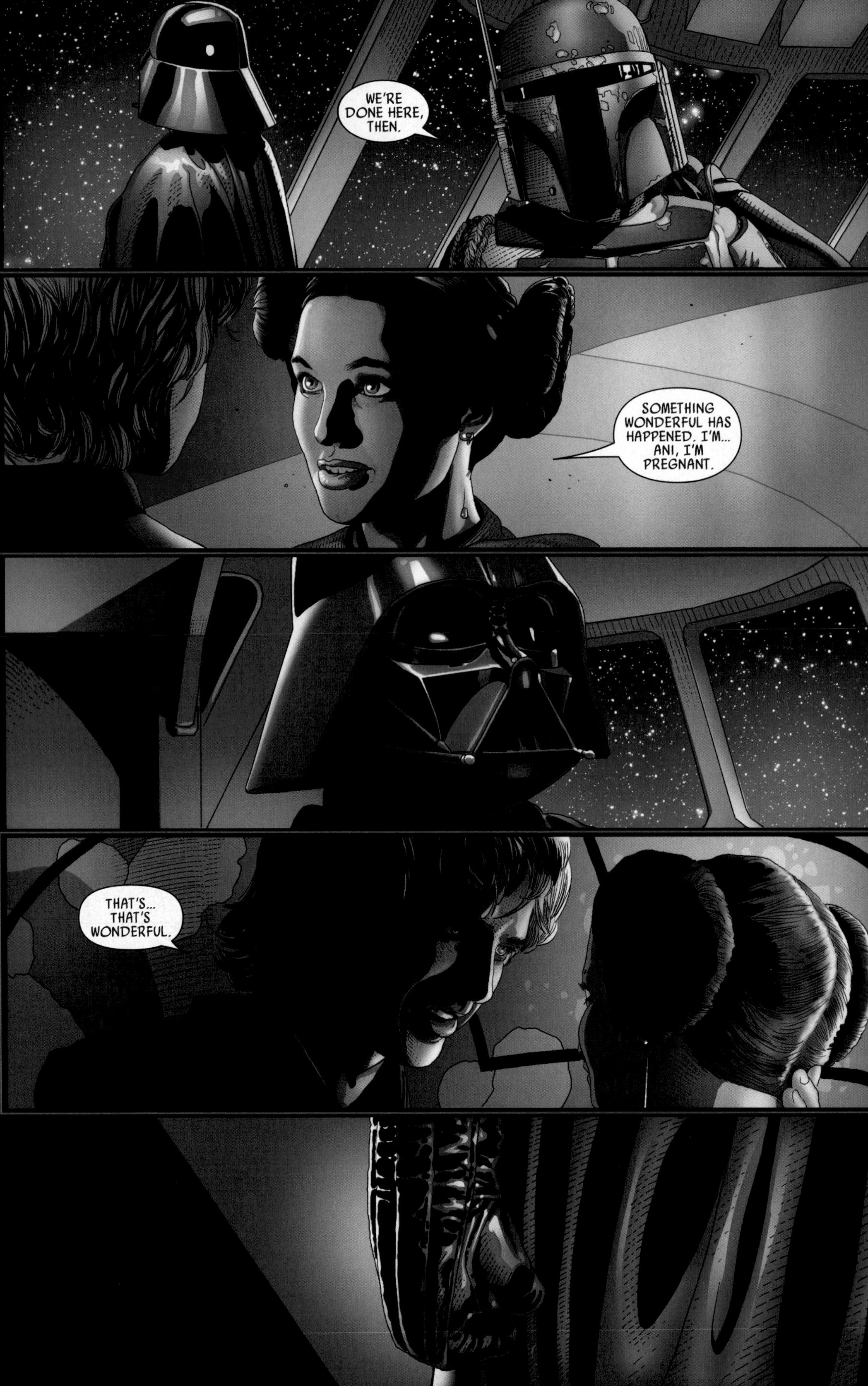
WE'RE DONE HERE, THEN.
SOMETHING WONDERFUL HAS HAPPENED. I'M... ANI, I'M PREGNANT.
THAT'S... THAT'S WONDERFUL.

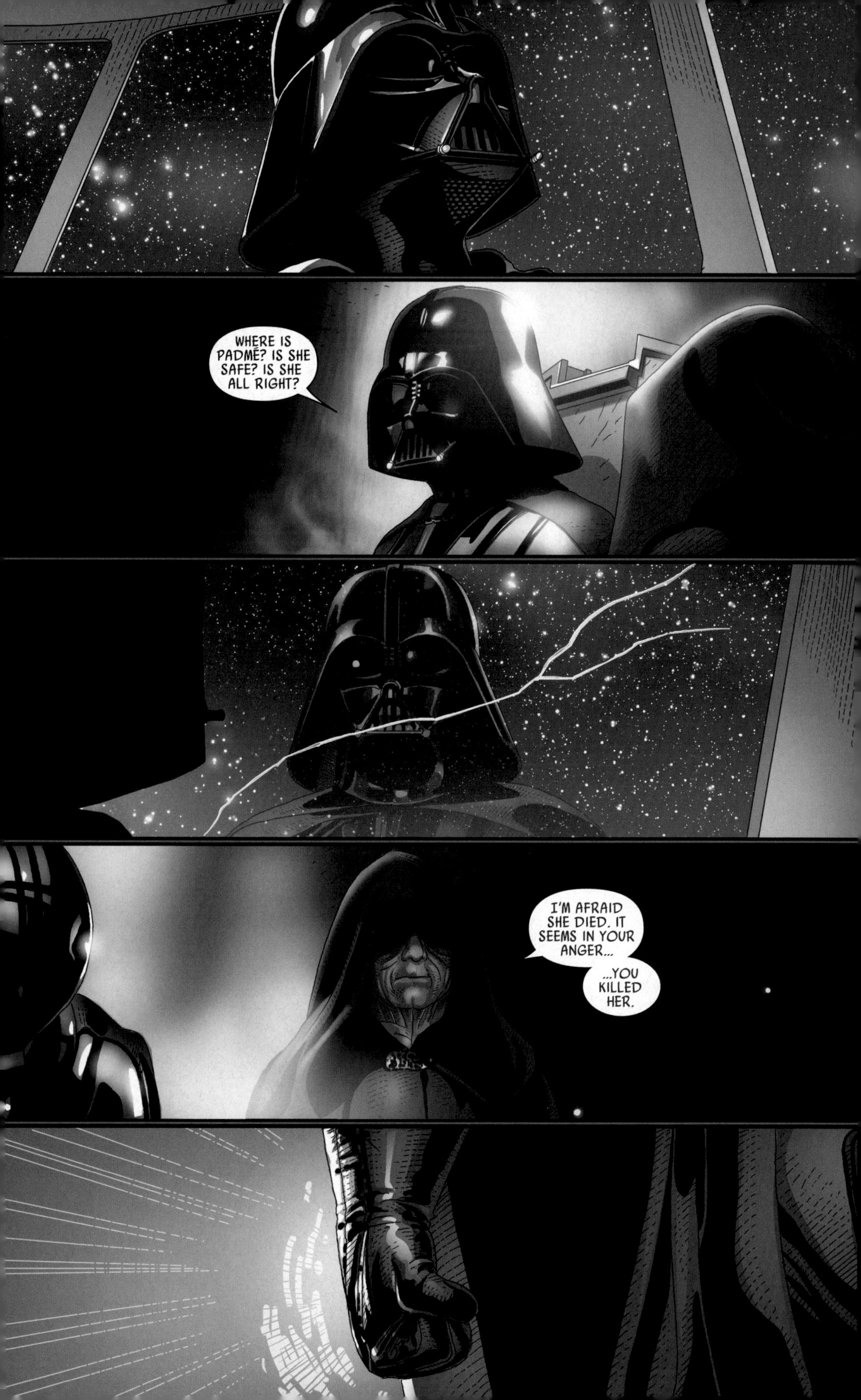
WHERE IS PADMÉ? IS SHE SAFE? IS SHE ALL RIGHT?
I'M AFRAID SHE DIED. IT SEEMS IN YOUR ANGER...
...YOU KILLED HER.

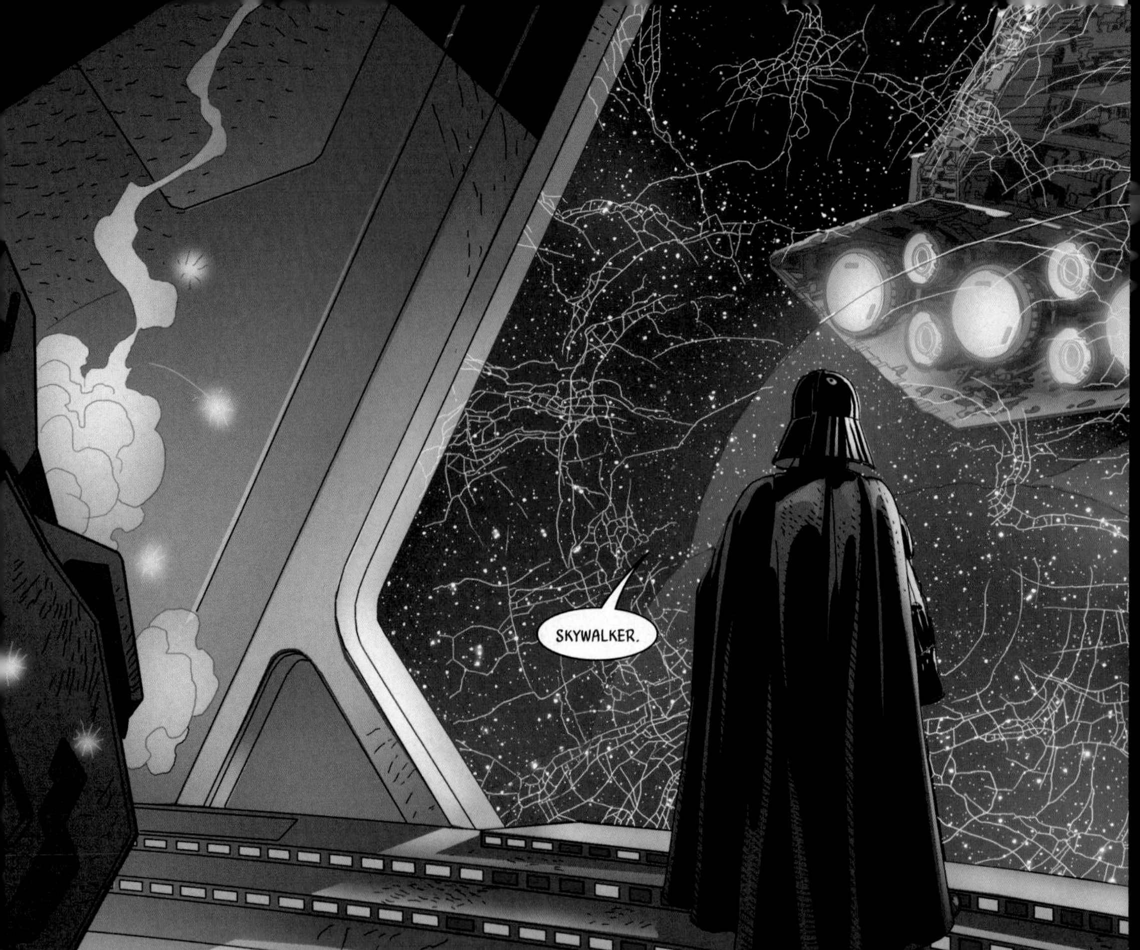
SKYWALKER.

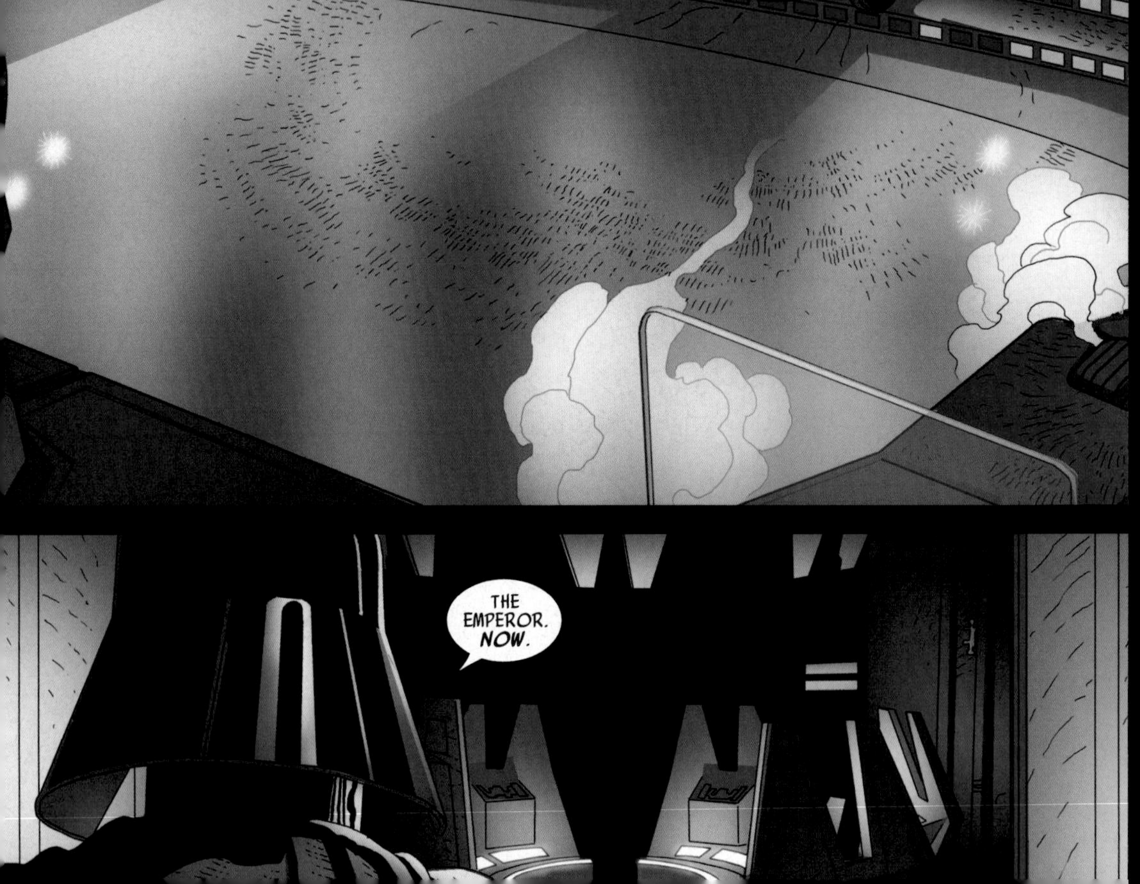
THE EMPEROR. NOW.

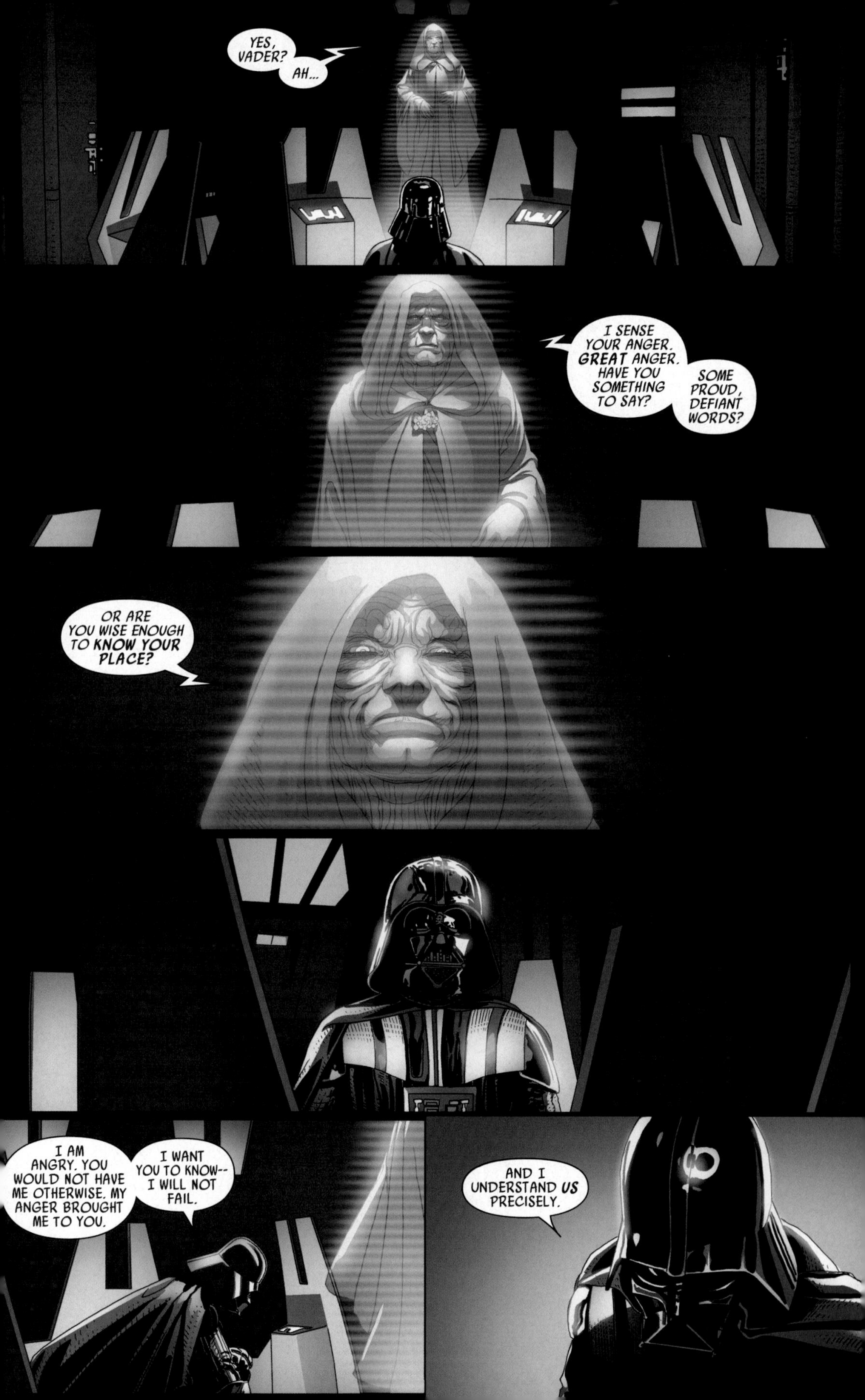
YES, VADER?
AH...
I SENSE YOUR ANGER. GREAT ANGER. HAVE YOU SOMETHING TO SAY?
SOME PROUD, DEFIANT WORDS?
OR ARE YOU WISE ENOUGH TO KNOW YOUR PLACE?
I AM ANGRY. YOU WOULD NOT HAVE ME OTHERWISE. MY ANGER BROUGHT ME TO YOU.
I WANT YOU TO KNOW-- I WILL NOT FAIL.
AND I UNDERSTAND US PRECISELY.

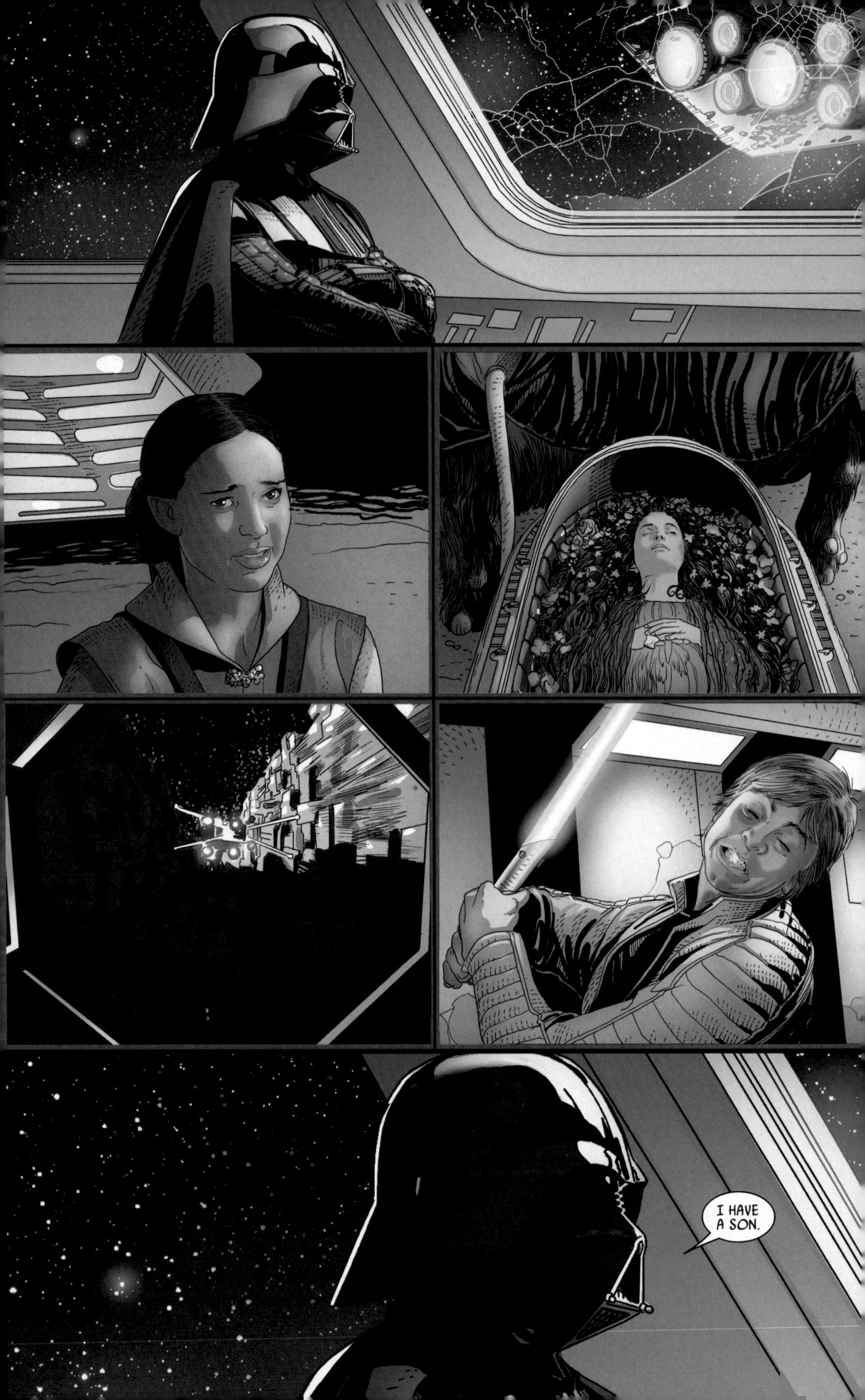
I HAVE A SON.

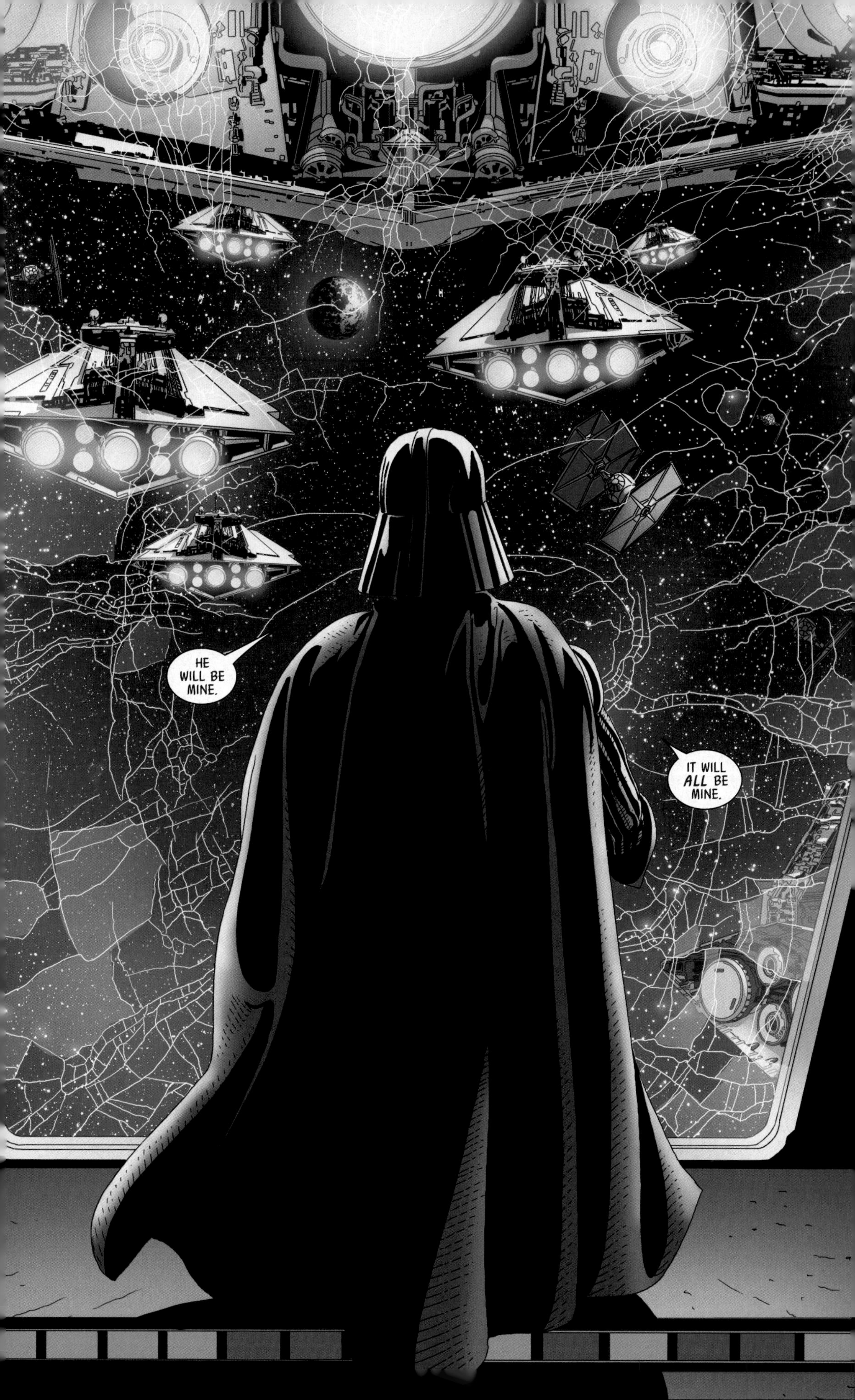
HE WILL BE MINE.
IT WILL ALL BE MINE.

ADI GRANOV COVER SKETCHES

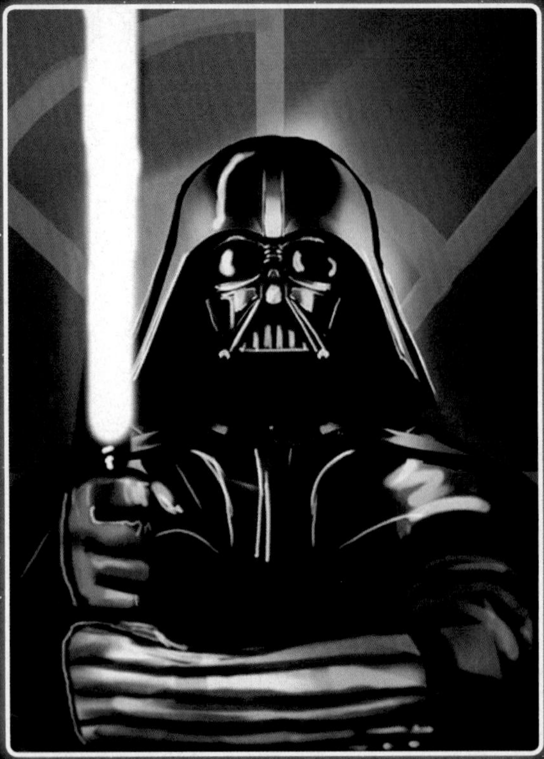

DARTH VADER 1

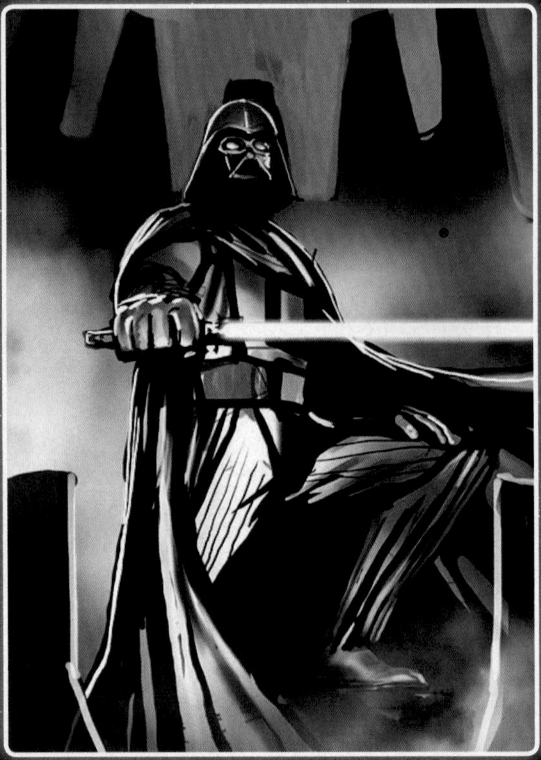

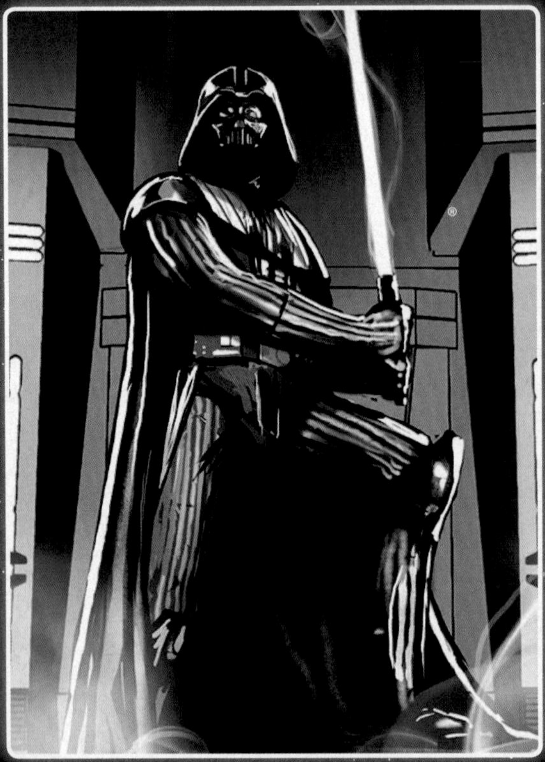

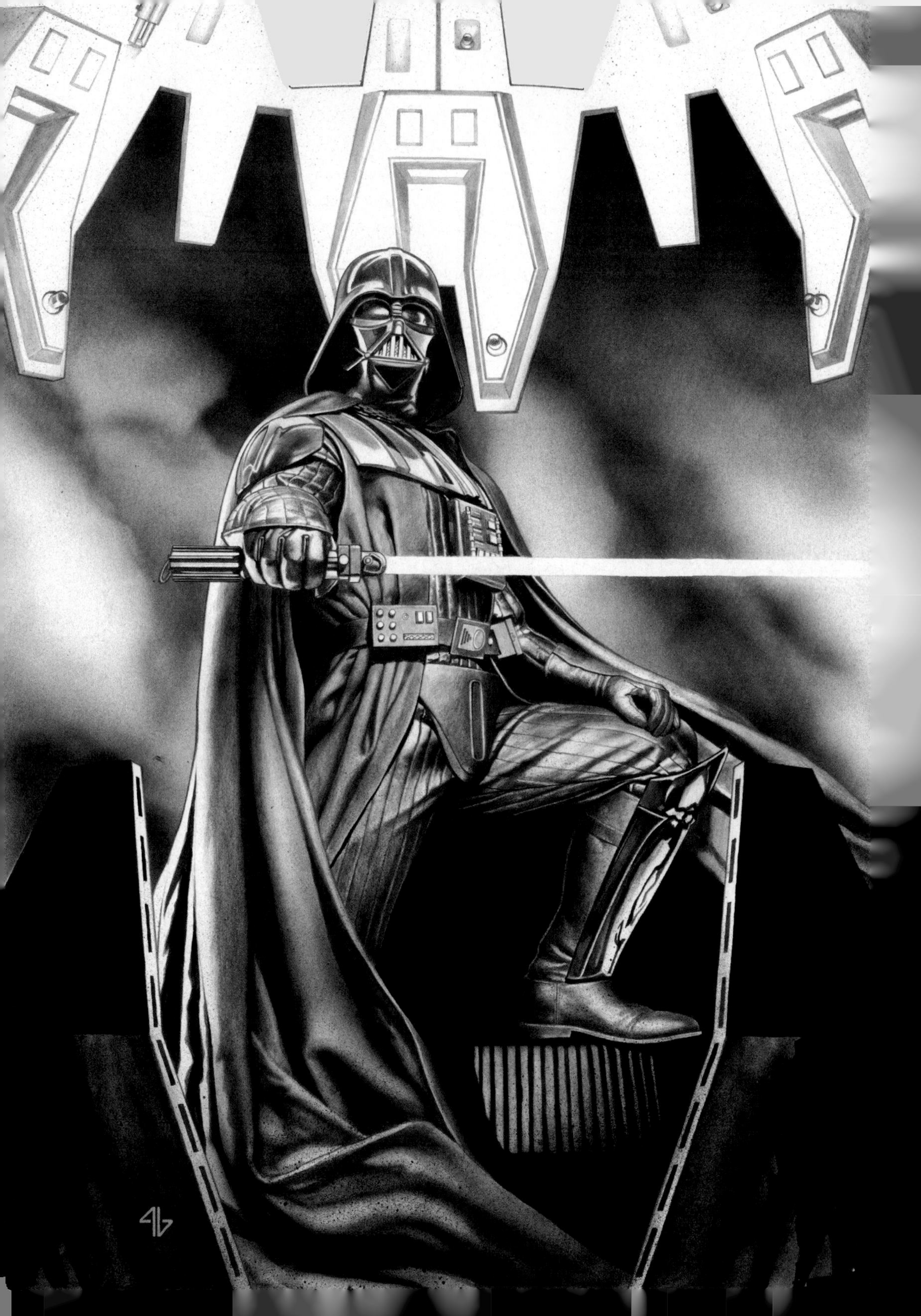

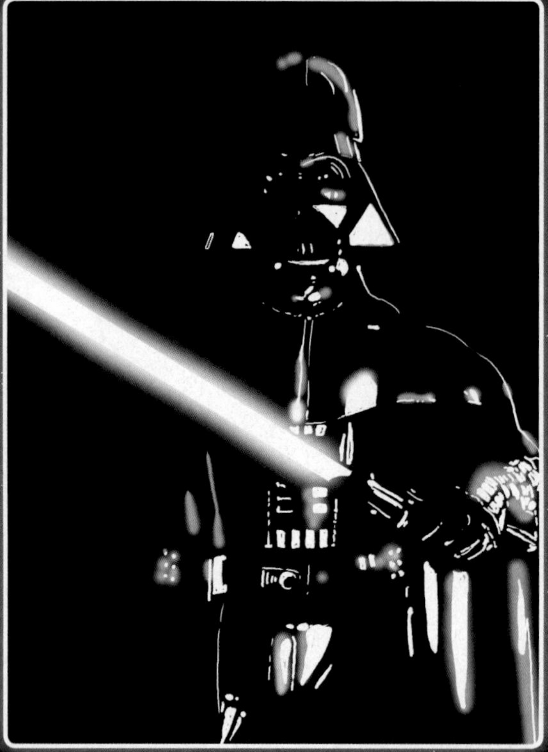

DARTH VADER 4

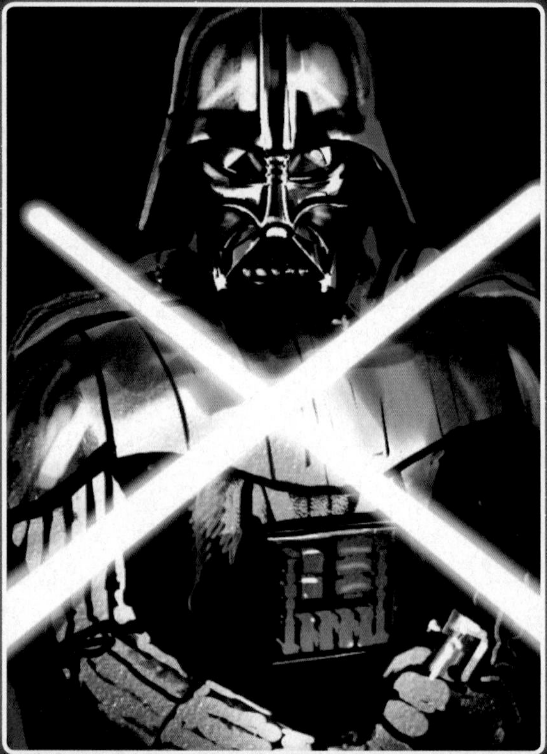

DARTH VADER 5

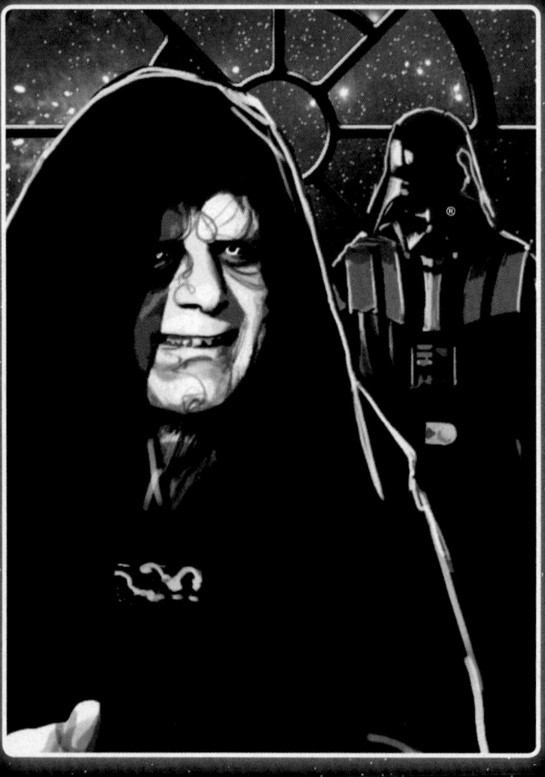

DARTH VADER 6

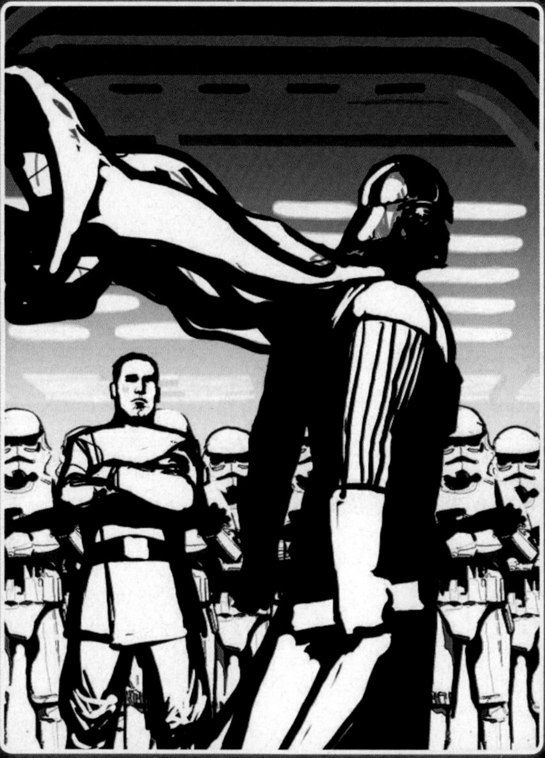

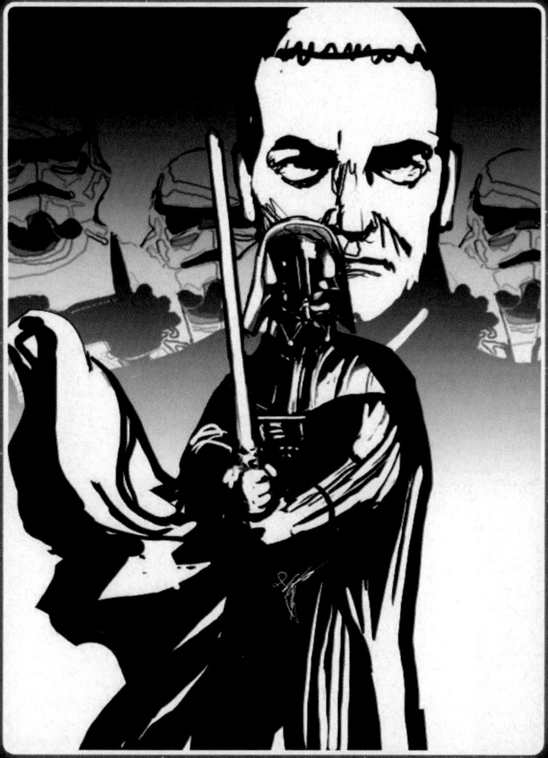

DARTH VADER 2

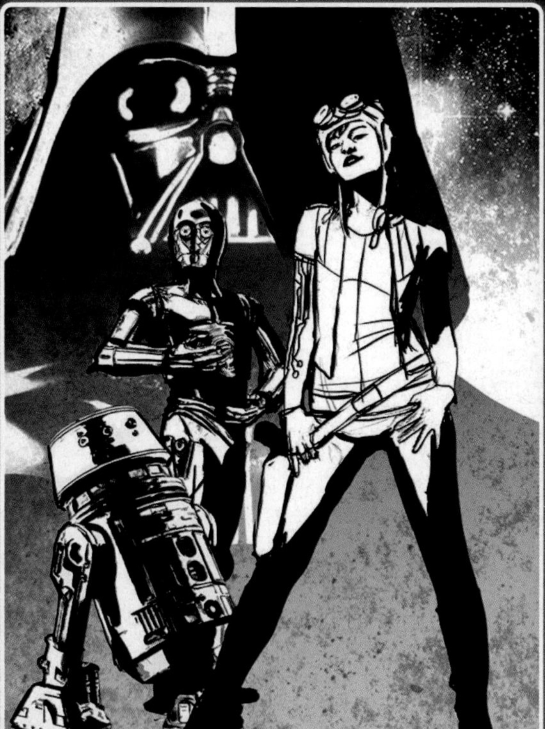

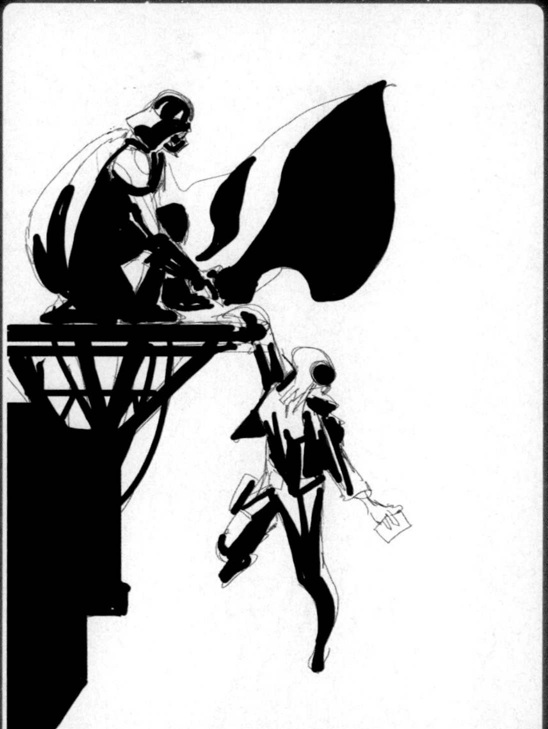

DARTH VADER 3

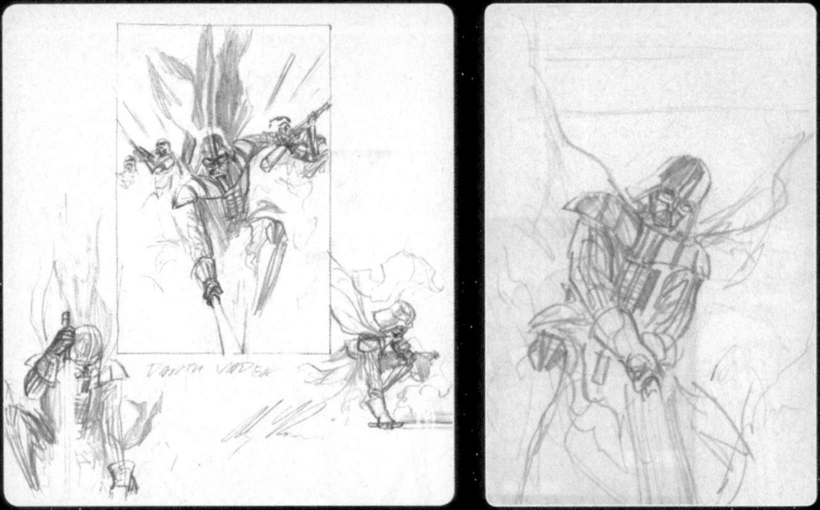
DARTH VADER

DARTH VADER 1
Ross Cover Sketches

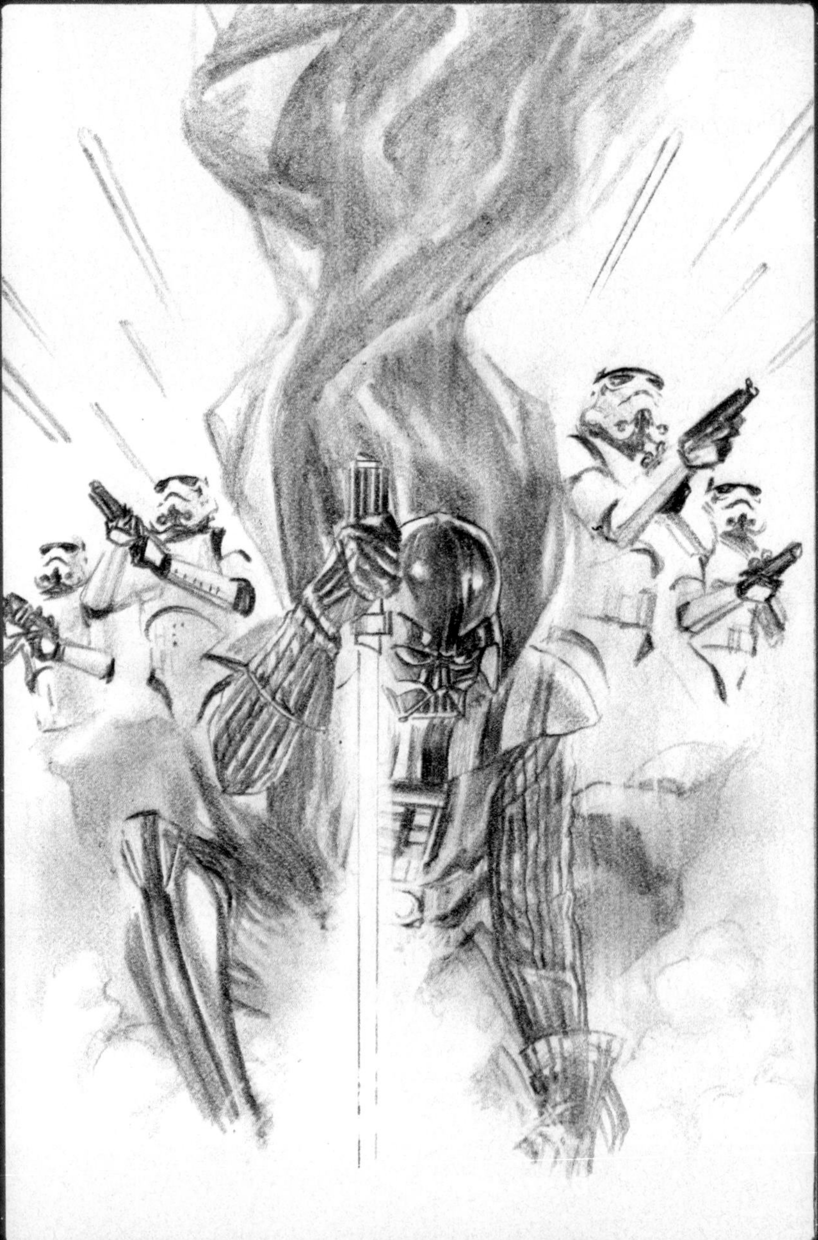

DARTH VADER 1
Ross Sketch Variant

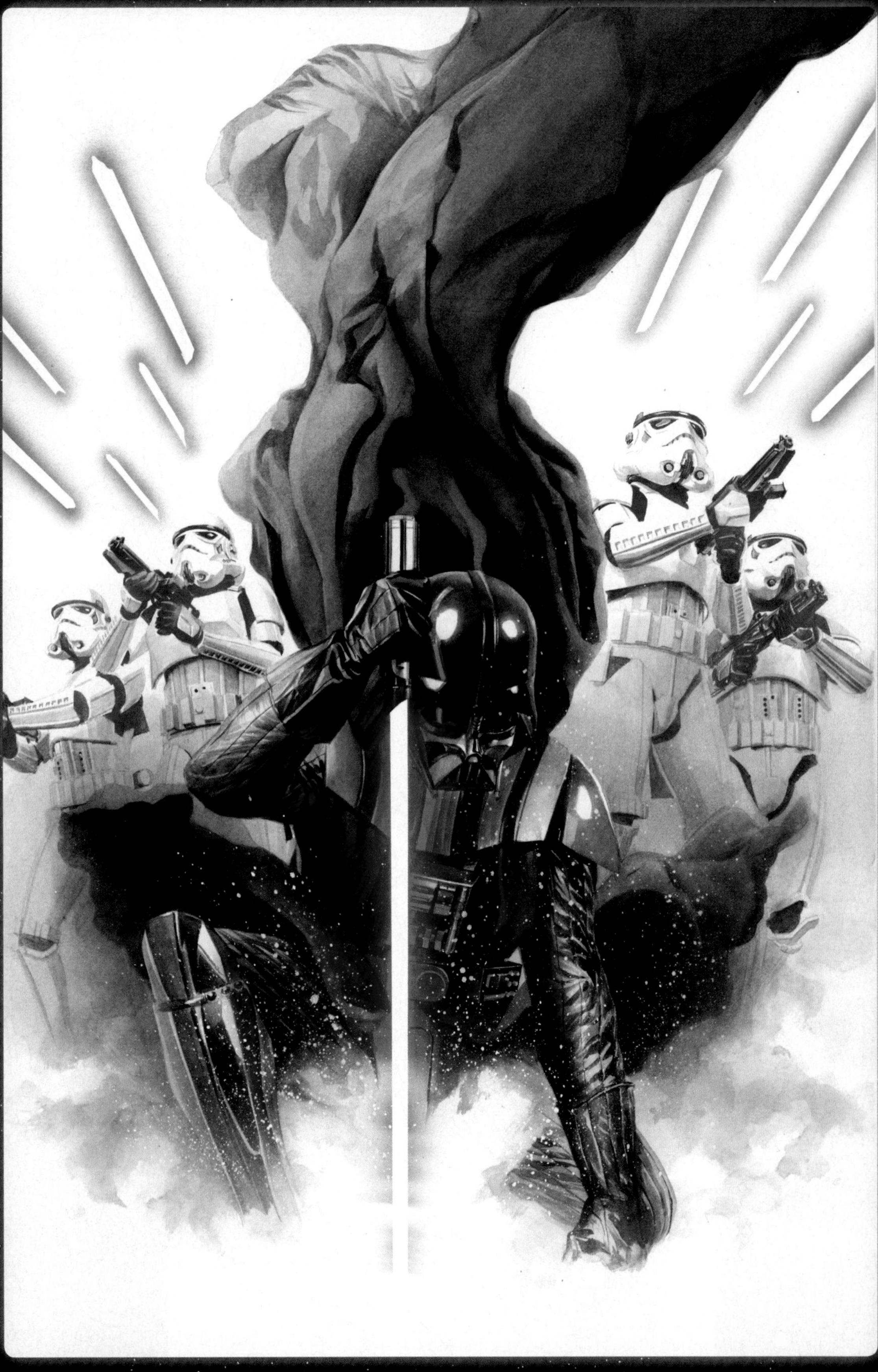

DARTH VADER 1 **Ross Variant**

SALVADOR LARROCA CHARACTER DESIGNS

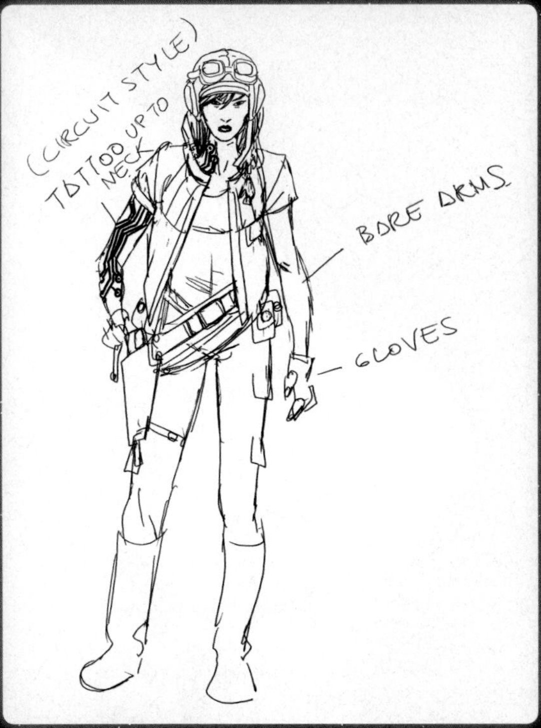
(CIRCUIT STYLE)
TATTOO UP TO NECK
BARE ARMS
GLOVES

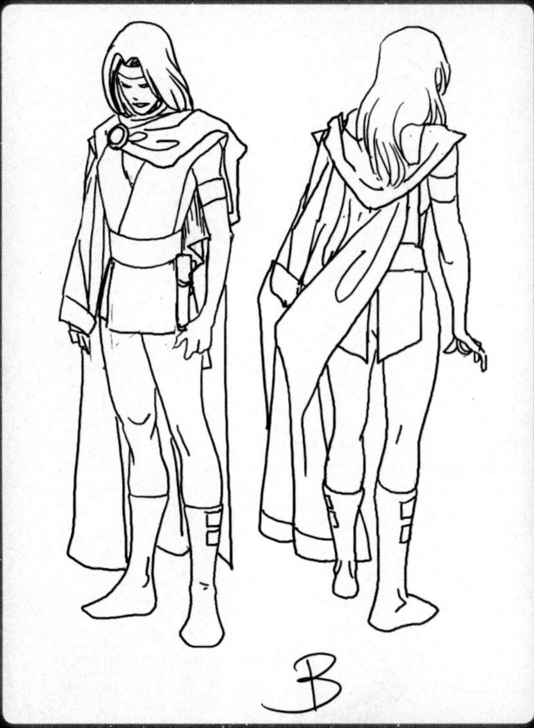
B

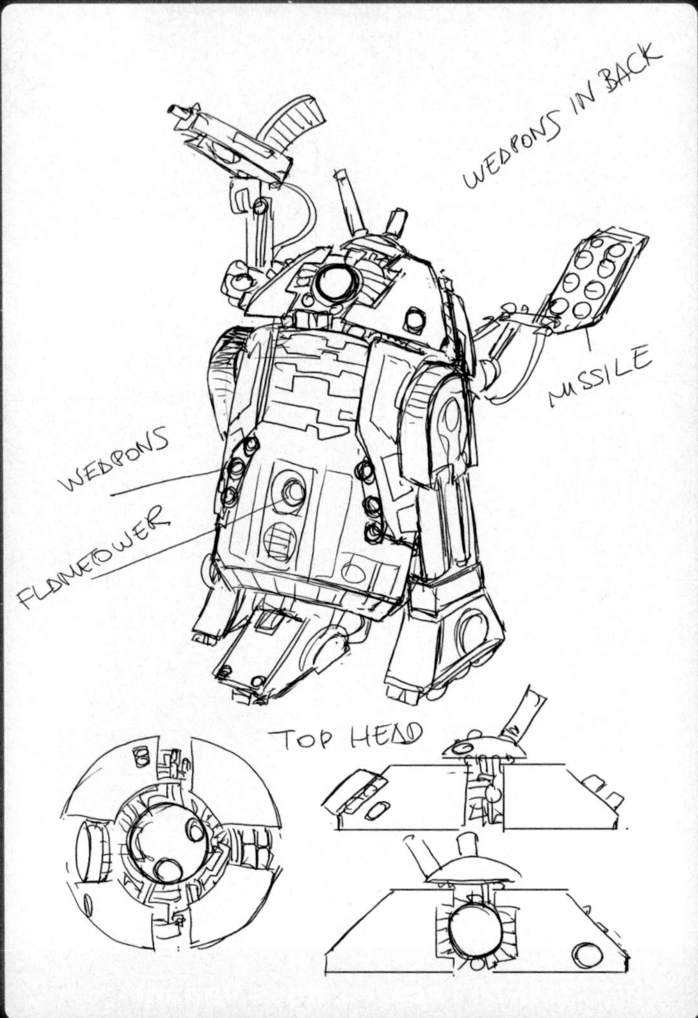
WEAPONS IN BACK
MISSILE
WEAPONS
FLAMETOWER
TOP HEAD

SENSATIONAL *STAR WARS* ARTWORK RETELLING THE STORY OF *A NEW HOPE!*

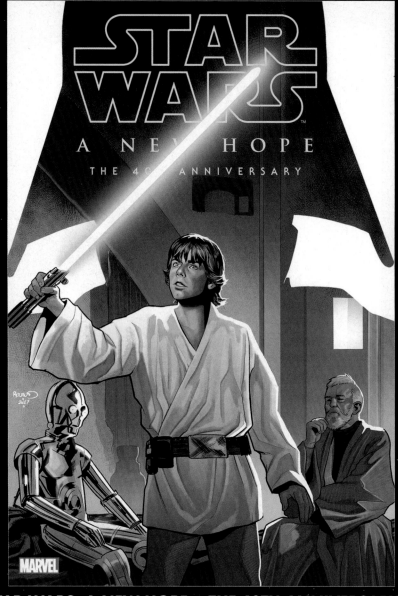

STAR WARS: A NEW HOPE — THE 40TH ANNIVERSARY HC
978-1302911287

ON SALE NOW
AVAILABLE IN PRINT AND DIGITAL WHEREVER BOOKS ARE SOLD

TO FIND A COMIC SHOP NEAR YOU, VISIT COMICSHOPLOCATOR.COM

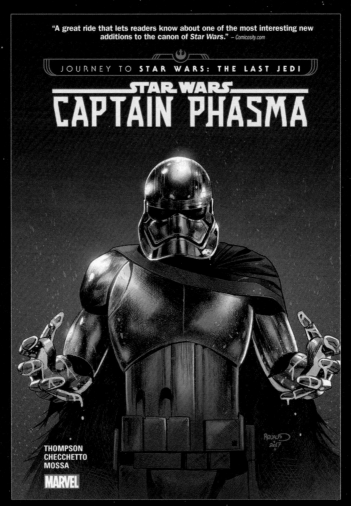

ACE PILOT POE DAMERON AND HIS BLACK SQUADRON TAKE ON THE FIRST ORDER!

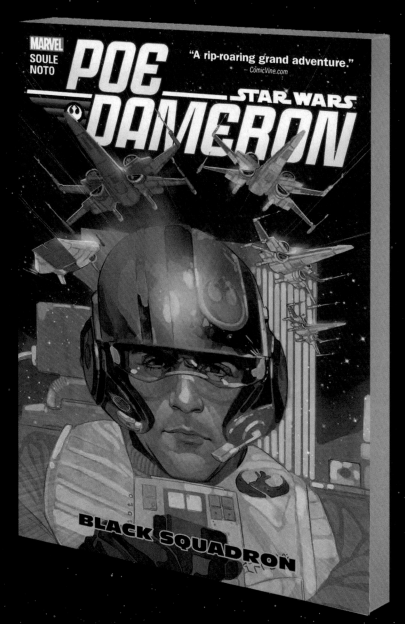

STAR WARS: POE DAMERON VOL. 1 — BLACK SQUADRON TPB
978-1302901103

ON SALE NOW

AVAILABLE IN PRINT AND DIGITAL WHEREVER BOOKS ARE SOLD

TO FIND A COMIC SHOP NEAR YOU, VISIT COMICSHOPLOCATOR.COM

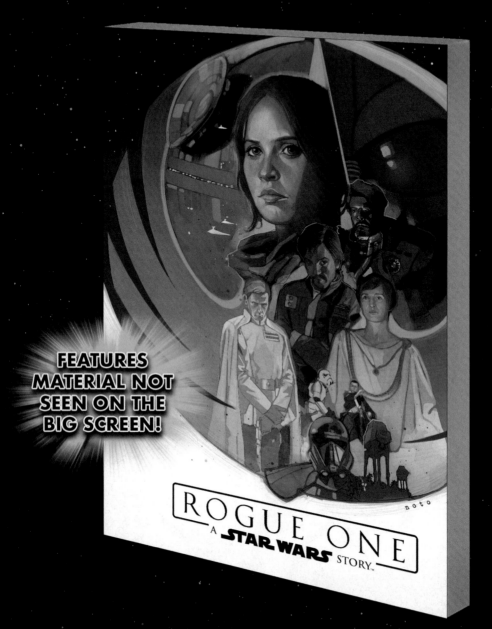

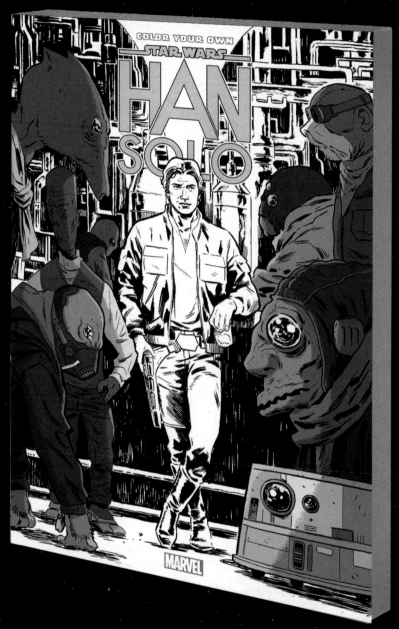

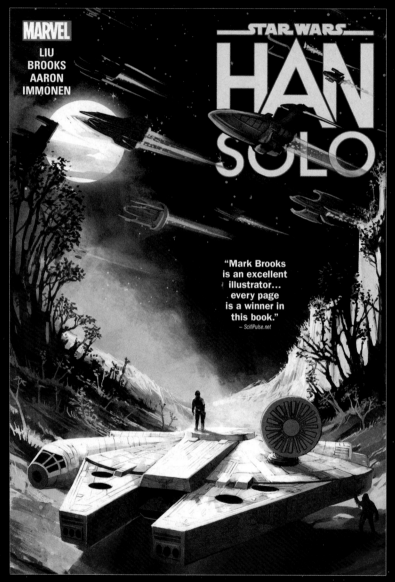